THE STORY OF ENGLAND

History Hit makes history more accessible in the digital age. Their podcast *Dan Snow's History Hit* has been broadcasting since 2015, and has over 1,500 episodes. They now have eight regular podcast shows, exploring topics from ancient history to the present day. Their online TV channel and app, History Hit TV, is a library of documentaries and interviews, and they create new and original history documentaries for their subscribers weekly. You can subscribe to access all History Hit podcasts and history documentaries at historyhit.com/subscribe.

History Hit have published two books: the *History Hit Miscellany* and the *History Hit Guide to Medieval England*.

THE STORY
OF ENGLAND

Making of a Nation

Dan Snow and the History Hit team

**HODDER &
STOUGHTON**

First published in Great Britain in 2024 by Hodder & Stoughton Limited
An Hachette UK company

3

Copyright © Hit Networks Ltd 2024

The right of Dan Snow and History Hit to be identified as the
Authors of the Work has been asserted by them in accordance
with the Copyright, Designs and Patents Act 1988.

Maps © Joanna Boyle 2024

A CIP catalogue record for this title is available from the British Library

Hardback ISBN 9781399726160
ebook ISBN 9781399726177

Typeset in Scala Pro by Hewer Text UK Ltd, Edinburgh
Printed and bound in Great Britain by Clays Ltd, Elcograf S.p.A.

Hodder & Stoughton policy is to use papers that are natural, renewable
and recyclable products and made from wood grown in sustainable
forests. The logging and manufacturing processes are expected to
conform to the environmental regulations of the country of origin.

Hodder & Stoughton Limited
Carmelite House
50 Victoria Embankment
London EC4Y 0DZ

The authorised representative in the EEA is Hachette Ireland, 8 Castlecourt
Centre, Dublin 15, D15 XTP3, Ireland (email: info@hbgi.ie)

www.hodder.co.uk

For My Ever Observant Orla, there are so many more smashed houses for us to explore.

Contents

Introduction

The English cannot escape their history. We commute in the shadow of towering cathedrals, and of castles that still dominate skylines. We drive on roads that follow Roman routes. We travel across Victorian bridges and viaducts. We dog-walk by Georgian canals. Every weekend more of us visit stately homes, battlefields and other heritage sites than attend football matches. Heritage is a national hobby. When we go abroad, we absorb – mostly – light-hearted jibes about forts overlooking the beach that were destroyed by the Royal Navy; we are chided for treasures looted. We listen politely as the heroes of our grandparents' schooling are decried as villains. We fend off questions from people obsessed by our ruling family, invariably described as English despite being drawn as much from Scotland and the Continent as England. We move through a world that speaks our language and plays our sports. There are 'parliaments', with 'speakers' and 'political parties', on every continent. It is entirely natural to stumble across familiar place names in unfamiliar surroundings. Wellington and Marlborough in New Zealand, Chipping Norton, Paddington and Sheffield in Australia and Birmingham, Boston, New York, and of course New England itself in the USA. Magna Carta is displayed with great reverence in

Canberra and Washington DC. Prayers are said to the health of the king every Sunday across the globe to the most observant of the over 100 million people who identify as members of the Church of England.

English history is complex. It extends far beyond our current borders; it has no neat end nor a beginning. Today England has a football team but not a nation state. We boast of our parliamentary tradition, yet England is a country with no parliament. It has not existed as a sovereign state for over 300 years, yet it feels alive. Millions of its inhabitants still identify predominantly as English. England's beginning is diffuse; so too is its end.

There was no champagne smash on the bows of England. No proclamation brought it into existence. It was a generational project, forged in war. A combination of the vision of a few, the luck of battle, a fortuitous run of competent kings (and one particular queen), and demographics. The catastrophic arrival of the Northmen, the seaborn 'Vikings' obliterated nearly all the long-standing, loosely English kingdoms. The crushing of the English made way for England. This crisis of the 9th century was an opportunity for the southernmost kingdom, Wessex. After centuries of internecine warfare against Northumbria, East Anglia, Mercia and the other statelets set up by the Saxons, Angles, Jutes and other Germanic peoples following the disintegration of the Roman Empire in the west, Wessex found that it was the only one left standing. Its old rivals had been extinguished by the pagans, their royal families butchered, their holy places sacked and despoiled. Once Wessex had – narrowly – ensured its own survival, its canny monarch, Alfred, switched to the offensive. He knew that the sword was not enough. Some bigger idea was required that could excite the loyalties of

Mercians and East Anglians who might otherwise be ambivalent about exchanging the Viking yoke for that of Wessex. So Alfred and his martial heirs – his children Edward and Aethelflaed, and his grandson Athelstan – framed the northern march of Wessex's spearmen as a national effort of liberation. This was to be a joint enterprise and anyone who shared a language and religion was invited to join, as Englishmen, to forge a new kingdom, England.

England proved durable. It survived a remarkably coherent effort by Britons, Scots and Vikings to strangle it. It overcame an unwillingness by many to subsume themselves in a political project obviously run from the far south of the island. It survived conquest by Scandinavians in the 11th century. Under the Danish king Cnut, England was just part of a vast North Sea empire. Had Cnut's heirs been of the calibre of Alfred's, England might have remained cemented into that maritime kingdom, one of the great what-ifs of our history. As it was, his hapless sons proved unequal to that admittedly giant task. England was sufficiently entrenched by the late 11th century to survive another conquest, this time by the Normans, who again bound England into another trans-maritime empire. It took centuries, but slowly the Norman kings, their Plantagenet successors and the wealthy landowning elite gradually came to identify as English, and by the 15th century they were even using English as the language of court. As other European states split, adapted or were defeated or absorbed, England survived. The southern and eastern boundaries were defined by the sea. The northern and western limits were far more ambiguous. The Britons, or Welsh, had been pushed into the peninsula today called Wales, and centuries of warfare were only conclusively resolved with the English conquest of the 13th century and the revolt and reconquest of the early 15th century. To the north, Scotland proved to be as much of an intractable challenge for the English as the region had been for the Romans. Expensive and logistically demanding to conquer, its climate and rugged landscape devoured armies like insects in a fly trap. But unconquered, its warlike lords scoured the northern marches of England. The burnt crops, slaughtered inhabitants, stolen herds, were insults no medieval king could endure. The English lurched from outright conquest to compromise. The rulers of Scotland were sometimes clients, at other times equals; they were occasionally prisoners, but could also be dominant. In the end England and Scotland were fused together, a gradual, uneven process, attended by plenty more violence.

Rather late in the story of England we find one of the foundational texts of Englishness. It is the mission statement for English exceptionalism, penned – obviously – by William Shakespeare, England's greatest wordsmith. In his play *Richard II* he puts a speech into the mouth of John of Gaunt, the powerful son of Edward III and father of the usurper Henry IV. John was a slightly odd vessel for this vision. He was born in Ghent, in the Low Countries – then known as Gaunt – to a French mother. He spent much of his time campaigning to assert his father's claim to the crown of France, while also making time to press his own claim to rule Castile. Yet Shakespeare has him waxing lyrical about England, 'this other Eden . . . This fortress built by Nature for herself'. England, he exalts, was a 'little world', it was a 'precious stone set in a silver sea'. Shakespeare was making a very deliberate point about the sufficiency of England, rooted in his own time and certainly not that of John of Gaunt's 14th century. He was writing at the end of a 500-year period in which the kings of England seemed not at all content with this 'little world'. They had dragged the flower of English manhood again and again to die on the Continent. They bled out in muddy siege works, they took crossbow bolts to the guts in breaches, they dropped by the wayside on barefoot marches across enemy terrain, all to slake their monarch's ambition to rule over swathes of France. That effort had failed, decisively, and irreversibly, by the 16th century. Shakespeare's job was to convince the English that England was enough, an earthly paradise over which even an Alexander would consider himself lucky to rule.

Yet it was evidently not enough. As Shakespeare's players spoke these words, England was expanding. English adventurers had pivoted to the west. Armies marched across Ireland, enforcing their monarch's flimsy claim to the Lordship of Ireland. England was locked in an expensive, generational struggle for control and colonisation. Schooled in the savage nursery of Connaught and Ulster, those same adventurers were making the first steps to plant the flag on the shores of North America. John Dee, Elizabeth I's alchemist, astrologer and adviser, convinced her that she was the heir to Arthur, fated to resurrect his empire. He even coined the phrase 'British Empire' while encouraging her with mystic justifications for a new Imperial project. Her refusal to marry and produce an heir, and the accident of inheritance, saw the King of Scotland, James VI, succeed her as James I of England. The vagaries of primogeniture did more for the building of a British Empire than the urgings of Elizabeth's mystic. James obviously had a vested interest in exalting Britishness. Just as Alfred used the idea of England to win the loyalty of his new subjects towards his expanding kingdom, so James and his successors emphasised Britishness to legitimise their rule. After a turbulent century, Britain was legally voted into existence in Edinburgh and London in the reign of his great-granddaughter, Anne. The debate around identity still rages 300 years on.

*   *   *

In 2023 History Hit teamed up with English Heritage to try to tell England's complex story. There is no substitute for visiting the places where that history was forged. In this era of satellite maps, digital image searches and endless drone shots, you might assume that you can learn everything about a place from the comfort of your laptop. But when you stand in a Neolithic circle, and watch as the light changes on the stones as a summer dawn gathers strength, or walk through the magnificence of an 18th-century stately home feeling the opulence through every sense, you appreciate them in a visceral way. True understanding lies in the combination of the reading that precedes the visit and the seeing, smelling and touching that physical presence allows. This book is built out of that adventure. It is born from the hundreds of sites that we have visited on our journey to make history fun, instructive and important. You will learn of the earliest human steps taken on these shores. You will chart the coming of bronze and iron. We will take you to places of burial. The places where our ancestors tried to protect themselves from other men with massive ramparts and from the supernatural with sacred enclosures. We will visit the battlefields and fortresses where the great men and women made epochal decisions, and the farms and foundries where the vast majority of us attempted to carve out a corner of the world in which to survive. In the book you will find there are over 40 QR code links to podcasts that will enhance your knowledge of the story of England, as well as more than 40 accompanying descriptions of the remarkable historical sites that helped direct this story.

I am often asked to recommend the best historical sites that I have visited. I can sense that people are looking for exotic descriptions of Maori forts, whaling ghost towns in the Antarctic or jungle-covered pyramids. My answer usually disappoints. My greatest joy is that I have been able to visit so much of my own country. I have seen so many of the places where our own story was forged. I have operated furnaces that still pour molten iron in the birthplace of the Industrial Revolution, I have gazed across the Channel from the roof of Dover Castle, I have walked for miles along Hadrian's Wall. I have crawled through Bronze Age copper mines and through the roof space of cathedrals. I have rowed on the arterial rivers that make England, the Thames, Trent, Severn and Mersey. I have visited and explored; and in doing so have tried to gain a richer and deeper understanding of England and us English. In the pages that follow, I hope that you will too. Enjoy.

Dan Snow

The Sycamore Gap at Hadrian's Wall

PART ONE

ANCIENT ENGLAND

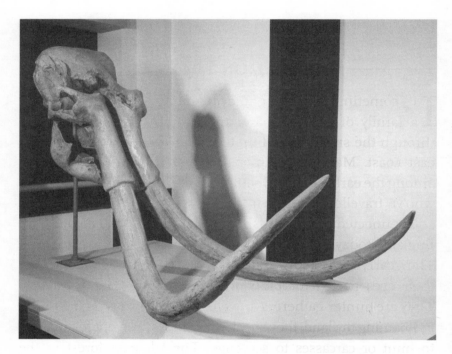
The cranium and tusks of a steppe mammoth found at Ilford, Essex

Chapter 1

Palaeolithic to Mesolithic

―――――――― **ONE MILLION YEARS AGO** ――――――――

I t's sometime between 950,000 and 850,000 years ago and a family of early humans are carefully picking their way through the storm-lashed mudflats on what is now England's east coast. Made up of men, women and children, they're among the earliest known settlers of England. They're pioneers who've travelled here from the European continent, which is still connected to the British Isles. It's cold. Much colder than England today. They wear heavy animal skins for warmth. They carry basic tools and weapons for hunting. They keep their eyes peeled for prowling hyenas and other predators. They are hunter-gatherers, travelling light, always on the move.

Roaming the land, they are on the constant lookout for animals to hunt or carcasses to scavenge. The tall pine forest in the distance provides shelter and sanctuary for animals like elk, horses and mammoths. The children pick through the under-growth as they move, looking for edible roots and vegetation. There aren't many creature comforts for them.

This was a time of survival. Dramatic changes in climate across the millennia broke apart and reshaped the land. Water and ice contoured the hills and mountains, carving out rivers and coastlines. The inhabitants of this land were forced to adapt or flee, and many of them would vanish altogether.

There may have been as many as ten waves of human occupation in England, where people migrated here only to be forced out again by extreme changes in the environment. But they've left fascinating and revealing traces across the landscape, if you know where to look.

PALAEOLITHIC ENGLAND

The evidence for Britain's prehistoric habitation is mainly scattered thinly through southeastern England. For much of the vast timespan of the Palaeolithic era (the Old Stone Age), which stretches back some three million years, the British Isles was still connected to mainland Europe. At that time the early humans may have found it difficult to cross or get round the vast water barrier of the Ancestral River Thames, which flowed into the North Sea.

Britain was really at the edge of the inhabited world. In modern terms, our human ancestors would be an endangered species, with one estimate being that at this point, some one million years ago, as few as 20,000 individuals were spread across the world. If small groups crossed over the land bridge to Britain, as a few did manage, they would have encountered a heavily forested landscape. If they could navigate this and get round the Ancestral Thames, then the climate would have become increasingly inhospitable.

The British Isles are on the same latitude as Labrador in modern-day Canada. This is

LISTEN TO THE
PODCAST

Stone Age England

PREHISTORIC SITES IN ENGLAND

SCOTLAND

CASTLERIGG STONE CIRCLE

STAR CARR

CRESWELL CRAGS

WALES

STONEHENGE

AVEBURY

THE RIDGEWAY

MAIDEN CASTLE

OLD SARUM

BOXGROVE SUSSEX

a place of frozen seas in the winter, and snow on the ground for months. The Atlantic Gulf Stream warms Britain up, bringing the tropical waters of the Gulf of Mexico into the Atlantic, which leads to ice-free seas and often mild winters. But when the Gulf Stream switches off, as it has done numerous times over the millennia, the temperature drops to what it should be according to latitude – closer to that of modern-day Labrador. So climate determined the story of early humans in Britain.

There is very little, if anything, in the deep prehistory archaeological record north of the Thames, simply because there were unlikely to have been many people active in northern England or Scotland at all at this time. Indeed, long periods of the archaeological record suggest that the British Isles were completely abandoned for tens of thousands of years on numerous occasions.

Many of the great prehistoric discoveries of England also have something else in common – their proximity to the coast; and the process of erosion over the many thousands of years has resulted in some fantastic finds.

'If you're a hunter . . . being near a lake or river means you're also going to get opportunities to hunt the animals that are coming to that river to drink or possibly try to cross the river. So humans have always been not too far away from water. There are some people who think that it was very important that it was, in a sense, part of our evolution that we waded in the water. I think that's unlikely, but I think water was always important to us. There always had to be sources nearby.'

Chris Stringer, Natural History Museum

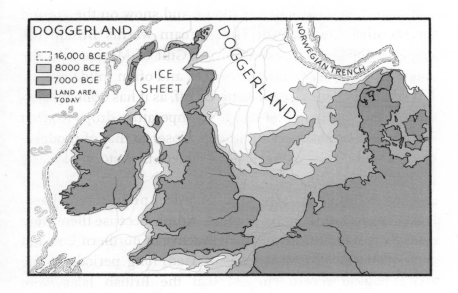

------ **THE HAPPISBURGH FOOTPRINTS** ------

The story of England, or at least of people living in what is now England, really begins at Happisburgh, Norfolk. The high level of coastal erosion here has proven a rich site for archaeological discovery, dating back to 1820 when fishing nets began dredging up the skeletons of large prehistoric animals.

In the year 2000, a black flint hand-axe was discovered on the beach by a man walking his dog. After studies by archaeologists, it was estimated that the tool dated to between 800,000 and 600,000 years ago, bringing known human presence in England back by at least 200,000 years based upon previous discoveries.

Happisburgh quickly became an important archaeological site, and between 2005 and 2010 a further 80 flint tools dating to the same timespan were found.

In May 2013, after a period of high seas, much of the beach sand beneath an eroded cliff was washed away to reveal ancient estuary mud, and there were some intriguing shapes within – they looked like footprints.

Analysis confirmed the discovery, before the footprints were washed away a couple of weeks later. Radiocarbon dating is useless at Happisburgh, it is only accurate within the last 50,000 years. Instead, analysis of the magnetic signatures in the sediment indicated the prints were made between 780,000 and one million years ago.

We don't know exactly which species of human they belonged to, but they could be members of the species *Homo antecessor*, who inhabited parts of Europe, notably northern Spain, in this period. The discovery confirms that humans lived in what is now England to around 900,000 years ago – the oldest evidence that we can point to. They are also the earliest hominid footprints to be found outside of Africa.

Prehistory Timescales

Palaeolithic	3.3m to 11,700 BCE	Humans begin using stone tools
Mesolithic	11,700–8000 BCE	More sophisticated tools with some pottery and textiles
Neolithic	8000–2000 BCE	Humans begin relying on agriculture, building more complex settlements

———————— THE HUNTER-GATHERERS ————————

For the vast majority of the 900,000 years when there was some form of human feet walking on this island, our ancestors were hunter-gatherers. They were also nomadic, moving from place to place in search of food and shelter. A change in the Mesolithic era saw humans move from large groups hunting big animals to smaller-scale hunting and gathering. But even then, they didn't grow their own crops or domesticate animals – this only occurred from the Neolithic period. Early on, groups would have hunted large animals like mammoths and collected plants. They probably wouldn't have turned their nose up at a recently dead carcass either. Later on, there is evidence of fishing.

To help them hunt and butcher animals, early humans used very simple stone tools such as hand-axes. From around 400,000 years ago, there is evidence of more sophisticated spear points, and tools to bore into animal skins to make cloth-ing. Bows and arrows were developed in the Neolithic era. The sharp points and heads of these surviving tools are most often shaped from flint. If you break off some flakes from this stone it's possible to get a sharp cutting edge.

Boxgrove

Some 200 miles to the southwest of the Norfolk coast is the village of Boxgrove, Sussex, and its Eartham Pit quarry. Excavations at the site began in 1982, uncovering hundreds of hand-axe tools, often almond- or teardrop-shaped, tools that were good for butchery. They were found alongside the bones of animals like deer, horses and even rhinoceros, some of which show traces of meat having been cut from them.

While flint and similar rocks were the preferred resource to make tools, and stone survives well over hundreds of thou-sands of years, our ancestors would have used other materials too, but the archaeological record is scarce. The best-preserved area of the site is the 'Horse Butchery Site', named for the fact that a large horse was slaughtered and butchered there approximately 480,000 years ago. In 2020, bone tools created from the skeleton of this animal were identified, making them the earliest known bone tools in the European archaeological record.

THE CLACTON SPEAR

An exceptional artefact was discovered at Clacton in 1911 – the end of a wooden spear made of yew wood, possibly for stabbing into an animal. It dates from 400,000 years ago (around the same time that fire became integral for early humans), making it the oldest working wooden implement ever discovered. The Clacton Spear is on display in the Human Evolution gallery at the Natural History Museum in London.

Homo heidelbergensis

Along with the numerous flint tools and animal bones, the oldest human remains in Britain were found at Boxgrove. But there's not a huge amount to go on – only a shinbone and a couple of teeth. This was a very big individual, and it was possibly a *Homo heidelbergensis* – an early human related to *Homo erectus* and the most recent common ancestor of modern humans and Neanderthals. There's just not enough of it to be absolutely sure.

Around the same time, there's evidence that the Neanderthals may have even been beginning their evolution, and it's possible that the Boxgrove material could be the beginning of the Neanderthal line.

Habitation by Neanderthals is seen more strongly at Swanscombe, on the south side of the River Thames, dating from around 400,000 years ago. Thousands more hand-axe tools have been excavated from the river gravel. So it seems there may have been early Neanderthals living in Britain as long as 400,000 years ago.

Evidence of Early Humans in England

Possible Human	Evidence	Dating	Location
Homo antecessor	Footprints	900,000 years	Happisburgh, Norfolk
Homo heidelbergensis	Shinbone and teeth	500,000 years	Boxgrove, Sussex
Neanderthal	Skull fragment	400,000 years	Swanscombe, Kent

—————— THE ANGLIAN GLACIATION ——————

Around 450,000 years ago, there was a severe cold snap and the northern ice sheets rolled over two-thirds of Britain, pushing down to just north of London. This was the Anglian Glaciation. Before this, the River Thames flowed through north Essex, Suffolk and Norfolk and into what is now the southern North Sea near Happisburgh. The vast ice sheet pushed it south, down to its present course through what is now London.

During glacial periods, the climate was similar to present-day northern Siberia's, and animals such as woolly mammoths, woolly rhinos, reindeer, musk ox, and even possibly polar bears would have roamed the permafrost and tundra. It's likely that when it got that cold, everyone in Britain either died out or migrated. They could have been here during the summers, but we don't pick up their presence in the archaeological record.

Fossilised human remains in Britain don't come back until nearly 230,000 years ago. Several teeth, almost certainly from a Neanderthal, were found in North Wales at a site called Pontnewydd.

THE FORMATON OF THE ENGLISH CHANNEL

The Anglian Glaciation covered East Anglia, but a huge glacial lake built up on the east side of the British Isles. If we picture the White Cliffs of Dover today, then that chalk extended in a huge ridge, the Weald–Artois Anticline, across to France and Belgium. When the glaciers retreated, the lake overflowed and cut through the chalk and waterfalls began to fill the basin of the English Channel.

This process was repeated over hundreds of thousands of years with glacial freezing and thawing, the sea levels rising and falling, each time eroding the Channel until around 125,000 years ago, when the land bridge finally disappeared, the English Channel was here to stay.

Britain as an Island

There is no evidence of humans occupying Britain when it first became an island. Indeed, the whole landmass was abandoned from around 180,000–60,000 years ago, probably due to the harsh climate. 125,000 years ago, sea levels rose to the point where certain low-lying parts of England such as the Wash were submerged; it would have been even warmer than today's climate.

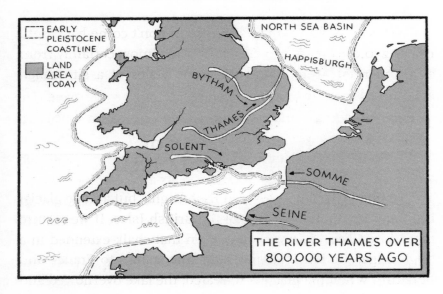

THE RIVER THAMES OVER 800,000 YEARS AGO

The bones of rhinos and elephants have been found under buildings at Trafalgar Square, and hippos were swimming in the River Thames. This would have been a warm and bountiful time for humans in southern England, but they missed out – the English Channel probably formed so quickly that they couldn't cross from Europe.

The Big Beasts of London

Some of the prehistoric animals that lived along the River Thames during the Palaeolithic:

Animal	Found at	Dating From
Woolly Mammoth	Ilford	200,000 BCE
Hippopotamus	West End	130,000–110,000 BCE
Rhinoceros	Old Bailey	60,000–24,000 BCE

——— RETURN OF THE NEANDERTHALS ———

Neanderthals (*Homo neanderthalensis*) are a hominid species whose evolutionary line split from that of modern humans. The earliest modern human (*Homo sapiens*) remains date back around 300,000 years since a 2017 discovery in a Moroccan mine. So we know that the line split at least 300,000 years ago, and possibly as far back as 800,000 years ago.

Neanderthals had a slightly more robust build than modern humans but shared many elements of human behaviour. The old view of these 'cavemen' was that they were unsophisticated and brutish, but they created tools, made simple clothing and were likely capable of some speech.

Neanderthals could have lived in England as far back as 400,000 years ago, but they made a limited return around 60,000 years ago, when sea levels dropped once again and a marshy land bridge known as Doggerland stretched from eastern England to what is now the Netherlands.

There were mammoths in Norfolk 60,000 years ago, and Neanderthals were probably hunting or scavenging dead mammoths at Lynford. The evidence left behind is through little hand-axe tools, which we assume were made by Neanderthals and were often found inside mammoth skeletons.

Enter Homo sapiens

It's most likely that our *Homo sapiens* lineage evolved in Africa over hundreds of thousands of years, and the oldest evidence we have for them reaching Britain is a piece of jawbone from Kents Cavern in Devon, discovered in 1927, which dates to just over 40,000 years old.

Modern humans may have arrived in England earlier, but the Neanderthals seem to have been dominant for most of the time before that. Then there was a period when we know the Neanderthals were being replaced by *Homo sapiens* in Europe, with a bit of interbreeding.

A set of teeth from a cave site in Jersey – La Cotte de St Brelade – gives us some clues. There were Neanderthals living in these caves around 45,000 years ago. But upon re-studying the teeth, archaeologists found that they actually showed mixed features of Neanderthals and *Homo sapiens*. So that might be evidence of a population with part Neanderthal and part *Homo sapiens* heritage.

About 2% of *Homo sapiens* DNA is from Neanderthals. So even though Neanderthals physically disappeared from England and the rest of Europe, a bit of them lives on in us. For the earlier species, such as *Homo antecessor*, there isn't evidence as to whether similar interbreeding was possible or not. By about 40,000 years ago Neanderthals had disappeared, and in Britain *Homo sapiens* became the only human species left.

MODERN HUMANS

Modern humans had more sophisticated tool-kits. Bone, antler and ivory tools, which are more difficult to work, became commonplace. With these tools came better clothing, so they could stand the cold better than Neanderthals. They also began to develop their culture through artwork. The best evidence for this in England is in the cave engravings of Creswell

LISTEN TO THE
PODCAST

Ice Age Britain

Crags, straddling the border of Derbyshire and Nottinghamshire, made about 15,000 years ago. There have also been musical instruments found, such as bone flutes, which have been replicated and played beautifully.

The estimated date of the Creswell Crag engravings coincides with the resettlement of Britain. Around 25,000 years ago, another glacial expansion forced humans out of Britain – the last Ice Age. When the Earth warmed up around 15,000 years ago, humans returned, and have remained here ever since. Then, from around 12,000 years ago, *Homo sapiens* began to adapt from a nomadic hunter-gatherer lifestyle into more settled farming communities through the Mesolithic era, and into the Neolithic.

Lanyon Quoit, a neolithic burial chamber in Land's End, Cornwall

Chapter 2

Stone Age to Bronze Age

The Neolithic ('New' Stone Age) era marked the dawn of agriculture and settled communities. These changes began around 10,000 BCE in the Fertile Crescent region of the Middle East, where humans first transitioned from nomadic hunter-gatherers to settled farmers. It's sometimes referred to as a 'revolution', but, like much of prehistoric progress, the changes came *very* gradually. The domestication of plants and animals, the development of pottery and weaving and the construction of permanent dwellings crept slowly westward across Europe.

Britain had once again become an island around 6200 BCE, when the marshy land bridge of Doggerland, stretching from East Anglia to the Netherlands, was submerged by rising sea levels. Doggerland now lies under some 20 metres of the North Sea (the Dogger Bank), providing rich modern fishing grounds. Britain has been cut off from the Continent ever since.

Partly due to this isolation, the Neolithic way of life reached the British Isles fairly late, in around 4000 BCE. Certainly, the new arrivals would have been boat builders and coastal-seafarers, but interestingly the earliest evidence of farming isn't found in southern England, but in Ireland and the Isle of Man.

The migration of Neolithic people across Europe from Anatolia (modern Turkey) appears to have taken two main routes. Some followed the Danube river into Central Europe, while another migration pushed westward across the Mediterranean basin into the Balkans and Iberia. This latter migration eventually found its way north through France and then to Britain, likely entering from the west. The Neolithic population in Britain, therefore, was most closely linked to Iberian migrants with some weaker links to Central Europe.

Of course, there is no writing left behind by these settlers; what we know of them is only provided through the archaeological record, but throughout southern and southwestern England are some of the most remarkable prehistoric sites in the world. These people were builders, and their most significant legacy comes from their megalithic monuments, some of which have been standing for more than 5,000 years. It is their burial practices, primarily, that form the Neolithic legacy in England. There are two distinct forms of early Stone Age tombs dotted around southwestern England – dolmens and long barrows.

DOLMENS

Dolmens are a type of chambered portal tomb, with a huge capstone, which has been dragged over a chamber and is held up by supporting megaliths. Experts believe they would have been surrounded by an earth mound, although most of these have been weathered away to leave a mysterious structure. The moorlands of Ireland house the largest dolmens in Europe, but these tombs are also common in southwest Wales, Devon and Cornwall, giving clues to the sea links of the western British Isles.

There's a remarkable prehistoric walk, seven miles from east to west, through the coastal moorlands of Penwith in Cornwall, at the very west of England. Dotted throughout this landscape, northwest of Penzance and west of St Ives, are numerous historical relics spanning millennia, including five notable dolmens: Sperris, Zennor, Mulfra, Lanyon and Chun Quoit. Among the dolmens (quoit being the Cornish term) is also the Men-an-Tol, an iconic little arrangement of standing stones and a circular stone with a hole in its centre. This was probably built in the late Neolithic or early Bronze Age, and it's not entirely clear what it was for, but in more recent centuries crawling through the doughnut-shaped stone was said to have healing powers.

Dolmens stretch into Dorset, with the Hell Stone Dolmen, and then into Wiltshire, with the similarly named Devil's Den. These macabre names tell their own story – that later Christians saw these ancient pagan tombs, so different from simple modern graves, as the mischievous work of the devil.

THE BARBER STONE, AVEBURY

To some Christians, the stone monuments left by England's prehistoric ancestors were too much to bear, and they faced destruction. There are instances of the huge stones at Avebury being pulled down and buried. One particularly zealous man, likely a barber surgeon, visiting Avebury was successful in felling one of the megaliths, but karma kicked in and the stone crushed him. His skeletal remains were found buried under the stone by an archaeologist in 1938, and dated to the early 14th century through a collection of coins, and his occupation assumed by a pair of medical scissors. Perhaps the inhabitants of Avebury were frightened by this 'omen' and were discouraged from any further destruction. The barber stone was restored to its upright position after the discovery.

LONG BARROWS

Dolmens are largely concentrated in the southwest of England, with an exception being Kit's Coty House in Medway, Kent, part of the 'Medway Megaliths'. It is also in the landscapes of Somerset, Gloucestershire and Wiltshire that the other type of early megalithic tomb, the long barrow, is common. There are around 200 known examples in what was labelled in 1937 the Cotswold–Severn Group. One of the most impressive, West Kennet Long Barrow, lies within the boundary of the Avebury World Heritage site. Visitors can walk right into the large burial chamber without having to crouch or crawl.

The construction of West Kennet would have been a more significant undertaking than any of the English dolmens. It has a massive barrier of megaliths at its front, and an ominous stone entrance with huge lintels that support the earth thrown over its top. Built around 3650 BCE, it was first a timber chambered barrow, and human bones were placed in the chamber. It appears that, over the subsequent centuries, it went through periods of disuse as a place of burial, but the stone chambers were incorporated into its structure around 3450 BCE. By the late Neolithic, when there was significant cultural development of the land around Avebury and Stonehenge, the tomb entrance was blocked up with large boulders.

The Ridgeway, said to be the oldest road in Britain, starts at Overton Hill near Avebury and snakes northeast for 87 miles through the North Wessex Downs to Ivinghoe Beacon in Buckinghamshire. This sometimes amounts to nothing more than a forest track, at others, it is aligned to busy modern highways. Travellers have used it for at least 5,000 years, and it was for a long time a major trading artery of southern England.

Heading 20 miles along the Ridgeway from Avebury, a traveller would arrive at Uffington in Oxfordshire. Here are the remains of a significant Iron Age hillfort, Uffington 'Castle', which sits on top of White Horse Hill. This hill gets its name from a remarkable geoglyph – the 110m-long Uffington White Horse, which was carved into the chalk during the Bronze Age.

The significance of Uffington as a seat of power and culture stretches further back in time with another of the most impressive surviving Stone Age long barrows: Wayland's Smithy, which was in use as a chambered long barrow around 3500 BCE. This barrow gets its quirky name from a mythical blacksmith called Weland by the Anglo Saxons, who in folklore used the tomb as his shop. One medieval story is that Wayland would reshoe your horse if you waited outside it. Like West Kennet, Wayland's Smithy has a front of huge megaliths with a haunting entrance, although those who dare can't get nearly as far inside it.

The transition from the Early Neolithic to Late Neolithic occurred around 3000 BCE, a change illustrated by the tradition of megalithic chambered tombs of dolmens waning and circular monuments and barrows becoming more common. There is no better example than the huge stone circle at Stonehenge, which stands 25 miles south of Avebury and West Kennet.

STONEHENGE

Stonehenge is England's best-known Stone Age site, and has iconic status all around the world. Over a million people visit the monument every year.

'It is spectacular. I think some people, when they first come, they wonder what all the fuss is about, but then they get to understand how unique it is. It's mainly the construction features in particular that make it unique for this period, but also the size of the stones. And there is definitely something magical about this place.'

Heather Sebire, English Heritage

It is truly unique. Not only for the vast size of the sarsen stone pillars, which stand seven metres tall, but also for the huge adjoining lintel blocks. While using supporting lintels is a common feature of Neolithic tomb building, and marks the entrances to some long barrows, there is no other surviving example of a prehistoric stone circle with adjoining lintels anywhere in the world.

The site was likely selected for it being in a large clearing in the otherwise forested landscape of the England of the time, with surrounding soft ridges looking down upon its setting on a sort of terrace. The visible horizon stretches for over ten miles in every direction. There is still a palpable atmosphere. It was likely built as a place of ceremony and spirituality.

Phase 1 (3000 BCE)

The creation of earthworks was part of the first phase of the monument, which was developed over generations beginning around 3000 BCE. Once the early monument builders had chosen a space, they dug out a ditch and threw up a circular bank. Given that the area is on chalky soil, this would have been gleaming white on the landscape. This ditch is one of the few parts of Stonehenge that has a secure date, and it has been about 50% excavated, although most of it not using the most modern techniques.

These ditch diggers would have used antler picks and scapulae (shoulder blades), which gave them a broad digging tool. It's likely that some of these tools were simply left lying about the site, but they also possibly deposited some of them, ceremonially, inside the circle.

Phase 2 (c.2900–2600 BCE)

Radiocarbon dating tells us that the antler picks were used around 5,000 years ago. That's at least 500 years before the main stones came in; but before that happened, inside the bank and ditch, a series of 56 pits were dug.

These were named after an antiquarian called Sir John Aubrey, who identified the holes in 1666. It was an autumn afternoon and he could see shadows caused by slight depressions inside the bank, which turned out to be pits that held cremation burials. So Stonehenge was definitely a place of burial and it's still the largest prehistoric cremation site known in Britain.

Next came a wooden structure. Around the same time as the pits were dug, there were probably some wooden posts erected.

Phase 3 (2500 BCE)

The sarsens arrive. These are huge 12-foot pillars – are shaped from very dense sandstone known as silcrete, and joined by lintels across their top. They form the outer circle, and they would have probably surrounded an inner formation of bigger sarsens entirely. This was a horseshoe of trilithons, which is the Greek word for three stones, the classic symbol of Stonehenge.

There are also smaller stones, known as bluestones. Some say these bluestones had healing qualities. If you knock that rock together, they give out a particular sort of ring. They're human sized. There was probably at least one concentric circle of bluestones, but what's left is in ruins.

Henge lingo
- **Henge** – a circular earthwork enclosure, often surrounding a stone circle.
- **Sarsen** – a large sandstone block, pillar or boulder.
- **Lintel** – a joining stone structure linking two or more pillars. Common in prehistoric doorways but not in stone circles.
- **Concentric** – circles, often in rings, that share the same centre point.

Transporting the Stones

The bluestones – which are not truly blue, although they have a bluey tinge when it's really wet – are rhyolites and diorites. They came from the Preseli Hills in West Wales, which is over 250 miles away. The bluestones would likely have been transported by boat and then dragged across western England. The giant sarsens were also not quarried at the site. Instead, they came from the Marlborough Downs, around 20 miles to the north.

It's not exactly known how these giant stones reached Stonehenge. Significant people power would have been needed. One estimate is that it would have taken about 200 people to drag a single sarsen, and the journey would have taken several days. They may have been pulled on a type of sledge, rather than just on rollers, but it would have taken a huge effort and somebody to give the orders.

How and Why Was Stonehenge Built?

After the erection of the sarsen stones and their lintels, the monument was rearranged rather than any major new features added. The inner circle of bluestones were re-erected, moved and possibly trimmed over almost a millennium from around 2400 BCE onwards.

A series of pits known as the Y and Z holes were dug outside the sarsen circle around 1600 BCE, but after this there appear to have been no further additions to the site. By this time Stonehenge, from its origins as an earthwork, had been in use for around 1,500 years.

The monument was built and adjusted over generations. The people were farmers, with periods of an abundance of food, which allowed them to do other things such as monument building. The moving and raising of the stones would have been a communal act, but it's likely that there were decades, even centuries, where the work stopped and little was added before the cycle might begin again; there is so much that we will never know for sure.

Stonehenge was certainly built to reflect the solar alignment of the midsummer sunrise and the midwinter sunset. No one was living at the site; the nearest settlement was around two miles to the northeast at Durrington Walls. So it's likely that it was a place of gathering and ceremony.

Although there were cremations before the stones came in, we do know that it was not a tomb. There are Neolithic barrows nearby in which generations of the dead would be carefully

LISTEN TO THE
PODCAST

Stonehenge

laid to rest. But Stonehenge seems to have had a bigger, more public purpose

We can learn a certain amount from the layout, and we can imagine the choreography. There is 'The Avenue', a processional way which goes down to the valley, over the King Barrow Ridge, and then drops down to the River Avon. It's thought that people probably travelled up the river (which is also possibly how the bluestones arrived), and would have made their way up a ceremonial avenue, a bit like a modern place of worship or civic centre.

'Stonehenge, in a way, was probably the equivalent, for prehistoric people, of Mecca, for example, or Santiago or Lourdes or somewhere of this sort from more modern times.'

Timothy Darvill, Bournemouth University

—————— AVEBURY AND SILBURY HILL ——————

Twenty miles to the north of Stonehenge is Avebury, where 180 unshaped standing stones originally formed what is the largest megalithic circle in the world at 347 metres in diameter. The outer ring encircles two smaller circles and is surrounded by an earthwork of just under a mile in circumference. Radiocarbon dating suggests that the digging of this huge bank, and the construction of the outer circle, took place around the same time as the creation of the sarsen circle at Stonehenge – around 2500 BCE. At the southwest of the monument is the entrance to West Kennet Avenue, where probably

100 pairs of standing stones lined a one-mile link between Avebury and The Sanctuary – a much smaller but quite complex concentric circle made of timber and stone.

Close to The Sanctuary sits Silbury Hill, the largest artificial mound in Europe. The hill is almost 40 metres high, and required 248,000 cubic metres of earth to construct, in several stages around 2400 BCE. While it has the appearance of a huge tumulus, no burial remains have been found at the site, and it is not clear what it was built for. Because of its height, it is visible from other surrounding monuments such as Avebury Henge and West Kennet Long Barrow, but it has been suggested that the process of building the hill was more important than the hill itself.

Metal

The giant constructions at Avebury, Silbury Hill and Stonehenge tell us that there were times of healthy agrarian economy and a labour surplus, meaning people could spend time on non-essential activities. The outer stone circle at Avebury, Silbury Hill and the main phase of Stonehenge were all similarly constructed, and all date from the mid-third millennium BCE. Eventually that age of monumental building came to an end as new materials and new people reshaped Britain.

The so-called Bell Beaker culture is named after an inverted bell beaker vessel which distinguishes them from what came before. The people of this culture had their origins in the Russian steppe and modern-day Ukraine, and migrated across Europe from 2800 BCE. They crossed over to Britain via the Netherlands between 2500 and 2000 BCE. They brought with them metal. Copper and bronze in particular gave them an enormous advantage in making tools, weapons and jewellery.

Prior to the arrival of the Bell Beaker, England would have been populated by olive-skinned and Mediterranean-looking people. They were gradually replaced by the new immigrants; until by around 2000 BCE their numbers had fallen to just 10% of the population.

BRONZE AGE

The Bell Beaker culture, unleashed the Bronze Age to England. Dartmoor, in South Devon, has the highest concentration of Bronze Age remains in the country; across its 368 square miles of undulating moorland there are more than 75 stone rows and 18 stone circles, along with the remains of over 5,000 Bronze Age huts.

Dartmoor was originally covered in woodland, but from around 10,000 BCE the first forest clearings began. There is some evidence of Mesolithic remains on the fringes of the moor, and a solitary Neolithic dolmen still stands at Spinster's Rock in the village of Drewsteignton to the north. Dartmoor's high soil acidity means that little pottery, bone or metal survives, but its relative remoteness and low human activity since the Bronze Age means that many of the stone structures and thousands of burial sites still remain.

On the western side of the moor, near the town of Tavistock, is the Bronze Age settlement of Merrivale. Sheltered in a valley

LISTEN TO THE
PODCAST

The Beaker
People

between the heights of Great Staple and King's Tor are the remains of over 50 roundhouses, some at around eight metres across, which supported a thatched roof. Perhaps the Bronze Age settlers were drawn to earlier heritage. Their settlement is also home to earlier monuments, dating from the late Neolithic – most notably two double stone rows, each comprising more than 150 stones, running east to west, with the southern row stretching 263 metres. There is a cist, or stone-lined burial chamber, with a huge split capstone, near the centre of the southern stone row.

TUMULI, BARROWS AND CAIRNS

Dotted throughout Dartmoor are thousands of Neolithic and Bronze Age burial sites. Some of these are underground burial chambers, known as cists or kistvaens, but the more noticeable are the many burial mounds. Tumuli (plural for tumulus) is a catch-all term for burial mounds, which can also be called barrows and cairns. Defining features of barrows and cairns (which can both be defined as tumuli) are that barrows are made of piled earth and cairns are made of piled stones. But, somewhat confusingly, many cairns on Dartmoor are in fact labelled 'Barrow', such as the Eastern White Barrow or the giant conglomeration of Three Barrows. On Dartmoor, these terms essentially mean the same thing.

Near to the Merrivale Stone rows is a small stone circle and a menhir, or standing stone. This is a fantastic spot for watching the sunset over the hills. Running to the west of the site is the Great Western Reave, a long stone field boundary, which stretches some six miles. It reminds us that the people who inhabited Merrivale were farmers, most likely keeping sheep and cattle.

Dartmoor

Near the centre of Dartmoor sits Grimspound, which is about 450 metres above sea level. Here a circular boundary wall of huge boulders encloses the remains of 24 roundhouses. On first visit, this may look like a defensive or ceremonial structure, and its name is probably derived from the Anglo-Saxon god of war Grim, more commonly known as Woden or Odin. But despite the depth of the wall it isn't particularly high, and its location, wedged between two hills, means it was unlikely to have been used as a fort. It is more likely that the boundary was used for keeping livestock from around 1500–800 BCE.

The southwest of Dartmoor contains the Upper Plym Valley, scattered thickly with Bronze Age settlements. Nearby are also some of the moor's most impressive ceremonial features. On a slope between the stream of Drizzle Combe and the River Plym is the Drizzlecombe complex, containing five enclosed settlement sites and huts, cairns and a cist. It is the three principal stone rows, each with an associated barrow and terminal menhir, that are most arresting to modern visitors. All three rows run uphill in a roughly southwest to northeast direction, with their terminal stones at the southern end and a cairn marking their northern limits. The tallest menhir (at 4.3 metres high the largest on Dartmoor) is on the eastern row and is known as the 'Bone Stone' due to its thin shape. At some point this must have fallen, as it was re-erected in 1893. A mile to the north of Drizzlecombe is the 350-metre-long Down Tor stone row and stone circle, which is often referred to as Dartmoor's most impressive Bronze Age feature. One hundred and eight stones lead west up the gentle slope of Hingston Hill, ending in a circle with a large megalith, within which is a cairn.

Dartmoor's intense Bronze Age activity may well have depleted its farmland and the soil became degraded and exhausted by around 1000 BCE. Its once thriving Bronze Age settlements seem to have been abandoned by 800–700 BCE. Falling temperatures added more pressure. They likely forced the communities to lower ground. But by this time the people living in England were learning a new and more sophisticated metallurgical process – how to smelt iron.

A victorious Constantius Chlorus rides towards London after
his defeat of Allectus

Chapter 3

Iron Age England and Roman Britannia

I ron is a much more abundant metal in nature than either copper or tin, which combine to make bronze. It's also stronger, making it more durable for weaponry and tools. Exactly where the technique of iron smelting was discovered is not known for certain, but it possibly originated in southeast Europe or the Caucasus beginning in 1200 BCE. By 800 BCE it had reached the shores of England. At Puzzlewood in the Forest of Dean, you can still see the pick marks left by Iron Age Britons as they extracted iron ore from the rocks of an Iron Age quarry.

There are no written records of pre-Roman England written by the people who lived here. 'Celts' has been used as a general label for these people and their culture, but historians now often refer to them as 'Iron Age Britons'. The Greek explorer Pytheas completed an exploratory voyage around Britain at the end of the 4th century BCE. He labelled the Iron Age Britons 'prettani' – 'painted people' – presumably referring to the tattoos that they covered themselves with. Later on, the Roman general Julius Caesar referred to their strange customs, such as Druidic human sacrifice. Greco-Roman writers divided the Britons up into different tribes across Britain – kingdoms such as the Catuvellauni, Trinovantes and Iceni – but there is no evidence for those groupings in earlier centuries.

It's through archaeology that we have the richest evidence for the lives of Iron Age Britons. Their craftsmanship is shown through the Waterloo Helmet and the Battersea Shield, both somewhat confusingly made of bronze, but probably melded in 350–50 BCE.

Only the highest echelons of these societies would ever see or own such objects. The legacy of the Iron Age is much more visible through sculpted hilltops throughout England – Bigbury, British Camp, Danebury and Carrock Fell to name a few of more than 1,000 hillforts identified across England.

MAIDEN CASTLE

Looming near present-day Dorchester, not far from the coast, Maiden Castle is one of the largest and most impressive hill-forts in Britain. Evidence suggests that the plateau where it sits was occupied back into the early Neolithic in c.4000 BCE – a millennium before Stonehenge was built. But it was during the Iron Age, over generations of occupation, that Maiden Castle was transformed into a powerful bastion. Its outer reaches were defended by four sets of banks and ditches, the innermost of which is still several metres tall.

'They look impressive today . . . but bear in mind this has been slumping for over 2,000 years. So the ditch was probably a good six or seven metres deeper; the ramparts might be six metres higher. And then originally on top of the ramparts you'd have a wooden palisade . . . and the ramparts of course were dug out of chalk. So (imagine) these big, gleaming white walls. Up against the green, grass background.'

Miles Russell, Bournemouth University

Maiden Castle was one of the largest engineering projects in England's prehistory, and would have taken an immense amount of manpower to build. Anyone approaching it 2,500 years ago would be funnelled through tight, winding passageways between the ramparts – valleys of death for any would-be attacker – before arriving at the great palisade that surrounded the plateau. Through the gateway, there would have been roadways dotted with rows of roundhouses – the classic Iron Age dwelling made of earth and timber with a thatched, conical roof. Maiden Castle had its own prehistoric suburbia, and was home to hundreds of people.

WATCH THE
VIDEO

Maiden Castle

These very early stages of 'urbanisation' evolved in Britain as the Iron Age progressed. By *c.*100 BCE more complex settlements called oppida had begun to appear, and the age of hillforts ended. Oppida were larger communal centres that were probably used as seats of power and places for ceremonial events. Archaeologists have identified several Iron Age oppida across England, with the most striking example being in Essex.

COLCHESTER

In late Iron Age England Colchester, or to give it its Roman name Camulodunum, was one of the most important settlements in the country. As with Maiden Castle, a series of big ditches and bank earthwork systems define Iron Age Colchester. But whereas Maiden Castle's earthworks – and those of hillforts more generally – formed a neat enclosure boundary around the hilltop, Colchester's earthworks – known as dykes – spread for miles and had a much more erratic design, with areas for agriculture, manufacture, elite residences and possibly rituals. Large burial mounds have been found around modern Colchester, alongside a wealth of impressive grave goods.

'Colchester, and burials elsewhere just outside Colchester but also around St Albans ... seem particularly rich. There are some other oddities around the country. Famously in Yorkshire you have the Arras burials where they have chariots ... and recently there was the famous warrior burial in Chichester [North Bersted Man] for example, which is really quite unique. But generally speaking, the number of very wealthy burials in this [Colchester] area seems to be quite special.'

Frank Hargrave, Colchester Museum

Colchester must have housed some of the wealthiest individuals in late Iron Age England. They were keen to show off their wealth and the connections they had established with a new, expanding power on the European continent: Rome.

THE LEXDEN BURIAL

In 1924 archaeologists excavated a vast tumulus in a suburb of Colchester – the Lexden Burial. An intact chambered tomb was found within, filled with objects dating to the late 1st century BCE. But most of these were not created in England – they were Roman. There were the remains of large storage vessels called Dressel 1 amphorae, designed for storing liquids such as wine, along with cups and plates that these high-status late Iron Age Britons had imported from the Continent. There was also an extraordinary medallion depicting the face of the Emperor Augustus.

ROMAN INTERACTIONS

In the late 1st century BCE, people living in the southeast of England would have become more aware of the expanding Roman world. Some Iron Age nobles even went to Rome and received a Roman education. Between 55 and 54 BCE Rome's most famous statesman, Julius Caesar, undertook two brief military campaigns in Britain. On the first expedition he didn't get much further than the Kent coast. During his second he possibly reached as far as Wheathampstead in Hertfordshire, a key centre of the Catuvellauni, before he had his forces turn round and return to the Continent. Caesar recorded how he led several victories over the Britons, and set up tributes to be paid to the Empire. But his campaigns were relatively brief and did not result in a lasting conquest.

The vast majority of Romano-British interactions at this time were mercantile. Goods and ideas flowed between the Roman Continent and southern England, with Colchester being a centre of exchange. Iron Age Britons were importing items from the Roman world such as the drinking and feasting equipment at Lexden, probably

LISTEN TO THE
PODCAST

Colchester: Britain's First Town

with more organic items like clothing that have not survived archaeologically. Woollen goods and hunting dogs headed the other way and were highly sought after on the Continent. England also became an important source of slaves; Britons fought Britons regularly, and enslavement was common for the defeated. With Romans being willing buyers for these captives, slave trading was big business in late Iron Age England.

THE CLAUDIAN INVASION

By 43 CE, the Roman Empire stretched from Brittany to the Levant. Over the previous few centuries, this empire had dramatically expanded from its Mediterranean heartlands. The newly ascended Emperor Claudius now sought his own military conquest. Further expanding the borders of Rome – a military triumph – was the perfect way for him to consolidate his power. Britain was the ideal target, and an army was sent across the English Channel. The force consisted of four Roman legions, around 20,000 men, commanded by one of Claudius' top generals Aulus Plautius.

Richborough Castle

Although there is still some debate as to where Plautius' army landed, it's quite likely it came ashore in east Kent. Richborough Castle is dominated by massive walls dating to later centuries, but within the walled enclosure are layers of defensive ditches and one has been dated to c.43 CE. These ditches likely belonged to one of the first (if not the first) fortifications that Plautius and his men built on British soil. Given that Richborough is situated a couple of miles from Kent's east coast today, it's difficult to envisage its strategic importance; but 2,000 years ago it was powerfully positioned on a small island at the end of a now silted waterway called the Wantsum Channel. It was a safe harbour for ships and an ideal base for Plautius and his soldiers, before they marched further inland.

After defeating an army of Britons at what was probably the River Medway, Plautius advanced to the Thames. There was no significant settlement near the mouth of the Thames at that time, just a few farmsteads spread thinly along its banks. The Romans recognised the strategic importance of a large settlement that could link the island to the Continent.

'It [London] only becomes a place where you want a city when you can cross the river and when you can unite what were previously competing territories into a single country. And that's what Rome does. Rome, by conquering Britain, makes London suddenly the middle of things rather than the edge of things.'

Dominic Perring, University College London

Plautius and his legions established a bridgehead on the river's northern bank and awaited Emperor Claudius' arrival with his own forces, which included elephants. Together, Plautius, Claudius and their armies headed northeast to Colchester, where British chiefs formally surrendered to the Emperor. The fledgling Roman province of Britannia was established.

Claudius quickly returned to the Continent, satisfied with the successful invasion. Plautius and his legions were left

LISTEN TO THE
PODCAST

The Origins of London

to expand the Roman province. The Second Legion, Legio II Augusta, commanded by the future emperor Vespasian, headed southwest. They first conquered the Isle of Wight, before marching into the West Country, passing by then largely abandoned hillforts such as Maiden Castle. The Second Legion would ultimately reach Devon, where they founded the fort of Isca Dumnoniorum – today's Exeter.

The Ninth Legion, Legio IX Hispana, marched north, founding forts at places such as Lincoln and Longthorpe. Meanwhile, the Twentieth and Fourteenth legions headed west towards Wales, ultimately defeating one of the last great resistance leaders, Caratacus, in 50 CE.

Londinium

By 60 CE, much of southern and central England was under Roman control. The heart of power lay at places such as Colchester, where the Romans had founded their first official colony, Colonia Claudia Victricensis, and erected a massive temple to the Emperor Claudius.

But another rapidly expanding settlement was better placed for connecting Britannia with the Continent: Londinium. Even though it was less than 20 years old, founded some time between 43 and 50 CE, Roman London was already becoming an important mercantile hub. The earliest surviving manuscript from London is a wooden tablet dated 8 January 57 CE, recording a deed of sale between two freedmen (freed male slaves in Roman society). Discovered as it was beneath the City of London, it's only fitting that this artefact is a financial document. London's position on the tidal River Thames also made it an important landing point for ships bringing supplies for the legions. From here, Rome was consolidating its supremacy over what we today call England.

But native disgruntlement was building into a massive revolt.

BOUDICA

The Iceni were an Iron Age tribe that lived in present-day Norfolk in East Anglia. Prasutagus, their king, had been an ally of Rome. He died 60 CE, having bequeathed half of his kingdom to the Roman emperor Nero and the other half to his two young daughters. The occupying Romans had other ideas. From their base at Colchester they stormed into Iceni territory, pillaging settlements and treating the locals as vanquished subjects. Prasutagus' two daughters were raped and his widow, Boudica, was flogged. This Iceni queen quickly rallied thousands of Britons to her side.

Her first target was Colchester. The Roman colony was home to several thousand Romans and native Britons. Walking along Colchester's high street today, the ancient Armageddon that befell this fledgling town is unseeable. However, just below the ground level there is a black, burnt soil layer that descends several layers. This 'Boudica Destruction Horizon' is the archaeological remains of a massive fire lit by Boudica and her warriors, which engulfed Colchester and razed it to the ground. No one was spared.

Within this burnt layer, archaeologists have discovered a wealth of artefacts:

- **Charred food** includes cereal grains, dates and hardtack bread the Romans called *bucellatum*.

THE STORY OF ENGLAND

- **Liquified glass** indicates that the temperature of this fire was nearly 1,000 degrees Centigrade.
- **Burnt Samian Ware pottery** was the Roman equivalent of fine china that traders, soldiers and colonists had brought to Colchester from the Continent.

Treasure at Colchester Castle Museum

Perhaps the most remarkable discovery is a set of gold and silver objects – rings, bracelets, earrings, an armilla and more. It's believed that these treasures belonged to a Roman family who buried them in the ground and never retrieved them. We know these items today as the 'Fenwick Treasure' as they were discovered under Fenwick department store on Colchester High Street. They are on display, along with many other objects from Boudica's sacking of the town, at Colchester Castle Museum.

Colchester was the first of three Roman centres that Boudica sacked. London and St Albans were next on her hit list. Similar burnt layers have been discovered under both. Boudica's rampage was halted at the Battle of Watling Street; near a Roman road heading northwest from Londinium through the Midlands, a heavily outnumbered Roman army commanded by Gaius Suetonius Paulinus routed her forces. What happened to this Iceni warrior queen we don't know for sure, but it's more than likely that she and her daughters didn't live long after this defeat.

——————— THE ROMAN RECOVERY ———————

The Boudican Revolt had ravaged the Roman province, but it quickly recovered. Colchester, London and St Albans were rebuilt with new defences and over the next century the Roman south and east of England began to prosper. In London, the new provincial capital, great public buildings were constructed in stone, including a basilica, forum and amphitheatre. At Richborough, now a flourishing Roman port town called Rupitae, a massive monumental arch was erected, commemorating the site as the start point for the Roman conquest of Britain. Towns were connected by a new network of long straight roads, such as Watling Street, Ermine Street and Fosse Way.

In the countryside, where the majority of Britain's Iron Age population still lived in small roundhouse farmsteads, the elite began to construct luxurious villas.

FISHBOURNE ROMAN PALACE

Fishbourne Roman Palace, situated just outside Chichester in West Sussex, was constructed in 75 CE. At around 130 square metres, the palace is the largest Roman residential building north of the Alps, and half of it still lies beneath the village of Fishbourne. The palace was divided into four wings, set around a square formal garden. It was incredibly Roman in its design, with little accounting for the British weather. There were luxurious mosaics, ornate topiary hedging, fruit trees, exotic animals, underfloor heating, blue decorations imported from as far away as Afghanistan. This luxurious palace was designed to impress and awe the locals.

LISTEN TO THE
PODCAST

Fishbourne Roman
Palace

'It's so Roman . . . You build this on the south coast of Britain and you are making a statement to everybody who sees it, including the local Iron Age population, that this is us now. This is what we're all about. We have access to technologies and resources that you can only dream of. The key thing was to stupefy people . . . To make an impression on them.'

Rob Symmons, Fishbourne Roman Palace

Villa estates such as Bignor, Chedworth and Lullington began appearing across southern England. But further north, things were still volatile.

THE NORTHERN FRONTIER

By the early 2nd century, Roman Britannia stretched as far as Cumbria and Northumberland in northern England. Roman forts slightly further south at places such as York (Eboracum) and Chester (Deva), only founded a few decades earlier, were slowly evolving into civilian settlements. But the Romans had not conquered what is now Scotland. In 122 CE, when the Roman Emperor Hadrian visited York during his travels across the Empire, northern Britain was 'barbaricum' – the land of the barbarians. Hadrian didn't stay in Britain long, but his legacy has endured through the construction of a huge stone barrier.

Hadrian's Wall

Stretching from the Tyne Estuary to the Solway Firth, Hadrian's Wall is one of the most visited ancient sites in England. Only parts of it survive today, but in its prime it stretched from coast to coast – 80 Roman miles (roughly 72 modern miles). The wall itself evolved significantly over nearly three centuries of Roman control. Originally, only part of it was built of stone, which was locally quarried. West of the River Irthing, the original wall was made of timber and turf. It was only later that this section of Hadrian's Wall was rebuilt in stone.

Along with the wall additional fortifications were built up:

- About 160 small and regular turrets, each about two metres wide and four metres high.
- 80 fortlets known as milecastles, built every Roman mile.
- 17 forts along the length of the wall, with the greatest surviving examples being Housesteads, Chesters and Birdoswald.

Layers of defences were laid out in front of the wall, including a ditch, a rampart and wooden obstacles that worked like ancient barbed wire. Behind the wall, too, there was another earthwork that archaeologists call the Vallum, which perhaps indicated the beginning of this militarised zone for anyone approaching the wall.

By the 2nd century, physical frontiers were nothing new to the Romans. But Hadrian's Wall was the first time they had made such a long fortified frontier. A formidable, physical barrier to deter any raiding 'barbarians' descending from the north, guarded by thousands of auxiliary (non-Roman citizen) soldiers and artillery pieces. But, just like previous great building projects such as Maiden Castle and Fishbourne, this was also a massive statement. Hadrian's Wall was a projection of Roman power.

Archaeologists have been able to deduce a lot about Roman life on Hadrian's Wall due to the wealth of objects and architectural remains that have survived. At the fort of Housesteads, dramatically positioned on top of a remote Northumberland slope overlooking sparsely wooded hills in all directions, the outlines of several buildings have survived, including barrack blocks, the commander's house, a building that is believed to have been a hospital and the greatest surviving Roman latrines in Britain. Housesteads is the best-preserved Roman fort in Britain.

A plethora of inscriptions also survive, revealing details about the soldiers who manned the wall and from where in the Roman Empire they originated. One unit that served on Hadrian's Wall came from as far away as Syria. Others came from places such as Bulgaria, Spain, Germany and the Balkans.

It's not just the soldiers we hear about from these inscriptions. Women, children and slaves also lived in and around the Roman forts, along with a large number of traders, craftsmen and other specialists who helped ensure the smooth day-to-day running of these front-line bases.

Vindolanda

At the fort of Vindolanda, just south of Hadrian's Wall, archaeologists have unearthed some of Roman Britain's greatest treasures. The complex was rebuilt nine times, with each community leaving a distinctive mark. More than 5,000 shoes have been excavated, while the world's oldest surviving boxing gloves are on display. Then there are Vindolanda's famous namesake tablets: letters containing personal messages, written by the fort's occupants in the 1st and 2nd centuries CE. They provide unique insights into the daily workings of frontier life, including some unusual requests for supplies.

LISTEN TO THE
PODCAST

Vindolanda

'I think what's most significant about the writing tablets is that it's everyday stuff. It's not kings and queens. It's about socks and underpants ... through to things like a birthday party invitation. These types of things, these real personal sorts of information. Things about festivals they're going to have, what kind of food they're getting in. Everyday things about real people.'

Barbara Birley, Vindolanda Trust

Naturally, during its three centuries of service, Hadrian's Wall experienced significant evolution. One of the biggest changes occurred in the early 3rd century.

SEVERUS IN BRITAIN

In 208 CE, the largest armada that had ever set out for Roman Britain crossed the Channel – roughly 50,000 soldiers and 7,000 naval troops. At its head was the warrior Emperor Septimius Severus. Born in North Africa, Severus had risen to power in 193 CE, during the so-called 'Year of 5 Emperors'. Over the next few years, he had consolidated his control, removing rival Imperial contenders and laying the foundations for his own Severan Dynasty. Years of military campaigning followed and in 208 CE Severus turned his gaze to Britain, with a focus on the far north.

Militarily, much of Severus' campaigning in Britain would occur in present-day Scotland. But his extended stay in Britain also left a massive footprint over the whole province of Britannia. In London, the 2.5-mile Roman wall that surrounded the town was built on Severus' orders.

By the early 3rd century, Eboracum, modern-day York, had transformed into a thriving settlement by the River Ouse. For Severus, seeking somewhere to base his forces, it was the perfect location.

> 'He doesn't just turn it (York) into his campaign headquarters. He brings senior members of the Senate. He brings his Imperial fiscus treasury. And he brings Julia Domna (his wife), Caracalla and Geta (his two sons). So he creates the capital city of the Roman Empire for this brief three-year period in York.'
>
> **Simon Elliott, historian**

Hadrian's Wall too was transformed as Severus marched his legions north. At Vindolanda, the recent discovery of round-houses dating to the time of Severus suggests that this fort might have housed Britons during this period – possibly captives or refugees from his campaigns. Meanwhile much further east, at the mouth of the River Tyne, Severus transformed the Roman fort of South Shields into one of his key supply bases through the building of 20 extra granaries.

LISTEN TO THE
PODCAST

Septimius Severus

Severus' campaigns north of Hadrian's Wall proved incredibly bloody, but ultimately he failed to conquer the north of Britain. By early 211 he was consigned to his bed in York, riddled with gout. He died there in February that year. His supposed last words to his two sons were, 'Look after yourselves. Pay the soldiers. Ignore everyone else.'

Severus was the first Roman emperor to die in England. He would not be the last. For three years, Roman York was elevated from a minor Roman city to the temporary capital of Severus' Empire. But with his death, York's prominence decreased. His two sons quickly abandoned any further campaigns in northern Britain and hurried back to Rome, taking the Imperial infrastructure with them. Eboracum faded back into the shadows and Londinium once again became the heart of Britannia. Southern England, which had enjoyed relative peace for more than 100 years, continued to boom with luxurious house building.

More villas were constructed in the countryside, built by elite Romans wanting to display their wealth and high status. At Bignor Roman Villa in West Sussex, the rooms are covered in colourful mosaics, depicting various mythological figures such as Venus, goddess of love, winged 'Cupid' gladiators and the gorgon Medusa. Many of these villas contained Roman underfloor heating systems, known as hypocausts. Slaves worked a nearby furnace pit that fed hot air through channels and into an open space, heating the room floor above. Today, you can usually spot hypocausts in villas from their pilae stacks – columns of tiles, around which the hot air flowed. Villas also had private bath complexes, where the owners and their guests could wash and relax.

Bathing wasn't just for the Roman upper class. Public bathing complexes could be found in almost every Roman centre in Britannia, including military outposts along Hadrian's Wall.

Aquae Sulis: *The Roman Bath*

Named after the Roman bath complex, the city of Bath contains one of England's most visited Roman sites. The complex was constructed around 70 CE, and originally contained three separate baths adorned with elaborate decorations. The main bath you can visit today is 1.6 metres deep and holds over a million litres of water reaching a temperature of around 45 Celsius. This bath is surrounded by Roman square pillars. The round pillars, open roof and statues looking down from above are all later Georgian additions.

> 'There are lots of hot springs in Europe. This is the only one, of course, in Britain . . . And of course where they do occur, that hot water, it's not just hot and free. It's also something for which the Romans didn't really have a proper natural explanation.
>
> 'You know, why does hot water come out of the ground? Why should it? And well, their answer was that they weren't quite sure. So therefore, it must be the work of the gods.'
>
> **Stephen Clews, The Roman Baths**

Believing the hot spring site was the work of the gods, the Romans built a temple next to it, where they worshipped a hybrid deity called Sulis Minerva. Sulis was an Iron Age deity, so this indicates that the hot spring was already sacred to Iron Age Britons. Minerva was a Roman goddess of wisdom, justice and victory. The head of Sulis Minerva's cult statue can still be seen today – a face made of gilt bronze that in Roman times was the holiest object at Bath. Fittingly, the Romans called this site Aquae Sulis – 'the waters of Sulis'.

Visitors to the hot spring viewed it as sacred. Some threw objects into it, hoping that Sulis Minerva would answer their needs. More than 100 curse tablets have been discovered in the spring, left by visitors seeking the goddess's help to right a wrong. With no lockers, theft was common at the Roman Baths. Many curse tablets were written by bathers asking Sulis Minerva to punish the unknown thief who had stolen items of their clothing while they were in the baths.

Sulis Minerva exemplifies how the Romans weren't afraid to embrace other deities and align them with their own pantheon of gods and goddesses. Atop Maiden Castle, for instance, are the remains of a late Roman temple believed to have been dedicated to another Romano-British god, their name unknown.

THE MITHRAEUM

Beneath Bloomberg's London headquarters and not far from the Bank of England are the remains of a narrow stone temple. Underground, probably with no natural light source, this space would have been lined with candles. In the 3rd and 4th centuries men would have gathered here to worship as part of a secretive cult that had slowly made its way to Britain from the eastern fringes of the Roman Empire, which centred on the god Mithras. Initiates of this cult were sworn to secrecy; we know little about the worship of Mithras today. Rediscovered after World War Two, the well-preserved London Mithraeum has been transformed into a unique and free visitor attraction.

──────── LATER ROMAN BRITAIN ────────

In the latter half of the 3rd century CE, the Roman Empire experienced a series of catastrophes. Civil war raged as dozens of generals vied for the Imperial throne at the point of a spear – the so-called 'barracks emperors'. There were devastating plagues and raids on Roman territory from external enemies: Picts, Saxons and Franks keen to take advantage of this '3rd-Century Crisis'. It wasn't a great century to be a Roman, with turmoil affecting every part of the Empire, including Britain.

For wannabe emperors, Britain was a powerful base. It was home to three Roman legions, around 15,000 men, with thousands more auxiliaries. During the latter half of the 3rd and early 4th centuries, Roman Britain saw multiple Roman usurpers:

1. **Postumus**, founder of his breakaway 'Gallic Empire'.
2. **Carausius**, who ruled in Britain between 286 and 293 before he was assassinated by another usurper called Allectus.
3. **Allectus** was in turn defeated by a Roman general called Constantius Chlorus, who brought Britain back into the Imperial fold.

A medallion on display at the Museum of London depicts the victorious Constantius Chlorus riding into the walled city of London. It's the first ever pictorial depiction of London in history.

Constantius Chlorus' Britannia story did not end there. A couple of decades later, in 306 CE, he died in York after campaigning north of Hadrian's Wall, following in the footsteps of

Septimius Severus almost a century earlier. By that time Constantius had also risen to become one of two senior Emperors in the Roman Empire – part of a new division of power aimed at ending the 3rd-century crisis called the Tetrarchy. Following his death, Constantius' soldiers proclaimed his popular son to be the new Emperor – Constantine – and a later statue of him can be seen outside York Minster today.

Constantine quickly left Britannia with his legions. His life is fascinating, albeit incredibly brutal; he fought his way up to ultimately become sole Roman Emperor. He became the first Roman Emperor to convert to Christianity in 312 CE. In the 4th century Christianity was not yet widespread in Britannia, but there is evidence of conversion. At the rich household of Lullingstone Roman Villa in Kent, archaeologists have unearthed a beautiful wall painting of the chi-rho, a Christian symbol.

THE END OF ROMAN BRITAIN

By the 5th century, Richborough was no longer a thriving port town with Domitian's massive marble arch dominating the skyline. Instead, it had transformed back into a military establishment.

Standing almost ten metres tall, Richborough's stone walls surround three sides of the fort. Some 1,700 years ago, they would have been even taller and encircled the central area. Locally quarried sandstone and limestone were the prime materials for making this 3-metre-thick wall. A close inspection finds several horizontal red ceramic bands running the length of the barrier. The Romans employed this masonry technique when building walls across the Empire. These bands helped to bind the structure together, making it more sturdy against earthquakes. Similar masonry is displayed in the Roman walls of London and Colchester.

The core of Richborough's wall was made from local flint, alongside some interesting Roman recycling. The impressive arch had been torn down and its materials and decorations reused in the building of the wall, as too presumably were the stone materials of other buildings in and around Richborough that were no longer in use. At the northern gateway (a heavily fortified entrance called a postern gate) are the remains of a lion statue stuffed into the wall.

Richborough may have transformed from thriving port town to military base in order to deter Germanic sea raiders, Frankish and Saxon warbands who were looting the wealthy coastal lands of southern and eastern Britannia at that time. But Richborough's walls might also have been erected by a usurper, maybe Carausius, determined to protect his rule from potential invading Roman armies.

Richborough was one of roughly ten Roman defensive coastal forts, commonly called 'Saxon Shore Forts', that we know of in England. The others, going from west to northeast, are Portchester, Pevensey, Lympne, Dover, Reculver, Bradwell, Walton Castle, Burgh Castle, Caister-on-Sea and Brancaster.

Despite its military revamping, Richborough remained a gateway into Britannia during its later years. But gradually the administration of Roman Britannia began to break down. The province was drained of military manpower, which reached its conclusion in 407 CE when Constantine III, another usurper, took a Roman army from Britain to the Continent in his bid for power. How many soldiers remained in Britannia after Constantine is unclear, but it's likely that some remained in the north, around Hadrian's Wall.

Some of our best surviving archaeological evidence for this very late period are coin hoards, including a massive hoard of coins that was discovered at Richborough. Some of these depicted early-5th-century Roman Emperors such as Honorius and Arcadius, confirming their very late date. These coins appear to be some of the last that Rome officially delivered to Britannia. Richborough was likely one of the last beacons of official Roman administration in Britain.

Within a few years it was all over. The Roman administration of Britannia was at its end. 'Look to your own defences' was the response (paraphrased here) Emperor Honorius sent to the Britons in 410 CE, when they appealed to him for help. In fairness to Honorius, with a Visigothic invasion of Italy under way and Huns closing in, his flailing Western Roman Empire was already stretched beyond breaking point. Roman Britain had ended and the Britons were forced to live without Roman support.

On Hadrian's Wall, forts like Vindolanda and Birdoswald slowly transformed into strongholds for local communities in the Northumbrian and Cumbrian landscapes. Further south, Roman London was completely abandoned, becoming a ghost town for centuries before it was finally repopulated in the 9th century. Outside the urban centres, what were once impressive forts and villas fell into disrepair. Roman customs and practices faded away. So the Roman impact on Britain faded; but its legacy endured.

'If you go to any town or city in England, you can look at the Classical columns being used. Look at the bourgeois arches being used in building techniques. If you go to any area where there's been a Roman settlement, you'll find reused Roman stone locally everywhere. If you go to most of the churches, especially in the southeast of Britain . . . they're almost always near sites of Roman villas and often have reused stone around them. You can look at place names; you can look at the Roman road network, which became the A road network of pre-modern Britain. You can look at nearly every town and city in Britain which was originally Roman in some way, shape or form . . . So the Romans are all around us.'

Simon Elliott, historian

The tomb of Queen Eleanor, wife of Edward I

PART TWO

MEDIEVAL ENGLAND

The decorated Anglo-Saxon helmet excavated at Sutton Hoo

Chapter 4

Angles, Saxons and Jutes

The Roman withdrawal left a power vacuum in England and Germanic tribes were drawn to cross the sea. The arrival of peoples known as Angles, Saxons and Jutes changed the face of England and forged the Anglo-Saxon period. Their homelands in northern Germany had not converted to Christianity, and written sources are scarce, both of which obscure how they arrived and became integrated into English society. But archaeological evidence demonstrates that this was far from being the 'Dark Age' that it has been contentiously labelled.

SUTTON HOO

In 1937 landowner Edith Pretty commissioned self-taught archaeologist Basil Brown to excavate a number of ancient-looking burial mounds on her property at Sutton Hoo in Suffolk. Little of value was found in the initial digging, but excavations of what became known as Mound 1 in 1939 led to one of the most spectacular archaeological discoveries of all time. A 27-metre longship contained the burial chamber and grave goods of a 7th-century noble, possibly

THE STORY OF ENGLAND

Raedwald of East Anglia, although this is uncertain. Various gold pieces and remnants of an ornate helmet and sword displayed the intricacies of early medieval metalwork, and hinted at trade connections to the Byzantine Empire and even as far as Sri Lanka. The Sutton Hoo discoveries are now the centrepiece of Room 41 at the British Museum.

There is debate about whether immigrants to England in the 5th and 6th centuries were primarily violent invaders or settling traders. Similar questions are asked of the Scandinavian Vikings, who arrived in later centuries. The traditional understanding of the Anglo-Saxon arrivals was that the Britons were violently driven from their lands into the west and across the sea to Brittany. An alternative premise suggests a degree of coexistence that afforded higher status to the Anglo-Saxon newcomers.

After the Romans left Britain, the remaining people appear to have largely reverted to small tribal groups. They fought among themselves as frequently as against the Anglo-Saxons, who began to build small kingdoms based on their military domination. The 6th-century historian Gildas wrote that the Britons defeated the Anglo-Saxons at the Battle of Mount Badon around 500 CE, temporarily stemming their expansion. In 577, the Anglo-Saxon ruler of Wessex, Ceawlin, reportedly led a campaign west that culminated in the Battle of Dyrham in Gloucestershire. Although Ceawlin was eventually forced to withdraw by disunity among his own men, this moment is often viewed as the final severing of the link between the Britons of Wales and those in the southwest of England.

THE HEPTARCHY

Power shifted among the numerous petty kingdoms as they vied for local power. The 12th-century writer Henry of Huntingdon highlighted the Heptarchy, the kingdoms that dominated England in the centuries after the arrival of the Anglo-Saxons. As the name suggests, he identified seven primary realms.

The Anglo-Saxon Heptarchy

Strongest Kingdoms	Less Influential
Northumbria	Essex
Mercia	Kent
Wessex	Sussex
East Anglia	

Despite the adoption of a Heptarchy, there were frequently many more kingdoms in England. For example, Northumbria was made up of two smaller realms, Bernicia and Deira. Power moved between these kingdoms as they vied for dominance. In the late 6th century Kent enjoyed short-lived superiority, followed by East Anglia. During the next century Northumbria rose in power, then entered a period of rivalry with Mercia, the central kingdom, who in turn became dominant until the rise of Wessex in the south.

When Bernicia and Deira were unified as Northumbria under King Edwin in the early 7th century, Bamburgh on the northeast coast served as its capital. Perched on an outcrop of solid volcanic rock, it was in a strong defensive position. An Iron Age hillfort had existed on the site for centuries, and Bamburgh was probably considered the capital of Bernicia at the time of the unification of Northumbria.

KINGDOMS OF THE
ANGLO-SAXON
HEPTARCHY

ENGLISH MILES

0 10 20   40   60   80

STRATHCLYDE

NORTHUMBRIA

NORTH
WALES

MERCIA

EAST-
ANGLIA

ESSEX

KENT

WESSEX

SUSSEX

Bamburgh's name is derived from the fact that it was previously gifted by King Æthelfrith to his wife Bebba. A burgh was an Anglo-Saxon fortified town, often surrounded by a wooden palisade that could protect the local population when attacked. Bebba's Burgh became Bebbanburgh, the root of the current name, Bamburgh.

The site of Bebba's Burgh is now occupied by Bamburgh Castle. In an area of sand dunes just to the south of the castle, a collection of graves were uncovered in what is known as the Bowl Hole. The space was used as a graveyard by the Anglo-Saxon burgh. Some female skeletons had notches worn in their teeth believed to be a result of holding thread in their mouth as part of the weaving process. Only one, a younger male, showed any signs of a violent death. The remains also showed that Bamburgh was engaged in trade with Continental Europe and that the links were strong enough for those from outside England to be buried in the graveyard.

THE RISE OF CHRISTIANITY

Christianity began returning to England in the late 6th century after Æthelberht, King of Kent, married a Christian princess, Bertha, from Frankia. Pope Gregory the Great sent Augustine, a Benedictine monk who later became a saint, to England in 596 to try to convert the island. King Æthelberht permitted Augustine to set up a base in his capital city of Canterbury. Within a few years, the king had converted. His daughter Æthelburg married King Edwin of Northumbria and took a Christian priest, Paulinus, with her. Paulinus became the first Bishop of York, though there were frequent pagan backlashes across the island, and when Edwin died his widow and Paulinus were driven back to Kent.

THE OLDEST CHURCH IN ENGLAND

St Martin's Church in Canterbury is the oldest church in England still in use. Parts of it were built during the Roman occupation, but in the late 6th century it became the private chapel of Queen Bertha. Augustine created his mission here in 597 and expanded it to its current size, before founding a nearby abbey and Canterbury Cathedral. Augustine was the first Archbishop of Canterbury and later recognised as a saint.

In 634 Oswald had become King of Northumbria. He had converted to a Celtic form of Christianity while in exile in northwest Scotland. Oswald asked the monks of the island of Iona for help spreading Christianity to his realm. The first candidate sent from Iona was a failure but was followed by Aidan, who proved highly effective. Oswald made Aidan the first bishop of Lindisfarne, also known as Holy Island. Lindisfarne is visible from Bamburgh and the two seats of power worked closely together.

Oswald was killed fighting Penda, the pagan king of Mercia, in 642. Bishop Aidan lived until 651. Their legacy was the Christianisation of the north of England. However, there were conflicts of doctrine between the Celtic Christianity of the north and the Roman Christianity of the south, such as the date of Easter being calculated differently. In 664 the two sides met at the Synod of Whitby, held at a monastery under the control of Hilda of Whitby in what is now Whitby Abbey. Eventually, King Oswiu of Northumbria accepted the Roman method of calculating the date of Easter, along with other Roman customs, formally ending the presence of Celtic Christianity in England.

THE VIKINGS

In the late 8th century, England entered a period of terror. The Vikings of Scandinavia began marauding down the coast. Although it was probably not the first encounter with these pagan raiders, the earliest dated attack came at Lindisfarne, the seat of Northumbria's religious life. Wessex may have encountered this new threat first in 789, when three ships reportedly landed and killed the king's reeve. But on 8 June 793, a raid on Holy Island sent shockwaves throughout Europe.

The Anglo-Saxon Chronicle, a great record of Anglo-Saxon England, kept by monks in various regions, recorded ominous signs:

'Dire forewarnings were come over the land of the Northumbrians, and miserably frightened the folk: there were excessive whirlwinds, and lightning, and fiery dragons were seen flying in the air.'

On 8 June, the dragons that emerged from the North Sea mist were at the head of Viking longships. The raiders found Lindisfarne packed with gold and treasure, and met little resistance. They stole all they could, killed many of the monks, and took the rest into slavery.

'Early medieval Northumbria wasn't a peaceful place. There's plenty of conflict going on. But the idea of attacking and sacking a monastery was something qualitatively different to the other kinds of battles that were endemic in this period.'

David Petts, Durham University

The news was heard at the court of the Frankish king Charlemagne. A Northumbrian monk named Alcuin, who was a tutor to Charlemagne's children, received word that, 'The church of Saint Cuthbert is spattered with the blood of priests of God, stripped of all its furnishings, exposed to the plundering of pagans'. Learning of the wealth of undefended religious sites, the Vikings began more frequent raiding, pillaging nearby Jarrow the following year. Clerics began assuming that such suffering at the hands of pagans was God's wrath.

'Is this the outcome of the sins of those who live there? It has not happened by chance, but is the sign of some great guilt.'

Alcuin of York

Over the decades that followed, the Vikings returned each summer. A larger-scale invasion came in 844, and soon Viking warbands were overwintering in England. The Anglo-Saxon Chronicle records the arrival in 865 of the Great Heathen Army, which spent several years in England attacking East Anglia, Northumbria and Mercia, before eventually being halted in Wessex. In 869, King Edmund of East Anglia was killed by Vikings. Whether he died in battle or was later martyred for refusing to denounce his Christian faith is unclear. His body was later moved to Beodricesworth, which

LISTEN TO THE
PODCAST

The Viking Raid
on Lindisfarne

became known as Bury St Edmunds in recognition of its saintly resident. Over the 9th century, Vikings also began to settle in England, establishing trading outposts and becoming integrated into local communities. Camps used by the Great Heathen Army have been discovered at Repton in Nottinghamshire and Thetford in East Anglia. Archaeologists have been able to reconstruct the movements of the Great Heathen Army by identifying traces of their encampments.

ALFRED THE GREAT

By the 870s, Viking forces had subjugated much of England. The final Anglo-Saxon kingdom that defied them was Wessex in the southwest. In 868, it provided support to Mercia when it came under a Viking attack led by Ivar the Boneless, and Wessex was soon threatened. Nine battles were recorded during the following year, although the forces of Wessex, under King Æthelred, retained control. When Æthelred died in April 871 he was succeeded by his brother, Alfred.

Over the years that followed, the Vikings made repeated incursions into Wessex but failed to defeat Alfred. In January 878, they launched a surprise assault on Chippenham, where Alfred had been celebrating Christmas. Many were killed, though Alfred managed to escape, retreating to a fort on the island of Athelney in the Somerset marshland. Here, Alfred is reputed to have been so preoccupied with the problems of his realm that he allowed cakes to burn that he had been asked to watch by a woman who had given him shelter. Regrettably, this story is almost certainly a work of fiction.

In May 878, Alfred ordered a muster of all his forces at Egbert's Stone, the supposed location of which is now marked by King

Alfred's Tower at Stourhead in Wiltshire. He met the Viking army at the Battle of Edington that month and won a decisive victory. Alfred then negotiated the Treaty of Wedmore with Guthrum the Old, the leader of the Danish Vikings. Guthrum agreed both to leave Wessex and to convert to Christianity.

At some point before Guthrum's death in 890 a further agreement was made, known as the Treaty of Alfred and Guthrum. This would divide England into two. In the south and west, the land would come under the control of Wessex and western Mercia. To the north and east, Guthrum would hold sway in what later became known as the Danelaw.

> 'Alfred's big job in his reign and certainly one of the reasons why you might consider him "great" is that he finds new ways of dealing with Vikings that don't simply involve having a battle or paying them off. And in doing that, he sets some of the stage for what becomes England.'
>
> **Justin Pollard, historian, television producer and writer**

Alfred started reshaping Anglo-Saxon military defences and tactics to prevent further Viking victories. He established 33 fortified sites across his lands, each within about 20 miles of another so a military response could be made to a threat anywhere within a day. Alfred also sought to improve Wessex's naval capabilities to protect the coastline. Alongside his military activities, he took a great interest in legal reforms, culture and art.

LISTEN TO THE
PODCAST

Alfred the Great

The capital city of Wessex, Winchester, therefore became an important seat of power as the influence of Wessex grew. Alfred reoccupied London, styling himself afterwards King of the Anglo-Saxons in recognition of the importance of that city and his position in it. Winchester retained a critical role for centuries more. King Alfred was buried there in 899, and the city remained the home of the royal treasury for centuries after his death.

THE BONE CHESTS OF WINCHESTER CATHEDRAL

The high altar area of Winchester Cathedral contains six mortuary chests within which are the partial skeletons of at least 23 important people from this period. It appears the bones in these chests were first mixed up in the 12th century, after the demolition of the old minster, while further confusion came after Roundhead forces ransacked the cathedral during the English Civil War. The oldest name mentioned is Cynegils, the first Christian King of Wessex, who died in 641. The bones of Alfred the Great's father Æthelwulf, Danish King Cnut, his wife Emma of Normandy and the Norman king William Rufus are all likely to be contained within the chests.

The Danelaw and Viking Jórvík

The Treaty of Alfred and Guthrum set the border between Anglo-Saxon lands and the Danelaw. The document stated the frontier would run 'up the Thames, and then up the Lea, and along the Lea to its source, then in a straight line to Bedford, and then up the Ouse to Watling Street.' The Roman road that had seen Boudica's demise thus served as the boundary of the newly divided England.

Part of the Danelaw is also known as the Five Boroughs. These represented the most significant towns in the Kingdom of Mercia that had fallen under Danish control. They were Derby, Leicester, Lincoln, Nottingham and Stamford. Each borough was ruled as a Danish jarldom under the control of the King of York.

As early as 866, Viking forces led by Ivar the Boneless and his half-brother Halfdan Ragnarsson had captured the city of York, called Jórvík by the Danes, which would become a centre for the Viking presence in England. Although Anglo-Saxons from Northumbria briefly recaptured the city, Halfdan returned in 875 and established himself as the first King of York. The city retained strong links with Dublin in Ireland, which had been established by the Vikings and used as a base for attacks on England. Halfdan was killed in 877 attempting to assert his claim to be King of Dublin.

Guthred became the first Christian Viking King of York in 883. When he died in 895, he was buried at York Minster. In 901, York accepted an Anglo-Saxon ruler from Wessex. Æthelwold was the son of King Æthelred, Alfred's older brother. On Alfred's death, Æthelwold led a failed uprising in Wessex before moving north to York, where he was recognised as king before being killed in 903 leading another assault on Wessex.

Several Viking rulers followed, but came up against increasing pressure from the Anglo-Saxon regions beyond the Danelaw. As the Danelaw shrank, those with Viking heritage who had settled there remained. Their presence and subsequent integration with Anglo-Saxons helped foster the idea of a north–south divide in England. The Viking presence in the region that fell under the Danelaw was not ended, and communities seem to have become intermingled, and fostered a sense of difference between north and south.

'The whole speech of the Northumbrians, especially that of the men of York, grates so harshly upon the ear that it is completely unintelligible to us southerners. The reason for this is their proximity to barbaric tribes and their distance from the kings of the land.'

William of Malmesbury, 12th century

OLD NORSE NAMES

The legacy of this connection remains to this day, found most clearly in place names. In the city of York, several streets end in '-gate', which is the Old Norse word for street. Coppergate translates from Old Norse as Woodworkers' Street. Across the region, place names ending in '-by' or '-howe' use Old Norse words for a town or a farm. '-thorpe' refers to a hamlet, '-thwaite' to a clearing, and '-toft' to a homestead.

– THE CREATION OF ÆTHELSTAN'S ENGLAND –

The Danelaw came under increasing pressure from two of King Alfred's children. Edward the Elder succeeded his father in Wessex. Alfred's daughter Æthelflæd was married to Æthelred of Mercia. When Æthelred died in 911, Æthelflæd ruled in her own right as Lady of the Mercians. A Viking incursion was decisively crushed in 910 at the Battle of Tettenhall, where three Viking kings, Ingwær, Eowils and Halfdan, were killed. It ended Viking aggression for a generation.

THE ANGLO-SAXONS
AND THE DANELAW

ANGLO-SAXON STATES
THE DANELAW TERRITORIES

ENGLISH
NORTHUMBRIA

DANISH
NORTHUMBRIA

DANISH MERCIA

THE
DANELAW

ENGLISH

MERCIA

KINGDOM OF
GUTHRUM

WESSEX AND ITS
DEPENDENCIES

As Edward made assaults into East Anglia and Essex, Æthelflæd targeted the eastern parts of Mercia that were under Viking control. In 917, Derby became the first of the Five Boroughs to fall back under the Anglo-Saxons. Æthelflæd died in 918, when Edward took control of Mercia until his death in 924. By the time of their deaths, they had completed their father's work of stemming the advances of the Vikings and had laid the foundations for a fightback that would see the creation of England.

Born in 894, Æthelstan was Edward the Elder's heir. After his father remarried, young Æthelstan had been sent to live with his aunt Æthelflæd in Mercia. When Edward died, Æthelstan was quickly recognised as the new ruler of Mercia, his upbringing there making him an acceptable candidate. In Wessex, Edward's son by his second wife was recognised as king but died almost immediately. After several months of struggle with his other half-brothers, Æthelstan was recognised as King of Wessex too.

On 4 September 925, Æthelstan was crowned at Kingston-upon-Thames, a site frequently used for Anglo-Saxon coronations. Just two years later, Æthelstan would deliver a result his father, aunt and grandfather could only have dreamt of. When Sihtric, the Viking King of York, Northumbria and Dublin, died in 927, it left the Danelaw wide open. Æthelstan wasted no time in marching an army north and laying claim to the vacant thrones. On 12 July 927, all of the northern lords gathered at Eamont Bridge in Cumbria and submitted to Æthelstan's rule.

The part of the British Isles that would become known as England was under the rule of a single king for the first time. King Constantine of Alba, which covered most of what is now

Scotland, and King Owain of Strathclyde, in the west of Scotland, were also present at Eamont Bridge to acknowledge Æthelstan as their overlord. On his way south, the king gathered all of the Welsh rulers at Hereford and took their homage too. With apparent ease, Æthelstan had taken control of most of Britain.

This development raised the question of what title Æthelstan should use. Alfred had been known as King of the Anglo-Saxons, but Æthelstan now sought to rule those of Danish heritage too. 'King of the Saxons' was considered, but rejected as also too narrow. Æthelstan began to sign charters as 'Rex Anglorum' – King of the English. Rather than rule a land or part of its peoples, he sought to include everyone. The reference to the English was new and referred to the common language spoken across Æthelstan's lands. It was a corruption of the word Anglish – the language of the Angles.

Æthelstan began to hold councils, requiring his subordinates in the north and Wales to travel to his court, a situation many must have resented. Soon, coins were naming Æthelstan as *Rex Totius Britaniae* – King of all Britain. There is even a reference to him as Ruler of the Whole World of Britain! By marrying several of his sisters to Continental royalty, Æthelstan also began to craft an international presence for his new, unified realm.

In 934, Æthelstan went to war with King Constantine of Alba. The reasons for this are not clear. Constantine may have refused to attend council meetings and publicly display his subservience to Æthelstan. In the same year, Sihtric's heir, who had tried to take control of Northumbria, died, as did Ealdred of Bamburgh, another significant northern ruler. Constantine may have spotted an opportunity to extend his own authority south.

Æthelstan gathered an army, reported to include four Welsh rulers, eighteen bishops and thirteen noblemen, six of whom were Danish, and marched north. There are no detailed accounts of the campaign that followed, but it was clear who won. In July, Æthelstan was at Chester-le-Street making an offering at the tomb of St Cuthbert. By September, he was back south in Buckingham, where he issued a charter witnessed, among others, by King Constantine. In the document, Constantine is described as a *sub-regulus* – a junior king – expressly subservient to Æthelstan.

In 937, Constantine was at the heart of a wide alliance against Æthelstan. He was joined by Owain of Strathclyde, and Olaf Guthfrithson, King of Dublin. The Welsh issued calls to arms to throw off the shackles of Æthelstan's rule. Olaf sailed from Dublin in August 937 to rendezvous with his allies, but the immensely significant moment that followed is frustratingly poorly recorded. The Welsh did not arrive, something their bards lamented.

Some time in late September or early October 937, the Battle of Brunanburh was fought. The location of the battle has proved hard to pin down, but there is strong evidence that it took place on the Wirral in northwest England, near Liverpool. The name Bromborough, a suitable open space, and archaeological finds there are compelling.

The battle was apocalyptic, remembered for generations. The Annals of Ulster describe 'a huge war, lamentable and horrible', noting that thousands of Vikings fell that day.

'There lay many a soldier of the men of the north, shot over shield, taken by spears, likewise Scottish also, sated, weary of war.'

The Anglo-Saxon Chronicle

Among the lists of those killed are five kings, seven Irish earls of Olaf's army, Constantine's son, and thousands of others. Olaf sailed back to Dublin, and Constantine fled back across the northern border. On the English side, two of Æthelstan's cousins, Ælfwine and Æthelwine, were recorded among the dead.

Just two years after Brunanburh, in 939, Æthelstan died aged around 45. His body was buried at Malmesbury Abbey. The 12th-century chronicler William of Malmesbury claimed to have seen inside Æthelstan's coffin. He said the body was slim and the hair blond, flecked with gold.

The Witan

The increasing unification of the nation that would become England led to questions about how it should be governed. Among the Heptarchy, there was a long-standing tradition of rulers summoning an advisory council of senior nobles and churchmen. This group of advisers were known as a Witan. The word refers to the group of people rather than an institution, and the gathering together of this body was known as a Witenagemot.

As England emerged, the obvious choice was to use the widely known and accepted model of government. Æthelstan ordered rulers from across England, and from Wales and Scotland, to attend his council meetings, and these were the earliest instances of the Witan gathering on a national scale. Although the Witan lacked formal, constitutional powers, it advised the monarch and could drive policy, since the king relied on the support of his nobility to deliver his plans. This system allowed for the flow of

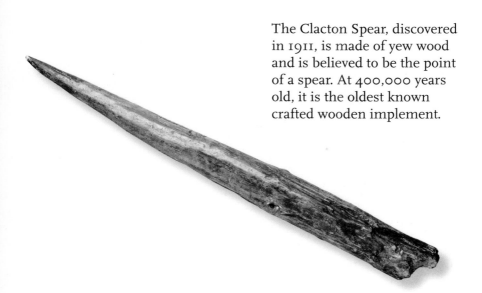

The Clacton Spear, discovered in 1911, is made of yew wood and is believed to be the point of a spear. At 400,000 years old, it is the oldest known crafted wooden implement.

Dating back to the late Bronze Age or early Iron Age, the Uffington White Horse can be found on a hilltop in rolling downland in Oxfordshire. Deep trenches filled with white chalk form the 110m-long image of a horse.

Dating back to 2400 BCE, Silbury Hill is the largest man-made mound in Europe. It is similar in height to the pyramids of Egypt, though it contains no burials. Why the mound was made remains a mystery.

Maiden Castle is one of the largest Iron Age hillforts in England and shows signs of occupation dating back over 6,000 years. It is surrounded by earthwork ramparts enclosing an area the size of fifty football pitches.

This silver medallion depicting the Roman Emperor Augustus was discovered in the grave of a chieftain buried around 15 BCE in the Lexden Tumulus, an Iron Age burial mound near Colchester.

On the 94th day of a dig in Colchester, archaeologists hit gold. They found a collection of jewellery and coins in a layer associated with Boudica's revolt in 61 CE. Perhaps they had been hidden as the uprising grew.

Bamburgh Castle was built on the site of an Anglo-Saxon burgh that once belonged to a queen named Bebba: Bebba's Burgh evolved into Bamburgh. The capital of the kingdom of Northumbria, it was a thriving trading hub.

Also known as Holy Island, Lindisfarne is within sight of Bamburgh and was the spiritual capital of Christianity when it was introduced into Northumbria. It was also here that the first major Viking raid on England was recorded in 793.

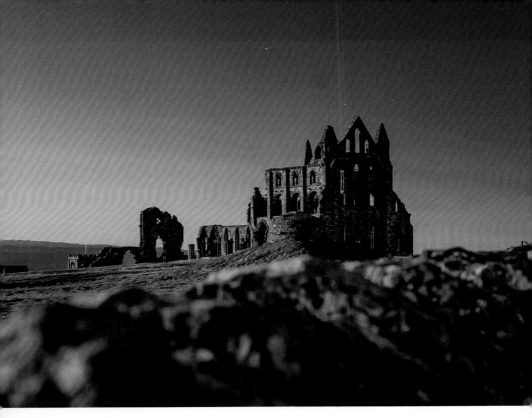

The Synod of Whitby, held in 664 in a monastery which later became Whitby bbey, was a definitive moment in English history. The ruins of the 13th-century abbey have continued to capture imaginations – Bram Stoker even had his Dracula arrive in England there.

Depicted here in the Bayeux Tapestry, Westminster Abbey was founded over 1,000 years ago. It was rebuilt by Edward the Confessor in the mid-11th century, although Edward fell ill and died just one week after it was consecrated in December 1065.

Æthelstan, a grandson of Alfred the Great, became King of the Anglo-Saxons in 924, later using the title King of the English. This image of Æthelstan from around 934 is the earliest surviving image of an English king.

When Henry II made Thomas Becket Archbishop of Canterbury, he planned to take control of the Church, but Becket blocked him. After six years in exile, Becket returned to England in 1170 only to be murdered at Canterbury Cathedral.

Salisbury Cathedral was built in the Early English Gothic style. Construction began in 1220 and was completed in 1258, during the reign of Henry III. Salisbury Cathedral holds one of the four surviving copies of Magna Carta.

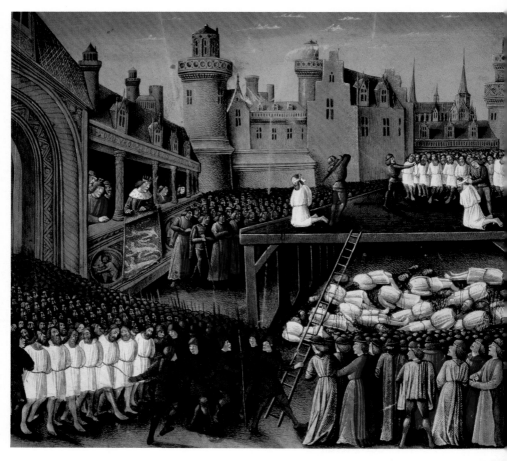

During the Third Crusade, King Richard I fought the forces of Saladin. In 1191 h ordered the ruthless massacre of 2,700 Muslim prisoners of war, depicted here.

The Tower of London was home to a royal menagerie from the early 13th century until 1835. Rulers often exchanged exotic animals as a display of their power. Henry III received three lions (or leopards), a polar bear and an elephant.

decisions down through the shires, as well as feedback to the ruler.

The Witan held a vital role in electing the next monarch. Among Anglo-Saxon ruling families, individuals were designated 'Ætheling', which meant throneworthy. It was a position that would later be denoted by the word prince. The next ruler would be drawn from the pool of the Ætheling. There was a preference for the succession of a brother or half-brother where possible, as this helped ensure that an experienced adult would take the throne. A monarch might associate a preferred heir with their rule, for example by causing them to witness documents second only to the king. This would indicate where the Witan might be expected to ensure the crown rested next, though there was room to select another Ætheling.

The Witan cultivated a conciliar, collegiate form of government. Many aspects of Anglo-Saxon England's government were common across Europe. Elective monarchy would endure for centuries in what became the Holy Roman Empire, which covered much of Central Europe. When it came, the end of Anglo-Saxon England saw the loss of the increasingly formal role of the Witan in electing a monarch. Kings would continue to summon councils of their leading nobility and churchmen. The name Witan faded into memory, but the role it had performed continued to be undertaken in other guises. Eventually, in the 13th century, these gatherings to advise and support kings would become known as parliaments.

——————— **THE DANISH KINGS** ———————

When Æthelstan died in 939, he was succeeded by his half-brother Edmund I. In 946 Edmund died, and his younger brother Eadred became king, followed in 955 by Edmund's son Eadwig. In 959 Eadwig died, and his brother Edgar became king until his death in 975, when he was succeeded by his son, Edward, known as the Martyr, who was around 13 years old. Edward was murdered three years later in 978 at Corfe Castle in Dorset. There was some suspicion that his death was arranged by his stepmother Ælfthryth in order to clear the path to the throne for her own son, Æthelred. There is no conclusive evidence that this was the case, but Æthelred did become king aged 12.

The re-emergence of a Danish threat in England dominated Æthelred's reign. After a Danish army defeated the English at the Battle of Maldon in Essex in 991, Æthelred fell back on the practice of offering Danegeld – effectively paying the Danes to leave his lands. In 1002, in response to perceived threats to his life, Æthelred ordered the murders of all Danes within his lands. Known as the St Brice's Day Massacre, it took place on the feast day of St Brice, 13 November. It remains unclear how many Danish people were killed, but murders in Oxford were described by Æthelred in a later charter as 'a most just extermination'. In 2008, during building works at St John's College, Oxford, the remains of 37 individuals were found. As they date from the right period and bear wounds suggesting they were killed by attacks from behind, they may be victims of Æthelred's attempted purge.

Some sources suggest that Gunhilde, the sister of Sweyn Forkbeard, King of Denmark, was among those killed. If true, it would help to explain Sweyn's invasion of England in 1003. He raided Wessex and East Anglia until 1005 when famine forced him to withdraw. Over the following years, Danish raids increased, and Æthelred increasingly relied on paying Danegeld to fend off the threat.

THE UNREADY

The king's response led to his epithet of Æthelred the Unready. Unready is derived from the Old English word unræd, meaning poorly advised. It was a play on the king's name; in Old English it was made up of Æthel, meaning noble, and ræd, meaning counsel. Æthelred the Unræd meant Well Advised the Poorly Advised.

'I think "ill advised" is a problematic one. In the end, his regime collapses under the weight of its own expectations, but I don't think that's any explicit fault of his. If anything, he took advice too often and too readily. And I think the conundrum that lies at the heart of his regime is precisely that he's following on from a very successful father and a very pious father.'

Levi Roach, University of Exeter

In 1013, Sweyn launched an invasion aimed not at raiding but at conquest. Sailing along the Humber, he found that the north submitted easily. As he moved south, Oxford and Winchester surrendered too. London held out under Æthelred and Thorkell the Tall, a Viking warlord who had

LISTEN TO THE
PODCAST

Æthelred the Unready

joined the English king. Sweyn moved to Bath, where the submission of the nobles caused London to give in. Æthelred spent Christmas on the Isle of Wight before joining his children in exile. Sweyn set about strengthening his grip over England, but died unexpectedly on 3 February 1014, having ruled for just five weeks.

Although the former Danelaw region recognised Sweyn's son Cnut as his successor, those further south sent word to Æthelred to return. Just two years after re-establishing his rule, on 23 April 1016 Æthelred died aged about 50, having ruled for a total of 37 years, the longest reign of any Anglo-Saxon king. Æthelred was succeeded by his son Edmund, known as Ironside, because he spent all of his brief reign in harness fighting Danish threats. In the autumn of 1016, Cnut and Edmund met and agreed to split England. Cnut would rule the portion north of the Thames, while Edmund would keep the south, to be succeeded there by Cnut. Edmund died on 30 November 1016, within weeks of the agreement, and Cnut was recognised as the new King of England.

Cnut ruled England for 29 years until his death in 1035 aged about 45. As King of Denmark from 1018 and King of Norway from 1028, he earned the epithet Cnut the Great and oversaw a large North Sea empire. He married his second wife Emma of Normandy, the widow of Æthelred, and was succeeded in turn by two sons from his first marriage: Harold I Harefoot from 1035 to 1040, and Harthacnut, who reigned from 1040 to 1042. When Harthacnut died aged around 24 without any children, Danish rule in England collapsed. The question was, who should be the new king?

—————— **EDWARD THE CONFESSOR** ——————

There is some evidence that Harthacnut sought to smooth the succession as his health failed. He invited his stepbrother, Emma of Normandy's son by Æthelred, back to England from his exile in Normandy. Edward was associated with Harthacnut's rule in ways that suggested an intention that he should become the next king.

On Harthacnut's death, Edward became king with the support of Earl Godwin of Wessex. Over the years that followed, Edward married Godwin's daughter Edith and promoted the family further, giving them earldoms that made them the most powerful faction in England. This reliance was in part the result of Edward's long period in exile, which resulted in a lack of a personal power base, and perhaps in the first Norman King of England.

In 1051, Edward used an opportunity to exile Godwin and his family after they refused to deliver justice as instructed. The following year Godwin and his oldest surviving son, Harold, returned with an army and succeeded in imposing themselves on Edward. Godwin died in 1053 and, although Harold became Earl of Wessex, Edward retrained the influence of the rest of the family as best he could. However, a series of deaths among England's earls meant that by 1057 a Godwinson controlled every earldom except Mercia.

Westminster Abbey

Evidence of Norman influence can be seen in Edward's construction of Westminster Abbey as a royal mausoleum. It was the first Norman Romanesque church in England. Edward spent more than the last decade of his life having the abbey built. It was consecrated on 28 December 1065, perhaps because of the king's failing health. It would not be finished until 1090, but Edward died on 5 January 1066, sparking a succession crisis that led to one of the most tumultuous and memorable years in English history and brought about the end of Anglo-Saxon England.

Battle Abbey, built on the site of the Battle of Hastings

Chapter 5

High Medieval England

———— THE NORMAN CONQUEST ————

The death of Edward the Confessor created another power vacuum in England. There were four candidates for the throne. Edgar Ætheling had been brought back to England by his great-uncle, Edward, as a serious contender for the throne, but in 1066 he was only about 14 years old. William, Duke of Normandy claimed that Edward had promised him the crown, though Edward would have been aware that it was not in his gift. There was a distant family link between them – Edward's mother, Emma of Normandy, was William's great-great-aunt – and Edward had spent his formative years in exile in Normandy. He was arguably England's first Norman king and had a close connection to the duchy.

Harold Godwinson was the most powerful nobleman in England and was Edward's brother-in-law. He claimed Edward wanted him to be king, a claim that was swiftly accepted by the Witan so that Harold was crowned at Westminster Abbey on the day of Edward's funeral, 6 January 1066. The fourth candidate was Harald Hardrada, King of Norway, a famed warrior who sought to bring England back under Viking control. Harald Hardrada landed first and was soundly, and probably unexpectedly, beaten by Harold Godwinson at the Battle of Stamford Bridge in Yorkshire on 25 September 1066.

Just a few days later William landed at Pevensey Bay and then moved east to Hastings, where he began constructing a wooden castle. Harold probably learned of this new threat as he sped back south to try to catch the Normans unprepared. William's scouts saw the approach of the English and Harold lost the element of surprise. The English army took up a position on top of Senlac Hill, dismounted and formed a shield wall. The Normans arrayed themselves with archers at the front, men-at-arms on foot behind and heavy cavalry at the rear.

Although Norman writers would later claim that the English had no skill whatsoever in warfare, the Battle of Hastings would last the whole day of 14 October 1066. Attacking uphill, the Normans found it impossible to break the English shield wall, and their most devastating weapon, their cavalry, was rendered useless. What happened next is unclear. Some sources say part of the Norman army decided to give up and began to trudge away. Others claim a rumour ran wild that William himself was dead, so that he had to remove his helmet and prove to his men he was still alive. In other versions, the withdrawal was a deliberate tactic.

Whatever the truth, the sight of Normans leaving the field caused the English to finally leave the safety of the hill and their shield wall and give chase. The Normans then turned and fought, bringing their cavalry to bear. The story that Harold was hit in the eye by an arrow sprang up later, and took hold. One near-contemporary source claims William gathered a group of his mounted knights and targeted Harold, mowing him down and hacking him to death. With the king dead, the English had nothing left to fight for.

BATTLE ABBEY

The bishops of Normandy ordered the invaders to do penance for the carnage at Hastings and their later conquest of England. William built Battle Abbey at the site as a way to atone for his sins, but also as a token of his victory. The high altar was placed at the spot where King Harold supposedly fell. Benedictine monks would reside at the abbey, which was dedicated to St Martin of Tours, for more than 500 years, and enjoyed special privileges granted by William. It was largely destroyed during the dissolution of the monasteries in 1538, and, while an impressive gatehouse remains, most of its buildings are in ruin. It is one of the sites to visit on the 31-mile 1066 Country Walk, which largely runs through the High Weald Area of Outstanding Natural Beauty.

Sibling Rivalry

The Witan tried to resist William's claim to the throne, electing Edgar Ætheling as the new king, but William proved impossible to ignore. He was crowned at Westminster Abbey on Christmas Day 1066. It was not an auspicious start to Norman kingship. When the English and Normans in attendance competed to shout their approval of

LISTEN TO THE
PODCAST

Medieval Invaders

the new king, William's guards outside thought trouble had broken out and set fire to the surrounding buildings. William had to complete his coronation in an almost empty Abbey, choking as it filled with smoke.

William ruled until his death in 1087. He left Normandy to his oldest son, Robert, and England to his second son, who became William II. His third son, Henry, got cash with which to make something of himself. This distribution of his lands and titles may have been a result of William not liking his oldest son. However, it also fits with Norman tradition, in which the oldest son received the patrimony (the father's ancestral lands – Normandy) and the second son anything added to it (England). In this case, it happened that what was added was more prestigious than the patrimony.

William II had a difficult relationship with the Church; much of his later reputation stems from clerical disapproval of him. William's relationship with Robert was just as uneasy. Barons with land on both sides of the Channel found their loyalties divided, and preferred to reunite England and Normandy. In 1088, a revolt was begun in England designed to replace William with Robert, but the duke failed to appear and William managed to defuse the situation. In 1091 William invaded Normandy, but made peace with Robert. The two agreed that, if either died without an heir, the other would inherit his lands and titles.

In 1096, Robert went east to take part in the First Crusade. To raise funds, he mortgaged Normandy to William for 10,000 marks, about a quarter of England's annual income. During Robert's absence, William acted as regent in Normandy. William died on 2 August 1100 after being shot by a stray arrow while hunting in the New Forest. Ever since, some have wondered whether it was really an accident.

William was in his early forties and unmarried. His lack of an heir should have seen Robert succeed him, but their younger brother Henry was present, and rushed to Winchester to seize the royal treasury before heading to London to be crowned King Henry I.

By the time Robert returned in September, his youngest brother was already King of England and with growing designs on Normandy, too. Henry invaded the duchy in 1105 and again in 1106. At the Battle of Tinchebray on 28 September 1106, Henry captured Robert, who would remain his brother's prisoner until his death in 1134, aged about 83.

--------------------- **THE ANARCHY** ---------------------

Henry I outlived his brother Robert by less than two years. Although Henry had a record number of recorded illegitimate children (probably around 24), he only had one legitimate daughter and one legitimate son. Henry's son and heir was known as William Adelin (Adelin was a Norman variant of the Anglo-Saxon term Ætheling); he drowned on 25 November 1120, aged 17, in the White Ship Disaster.

The royal court were travelling from Normandy to England. William and other young members of the court boarded the *White Ship*, got drunk, and tried to race the king across the Channel. The ship struck a rock before it left Barfleur harbour, and sank. The only survivor was a butcher from Rouen, whose cheap but warm clothing saved his life as those around him in expensive silks froze and drowned.

Henry's daughter, Empress Matilda, had been married to Henry V, Holy Roman Emperor, as a young girl. The king began to position Matilda as his heir, but female rule was problematic. A king's role was to lead armies into battle, but women were not permitted on the battlefield. There were more questions than answers, but Henry extracted oaths from his nobility that they would support Matilda. Henry's nephew, Robert's son William Clito (Clito was a Latin form of Ætheling), was viewed by Henry as a rival. After the death of Matilda's husband, Henry married her to Geoffrey, the son of the Count of Anjou, to try to neutralise the threat of William Clito, who promptly died aged 25 without an heir.

> 'When this marriage was arranged Matilda was 25 and Geoffrey was 13. So she's very unimpressed on a personal level. But what can she do? What are her alternatives? She can't just tell her father she's not going to get married because he's going to rescind the offer of her being heir to the throne.'
>
> **Catherine Hanley, historian and author**

When Henry I died on 1 December 1135, he was not succeeded by Empress Matilda as he had planned. Instead, Stephen, Count of Boulogne rushed across the Channel, and was crowned king on 22 December. Stephen was Henry's nephew, the son of Henry's sister Adela. His reign would be dogged by attacks on his lands and the challenge to his throne from his cousin Matilda. The peak of the conflict came in 1141. On 2 February, the Battle of Lincoln saw Stephen captured by Empress Matilda's forces, led by her half-brother Robert, Earl of Gloucester. The Empress moved towards London and was

LISTEN TO THE
PODCAST

Matilda: Empress,
Queen, Warrior

on the verge of a coronation when Stephen's wife, Queen Matilda, organised an attack on the city. Empress Matilda fled to Winchester and, when her forces were driven from there in September, Robert was captured.

By the end of the year, a prisoner exchange had been arranged and the political situation had been reset. The Crown was, if anything, strengthened by the proof that the institution could endure the captivity and absence of its current incumbent. Stephen ruled for 19 years, a period that has been remembered as The Anarchy due to the perceived lack of central control as the sides fought. England was divided between Stephen, Empress Matilda and King David of Scotland, though at no point was any part of it unruled or anarchic.

THE ANGEVIN EMPIRE

By 1153, the cause of Empress Matilda had been taken up by her oldest son, Henry. Known as FitzEmpress (son of the Empress), he was Count of Anjou, Duke of Normandy. He had also become Duke of Aquitaine by marrying Eleanor of Aquitaine following the annulment of her marriage to King Louis VII of France. Henry invaded England in 1153, and a series of stalemates ensued. When Stephen's oldest son unexpectedly died, and his other son renounced any claim to the throne, Stephen and Henry reached an agreement. The Treaty of Winchester was proclaimed at Winchester Cathedral. Stephen adopted Henry as his son and declared him heir to the throne.

Stephen died just a year later, on 25 October 1154. Henry, who was on the Continent at the time, succeeded unopposed. His accession marked the beginning of the Plantagenet dynasty, named for the sprig of broom plant – *planta genista* – that his father wore as a badge. Henry and Eleanor were a true power couple, controlling lands from Hadrian's Wall to the Pyrenees mountains. That Henry held more of France than the King of France made him and his descendants a grave concern to the French kings of the Capetian dynasty.

The Thomas Becket Affair

Henry was an incredibly capable man who became one of the most powerful rulers in Europe. He ordered the rebuilding of Dover Castle to create a fitting welcome for foreign dignitaries visiting England. From 1180 until his death in 1189, Henry oversaw the transformation of Dover into a luxurious royal residence fit to host fellow monarchs. The work would not be completed until the 1220s under Henry's grandson, Henry III, by which time Dover was the second largest castle in Britain, only outdone by Windsor. Its imposing position over the Strait of Dover meant it was used for defence throughout England's history, and it was garrisoned by the army during World War Two.

Dover's rebuilding came after a visit from Louis VII of France, who had come to pray at the shrine of Thomas Becket. The murder of the Archbishop of Canterbury on 29 December 1170 within the walls of Canterbury Cathedral had been the scandal of the age. Becket was the senior figure in Henry's government and an incredibly effective administrator. When Henry sought to gain increased control of the Church in England, he hit upon the idea of making Thomas Archbishop of Canterbury so that he could hand Henry the powers he wanted.

Once he was made archbishop, Becket refused to do as Henry instructed and was driven into exile for several years. When he returned to England, Becket caused fresh trouble, which led Henry to erupt in anger at the Christmas feast in 1170. Four knights took his rage as an instruction to kill the archbishop. They rode to Canterbury, where they confronted Becket within the cathedral. His resistance led to a struggle in which he was cut down and his brains spilled on the cathedral floor. Amid international outrage, Becket was swiftly canonised, and became the most popular saint in England for centuries to follow.

Unruly Sons

Henry travelled to Ireland to seek the Church's forgiveness by extending its authority there. During a rebellion in 1174, he visited Becket's tomb and prayed there all night, allowing the monks to beat him with birch sticks. By the time of his arrival in London afterwards, the rebellion had collapsed and the King of Scotland had been captured. God, his contemporaries concluded, had forgiven Henry and was back on his side. Later, as Henry became the most respected ruler in Europe, he would be offered, but would decline, the throne of Jerusalem.

The greatest threat Henry II faced came from his sons. His son, also Henry and born in 1155, is the only heir to be crowned in his father's lifetime in English history. This was a French tradition that was designed to remove uncertainty from the succession. Henry became known as the Young King. Richard was born in 1157, Geoffrey in 1158, and John arrived in 1166. Henry and Eleanor also had three daughters, Matilda, Eleanor and Joan, who proved much less troublesome.

Henry II and Eleanor's sons would argue among themselves relentlessly. The only thing that brought them together was opposing their father, urged on by the King of France. In 1173, Henry the Young King, Richard and Geoffrey began a rebellion with baronial support (John was too young to take part). Henry II managed to put the revolt down. His wife was implicated in the uprising, too, and would spend the rest of Henry's reign in England.

Old Sarum

Eleanor stayed primarily at Old Sarum in Wiltshire, one of her favourite homes in England. She was kept there with a good income and was frequently present at family events. Old Sarum had been a fortress from the Iron Age, and during the medieval period it became an important place for royalty. William the Conqueror had received the Domesday Book at Old Sarum, and built a motte and bailey castle on the site, to which was added a grand cathedral during the reign of Henry I. The cathedral was demolished during the 13th and 14th centuries to supply stone for Salisbury Cathedral. Today the site is still surrounded by Iron Age earthworks and the Norman walls.

Henry the Young King died in 1183 while rebelling against his father again. Geoffrey was similarly disaffected when he died in Paris in 1186. Henry II and Eleanor seem to have been close during these difficult periods. Perhaps Eleanor was not his prisoner after all but had taken the blame for the behaviour of their sons to allow Henry to forgive them quickly and defeat the games of the French. Richard continued to hound his father until, in 1189, Henry was too sick to fight any more. He was forced to meet Richard's terms and then discovered that

John had also joined in the rebellion. Within days, on 6 July 1189, Henry II died aged 56 after an incredible career.

──────────────── **THE CRUSADER KING** ────────────────

Richard became King of England following his father's death. His coronation took place at Westminster Abbey on 3 September 1189 and was followed by outbreaks of violence against Jews. Richard tried to restore order, but persecution and murders continued in London, and the following year there was a massacre of Jews who had taken refuge in Clifford's Tower in York. The growing antisemitism and Richard's desire to end the unrest was partly caused by a new crusade. Richard had sworn to take part, and immediately after his coronation he began to sell offices and property in England to raise money for the campaign.

Richard managed some successes on the Third Crusade, though his brutal execution of captives also caused long-term damage to his reputation. On his way back from the Holy Land, he was taken captive by Leopold of Austria, who claimed Richard had been responsible for the death of Conrad of Montferrat, Leopold's cousin, during the crusade. Leopold sold Richard's custody to his overlord, Holy Roman Emperor Henry VI. As Richard tried to negotiate his release, King Philip II of France encouraged the Emperor to keep his prisoner longer.

Philip was supported by Richard's scheming little brother John. He had been banished from England just before Richard left due to his plotting. John had been allowed to return, but had been causing trouble in his brother's absence. When news arrived that Richard had been captured, John began to position himself to take his brother's crown. He sought support from

Philip, who was assaulting Richard's Continental lands during his absence.

Eventually, a ransom was fixed. The demand was for 150,000 marks, more than double the English Crown's annual income. Richard's mother, Eleanor of Aquitaine, set about raising the huge sum and then took it to Germany herself to secure her son's release. Once Richard was freed, on 4 February 1194, King Philip sent a message to John warning, 'Look to yourself; the devil is loose'. But Richard quickly forgave John and focussed his energies on recovering the lands Philip had taken.

On 26 March 1199, Richard was laying siege to a castle at Châlus-Chabrol when he was struck in the shoulder by a cross-bow bolt. The wound quickly turned gangrenous, and the king died on 6 April. Despite his fame as a warrior, which earned him the epithet of the Lionheart, Richard I only spent around six months of his ten-year reign in England. He appears to have spoken no English, having been raised primarily in Aquitaine in the south of France. As well as this lack of attention and the crippling ransom for his release, Richard left England in a crisis: he had no legitimate children. There was a dispute about whether the greater right to the throne rested with Henry II's youngest son John, or a grandson by an older child, Geoffrey's son Arthur of Brittany. With the support of Eleanor of Aquitaine, John was crowned the next King of England.

BAD KING JOHN

There had been plenty of warnings about John's character, from pulling out the beards of Irish lords to his betrayal of his father and his brother. As king, John set about exceeding all expectations, but not in a good way. He alienated his barons by developing a reputation for greed, cruelty, and for sleeping with their wives and daughters. Perhaps John's greatest failing in the eyes of his nobility was his unpredictability.

When John fell out with the monks of Canterbury over the selection of a new Archbishop of Canterbury, it led to a rupture with the Pope. As John and the monks argued over their preferred candidates, the Pope appointed Stephen Langton to the post. John refused to recognise the new archbishop, and in 1207 England was placed under an interdict, which meant that all church services were ceased. In a deeply spiritual age, this was devastating to the population. For John, it meant more cash, as he pocketed funds that would otherwise have gone to the Church.

In 1212 there was an unsuccessful plot to murder John, and in 1213, as he prepared to invade France to reclaim lands that had been lost, Philip II turned the tables and tasked his son, Louis, with the invasion of England. John panicked, and on 15 May 1213 he met with a papal legate, a representative of the Pope, and effectively handed the kingdom of England over to the Pope for ever. This brought papal protection for John's crown, but also meant that England was a vassal state of the Pope, who was now its ultimate ruler.

John continued to be an unpopular and erratic ruler. Many of the barons, particularly from the north, decided something had to be done. Using tournaments as cover for their meetings, they began to draft a document that aimed to bring the king under the rule of law to ensure some certainty in his actions. In 1215, they presented it to John. The two sides met at Runnymede, a water meadow alongside the River Thames around 20 miles west of central London. Under threat of revolt,

John acquiesced to their demands and placed his seal on the document that would later become known as Magna Carta – Great Charter.

> 'What's so striking about Magna Carta is two things. First, it's the assertion of a general principle that the ruler is subject to the law, but in a way that's an old principle, there's nothing novel in that. Secondly, what's novel about Magna Carta is the sheer detail in which that principle is asserted across the whole range of royal government. So it's a detailed, granular, nitty-gritty charter trying to regulate the operations of kingship across the whole spectrum.'
>
> **David Carpenter, King's College London**

As soon as John had agreed to remedy his behaviour, he displayed his unpredictability once again. Writing to the Pope, his overlord, John secured permission to set aside Magna Carta. The barons refused to have their complaints set aside and sent word to Louis in France to come to England and be their new king. Civil war was set to erupt. By the autumn of 1216, forces loyal to Louis and the northern barons controlled most of the southeast and north of England. John tore around his realm, trying to put out the fires of rebellion. While crossing the Wash, an inlet of the North Sea, he reportedly lost part of his baggage train that included the crown and a vast amount of treasure. On 19 October, sickness overtook John, and he died at Newark Castle, aged 49. Once more, the question of who would rule England next hung heavy over the realm.

LISTEN TO THE PODCAST

Magna Carta

——— THE FRENCH KING OF ENGLAND ———

Louis was in England and had control of London, as well as the support of a large portion of the barons. He had been invited as a viable alternative to John not only because he was heir to France, but because his wife Blanche of Castile was a grand-daughter of Henry II. There was still a belief that a blood right to the throne was important – not just anyone could be King of England.

John left behind several children, the oldest, Henry, just nine years old. Although Louis had appeared to be winning the civil war, he had not taken the step of having himself crowned king, for reasons that remain unclear. In a demonstration of the power of the ceremony of coronation, those who supported Henry had the young boy crowned at Gloucester Cathedral, the most suitable location still in royalist hands, on 28 October 1216. A coronation transformed a person into a king, was laced with religious significance and could not be undone. At the same time, Magna Carta was reissued in the new king's name. The removal of John from the political scene took away the primary cause of the revolt of the barons in England. It imme-diately caused many to wonder whether they really needed, or wanted, Louis.

Louis continued to wage the war. He laid siege to Dover Castle, but the fortress resisted under the leadership of Hubert de Burgh. Even when the outer defences were breached, the castle managed to hold out. Louis made the decision to return to France to gather reinforcements, and the royalist forces seized the opportunity this presented. They travelled to Lincoln, where rebel forces were besieging the castle, a siege that was resisted under the command of Nicola de la Haye.

When the royal army, led by William Marshal, attacked, the barons and their French allies were caught between the castle and the royal army and were defeated at the Battle of Lincoln on 20 May 1217.

As Louis sailed back from France, his fleet was intercepted by royal ships and routed in the naval Battle of Sandwich on 24 August 1217. A striking element of the fight against Louis was an emerging idea that there was an English identity, distinct from the connection with the Continent that had existed since the Conquest, that was worth fighting for. Louis was forced to give up his efforts and return to France. A few years later, on 17 May 1220, Henry was re-crowned at Westminster Abbey. Magna Carta was reissued as a basis for government within the rule of law. Among these new beginnings lay the birth of an English identity.

THE PACIFIC KING

Henry III's reign would be the longest of any medieval King of England, and would only be surpassed in the early 19th century. His 56-year rule saw many changes for England. Henry himself was described by one contemporary as 'simplex', a word that might mean simple, foolish, or something more like naive and unworldly.

THE TOWER OF LONDON AND MENAGERIE

Henry III was interested in building, and much of the Tower of London as we see it today is a result of his work. At the time the Tower maintained a royal zoo, or animal menagerie, and lions had likely been kept there since King John's reign. Henry III received three 'leopards' from the Holy Roman Emperor Frederick II in 1235, although these were probably lions. A polar bear was added in 1252, and an African elephant in 1255. Edward I gave the menagerie a permanent home with the building of the 'Lion Tower' during his reign. The Tower of London menagerie continued to keep animals until 1835, when the Lion Tower was demolished.

Henry was also fascinated by Edward the Confessor and rebuilt Westminster Abbey, placing his idol at its heart. With no aptitude for war, Henry found peace with his neighbours in France, Scotland and Wales. The reissue of Magna Carta several times in his reign paved the way for the emergence of Parliament as a body that both advised the monarch and held the Crown to account, demanding reform where required. The word parliament first appears in 1236 to describe a gathering of barons and senior clergy that might once have been recognised as the Witan. The first elected members recorded attending Parliament appeared in 1254.

'The Abbey was a tremendous success for Henry III, and broadcast his kingship very widely because you've got to remember, location, location, location, it's at the centre of the realm, it's at Westminster, not tucked away in the countryside, and so everyone sees this great building going up.'

David Carpenter, King's College London

Henry had a problematic relationship with his brother-in-law Simon de Montfort, Earl of Leicester. Simon's family were from

France and had been involved in the Albigensian Crusade against heretics in the south of that country. As a younger son, he came to England to forge a career, acquiring the earldom of Leicester via his paternal grandmother. Simon drove the Jewish community from his lands, demonstrating an enduring vein of antisemitism that was not out of step with his contemporaries.

Simon became a focus for baronial opposition to Henry and, in 1264, led a revolt. At the Battle of Lewes on 14 May 1264, Henry and his oldest son, Edward, were captured by Simon, who set about ruling England in Henry's name. Having protested against the corruption and favouritism of Henry's regime, Simon soon fell into a similar trap. His Parliament in 1265 was not the first time elected representatives were summoned, but did mark a shift in the operation of Parliament. This was, for the first time, asked for its input on matters of policy. Edward managed to escape his custody and organise a fightback. At the Battle of Evesham on 4 August 1265, Simon was killed by Edward's forces and Henry was freed.

Another of the striking developments of Henry III's reign was his creation of a solution to the problems that had dogged succession in England. Before Edward left on crusade, his father changed the law of England so that the oldest son of the king would inherit the crown immediately on the death of his father. The idea of 'the king is dead, long live the king' was born, and enshrined in law.

LISTEN TO THE
PODCAST

Henry III:
The Pacific King

—————— THE CONQUEST OF WALES ——————

Henry III died on 16 November 1272, aged 65, while Edward was still on crusade. Edward was proclaimed king, as his father had planned. He did not return to England until 2 August 1274, almost two years after becoming king. Relations with his immediate neighbours soon began to unravel. By 1276, Edward had declared war on Llywelyn, whom his father had recognised as Prince of Wales. Llywelyn was the ruler of Gwynedd in North Wales and had established overlordship of the other Welsh kingdoms as well as recognition of his status by the King of England.

In July 1277, Llywelyn realised he could not fight Edward's forces and agreed to the Treaty of Aberconwy, which left him in control of only Gwynedd, though he retained the Prince of Wales title. Edward returned to Wales in 1282 and, by June 1283, Llywelyn had been killed and his brother executed. In 1284 Edward enacted the Statute of Rhuddlan, which brought Wales under English law, creating shires controlled by sheriffs.

The First English Colony

Over the years that followed, Edward ordered the construction of a series of castles encircling North Wales known as the Ring of Iron. Flint Castle, Hawarden Castle, Rhuddlan Castle, Builth Castle, Aberystwyth Castle, Denbigh Castle, Caernarfon Castle, Conwy Castle, Harlech Castle, and Beaumaris Castle enforced English rule, often importing English populations. Conwy was built as a royal residence with walls to enclose a new town, which was populated with

English families. The Welsh population was banned from being within the town walls at night.

Edward also focussed attention on Scotland. Inspired by Æthelstan and Henry II, he saw an opportunity to gain over-lordship of all of Britain. In the 1290s, a succession crisis gripped Scotland. Edward was asked to judge the titles of the rival claimants and asserted that this invitation recognised his authority over the Scottish Crown. When Edward found in John Balliol's favour, he continued to interfere until the Scots formed an alliance with the French and invaded northern England.

After this was driven back, Edward invaded Scotland in 1296. He took the Stone of Scone, on which Scottish kings were crowned, and had it taken to London and placed beneath a new coronation chair he had constructed. The chair, which is used to this day, represented the English king's control over the whole of Britain. War with Scotland would dominate much of the rest of Edward's reign. He faced uprisings led by William Wallace and then by another claimant to the Scottish throne, Robert the Bruce. Although he would later be dubbed 'The Hammer of the Scots', Edward failed to establish permanent control of Scotland. Alongside a reputation for war and conquest, he began the codification of English law in Parliament to clarify a legal system that could vary widely across regions.

THE ELEANOR CROSSES

When his wife died in 1290 in Nottinghamshire, her body was taken back to London. At each of the twelve places her body spent the night, Edward had a memorial cross constructed. Today, only three of the Eleanor Crosses remain, at Geddington, Hardingstone and Waltham. They are monuments to a complex figure's love for his wife.

Edward died in 1307, aged 68, while at war with Scotland. The question of England's relationship with its immediate neighbours remained to be settled.

Ludlow Castle, Shropshire, one of the first castles in
England to be rebuilt in stone

Chapter 6

Late Medieval England

──────────── **ROYAL FAVOURITES** ────────────

E dward II was the first heir to the throne of England to be styled Prince of Wales, as a mark of his father's conquest there. His rule is remembered as a catalogue of failures and favourites. In 1314, the loss against Scotland at the Battle of Bannockburn would prove a turning point toward the restoration of Scottish independence. Edward would indulge a string of favourites who were unpopular at his court, beginning with Piers Gaveston, who was executed by his enemies in 1312. The line concluded with Hugh Despenser the Younger, who proved so greedy and abrasive that, when Edward refused to distance himself from Hugh, matters came to a head.

Edward's wife, Isabel of France, allied with a rebel baron, Roger Mortimer, who had escaped from the Tower of London, and the two invaded England from France in the autumn of 1326. By mid-November, Edward and Hugh had been captured in Wales. While Hugh was hanged, drawn and quartered in Hereford, Edward was returned to London. At the beginning of 1327, Parliament opened at the Palace of Westminster to do something unprecedented. Edward was forced to abdicate in favour of his son, who on 25 January 1327 would become King

Edward III, aged 14. Roger Mortimer would act as regent until the king came of age.

Edward II – referred to in documents simply as Sir Edward of Caernarfon after the place of his birth – was sent to Berkeley Castle in Gloucestershire. The date usually given for Edward's death is 21 September 1327, while he was at Berkeley. The official story was that he died of natural causes. A later rumour emerged that he had been murdered by the insertion of a red-hot poker into his rectum, but there is no evidence to support this lurid story.

BERKELEY CASTLE

Sitting on the Severn Estuary northeast of Bristol, Berkeley Castle is part of the Welsh Marches, the border region between England and Wales that during the medieval period was often lawless and dangerous. It was, therefore, required to be defensible to repel raids from the Welsh. In 1470, a dispute over inheritance between Baron Berkeley and Viscount Lisle resulted in the Battle of Nibley Green, the last time two private armies fought against each other in England. The Berkeley family still own and live in the castle today. It is open to visitors and boasts an archive stretching back to the 12th century.

Not everyone was convinced Edward II was really dead. In 1330, his half-brother Edmund, Earl of Kent was executed for reportedly plotting to free him. Stories emerged on the Continent that the former king was in Italy, and even that he visited his son when Edward III was on the Continent. The reported death of Edward II at Berkeley Castle began the notion that deposed kings had to be killed. Whether he was, in fact, dead in 1327 remains a hotly debated mystery.

──────── **THE ENGLISH KING OF FRANCE** ────────

Edward III took control of his realm in 1330, aged 17, when he and some friends broke into Nottingham Castle using tunnels beneath it and seized Roger Mortimer. As he took control of his realm, Edward returned to his grandfather's war with Scotland. In 1332, at the Battle of Dupplin Moor, Scottish rebels and their English supporters defeated a Scottish army around ten times their size. Edward III's reign would be marked by the adoption of the Scottish tactic employed to great effect in 1332, which involved fighting on foot rather than on horseback, with a large number of archers integrated with the men-at-arms. Edward would take that tactic onto the Continent to devastating effect.

The Hundred Years' War began as a dispute over land on the Continent between Edward III and King Philip VI of France. In 1337 Philip confiscated Edward's lands, and Edward retaliated by laying claim to Philip's crown. Edward's mother was the daughter of Philip IV of France. Her three brothers had become king in turn, each dying without an heir. On the death of the last of these, Charles IV, in 1328, Edward was a candidate for the throne, but as King of England he was considered unacceptable. Instead the throne was offered to Philip, a nephew of Philip IV.

Edward enjoyed early success in France, most notably at the Battle of Crécy in 1346, and at the Battle of Poitiers in 1356, when King John II of France was taken captive by Edward's oldest son, also called Edward and known as the Black Prince. The focus on war across the Channel helped promote unity at home and sparked a growth in focus on chivalric ideals. Edward established the Order of the Garter, based at St George's Chapel, Windsor, as the highest order of chivalry in England. It is organised as two tournament teams of twelve, one led by the king, the other by the Prince of Wales.

There is evidence that Edward had put into action much grander plans at Windsor, his birthplace. Before the Order of the Garter was established, Edward had ordered construction of a huge round building that appears to have been intended as a home for a new Order of the Round Table made up of 300 knights. Victories in France caused Edward to alter his plans and create a tighter nucleus of loyal supporters around the Crown.

In 1360, Edward agreed the Treaty of Brétigny. In return for freeing King John II, Edward secured a huge ransom and recognition of his rights to lands in Gascony in southwest France. Edward also renounced his right to the French Crown, ending what is known as the Edwardian Phase of the Hundred Years' War.

The Black Death

Edward III's reign also coincided with the most devastating pandemic in world history. The Black Death, known by contemporaries as 'The Pestilence' and caused by the bacteria *Yersinia pestis*, originated in the Tien Shan region of China in around 1338. It spread along merchant routes to Europe, reaching the shores of England in the summer of 1348. Without an understanding of germ theory, it was believed that the plague was a punishment from God for sinning. It reportedly arrived at Weymouth, and the first major population centre affected was Bristol, but the plague spread rapidly throughout England. War with France was put on hold as the crisis grew across Europe.

> 'We can assume now that it killed somewhere between 50, possibly 60% of the population of Western Eurasia, the Middle East and North Africa. It was one of those points where at least, you know, part of humanity was actually on the verge of extinction.'
>
> **Philip Slavin, University of Stirling**

By the time infections subsided at the end of 1349, somewhere between 25% and 50% of England's population were estimated to have died. The plague would return to England with alarming regularity until the 18th century, including in 1361–2 and in 1369. Medieval medicine struggled to cope with the raging pandemic. Symptoms included large swellings at the lymph nodes, in either the neck, armpit or groin, which were called buboes. Medicine was still based on Galen's principles of the four humours – blood, bile, yellow phlegm and black phlegm – in which it was understood that illness was the result of an imbalance in these elements.

Bloodletting was an important treatment in medieval medicine, as it was believed to release excesses of humours. When it came to treating the Black Death, cutting the buboes open seemed a reasonable treatment, since it would release build-ups in the body. However, this rarely helped, and it

LISTEN TO THE
PODCAST

The Black Death

increased the chances of infection in the patient and further spread of the disease to those around them. People were rendered helpless, hopeless, and therefore terrified. On the wall of the Church of St Mary the Virgin in Ashwell, Hertfordshire is graffiti that reads '1350 Miserable, wild, distracted 1350. The dregs of the mob alone survive to witness.'

The Black Death caused fear and loss as it tore across England. As it subsided, its legacy became increasingly clear. A reduced population found they could command increased wages for their labour. The government reacted by capping wages at pre-pandemic levels. Ambition was created and fuelled by tragedy, but it was crushed by the government. A generation later, there would be a backlash that came close to a revolution in England.

GAMES IN ENGLAND

Medieval life could be hard, but it wasn't all doom and gloom. Sports and games were common in medieval England. For the elite, they often took the form of hunting, including hawking. For the common man, by the 14th century football was becoming an increasingly popular pastime. This was not football as it might be played today, but something closer to a mass brawl.

Medieval football involved the identification of a target, which might be a church, a boundary or another landmark, to act as the equivalent of a goal. Villages might also play against each other, attempting to get the ball to the centre of the other team's village. Early games on the Continent used solid balls of leather or wood; in England, that was replaced by an inflatable pig's bladder. The chances of this bursting may have led to it being encased in leather. How the ball reached its target appears to have been governed by no rules whatsoever, and violence was a part of the game.

In 1303, a student at Oxford University discovered his brother dead and blamed Irish students for killing him 'while playing the ball'. By 1314, the game was causing so much trouble that the Lord Mayor of London issued a ban due to the 'great noise in the city caused by hustling over large foot balls'. A case in 1321 explained that:

'During the game at ball as he kicked the ball, a lay friend of his, also called William, ran against him and wounded himself on a sheathed knife carried by the canon, so severely that he died within six days.'

Edward III enacted a law as part of the Hundred Years' War that every adult man in England was required to practise with a longbow. This contributed to the increasing militarisation of English society. To encourage focus on longbow practice, Edward issued a proclamation in 1363 stating:

'We ordain that you prohibit under penalty of imprisonment all and sundry from such stone, wood and iron throwing; handball, football, or hockey; coursing and cockfighting, or other such idle games'.

Although football would become increasingly codified, games of medieval football are still played in England, many around Shrovetide at the beginning of Lent. A game known as Scoring the Hales is begun each year at Alnwick Castle in Northumberland when the Duke of Northumberland drops a ball from the walls of the castle. At the other end of England, a game is played from Corfe Castle in Dorset. Other games still exist in Atherstone, Warwickshire, in Ashbourne in Derbyshire and in many other locations across England. Repeated bans have failed to completely eradicate the violent forerunner of what is today referred to as the Beautiful Game.

—————— THE PEASANTS' REVOLT ——————

Edward III died on 21 June 1377 after 50 years on the throne. His legacy lay in the crystallisation of English identity, but also in complex foreign relations and a tinderbox of social unrest at home. Edward's oldest son, the Black Prince, died a year before his father. Edward III was therefore succeeded by his grandson, the Black Prince's son, Richard II, who was just 10 years old.

In 1381, a revolt broke out in Kent and Essex in the southeast that would become known as the Peasants' Revolt. The term peasants did not refer to wealth or social status; it derived from the word rustic, and referred to anyone who lived outside a town or city. Some who became involved were wealthy members of the community.

When tax collectors arrived in Brentwood, Essex, in May to reassess the most recent poll tax, it provoked a violent reaction. Groups began to gather and then to coordinate their activities. Violence erupted, with rebels focussing their efforts on destroying documents that helped keep them under the control of landlords. On 9 June, a huge bonfire of these records was held in Rochester, and the castle was taken by the rebels. The following day, the rebels entered Canterbury in Kent, and trouble in Essex grew.

'The immediate trigger for it was the collection of the third poll tax in four years. It doesn't seem that it was a straightforward protest against the poll tax per se. Initially the poll tax was collected without too much opposition. What seemed to be the problem was the way in which various exemptions from the poll tax were implemented and an attempt to roll that back and that reassessment seems to have caused a particular anxiety and feeling like that was an unjust procedure.'

Andrew Prescott, University of Glasgow

BLACKHEATH

Then an open expanse just over six miles southeast of the centre of London, Blackheath was often used as the stage for events that involved huge crowds. Nearby Eltham Palace was a key royal residence from the 14th to the 16th centuries, and Blackheath was used for state events. In 1400, Henry IV greeted the Byzantine Emperor Manuel II at Blackheath. In 1415, Henry V was given a rapturous welcome home from his victory at Agincourt there. The heath has also provided a gathering place for rebels. It was a base for the Peasants' Revolt in 1381, and for Cade's Rebellion in 1450, both of which held London for a time. In 1497, Henry VII faced an army of Cornish tax rebels who had camped at Blackheath at the Battle of Deptford Bridge, which is sometimes known as the Battle of Blackheath.

On 12 June 1381, the Kentish force set up camp at Blackheath. They sent the Constable of Rochester Castle to see the 14-year-old King Richard II at the Tower of London to request a meeting. The king's advisers agreed to meet at Rotherhithe, halfway between Blackheath and the Tower, on 13 June. When Richard's barge was rowed along the Thames that morning, his advisers panicked as they made out more than 10,000 men waiting for them. The barge was turned round and the king taken back to the refuge of the Tower.

Furious, the rebels poured across London Bridge and were welcomed into the capital by a populace that shared many of their grievances. The Savoy Palace, the London home of Richard II's unpopular and vastly wealthy uncle John of Gaunt, was burned to the ground, but the rebels supposedly left all his riches inside, insisting they were not thieves. Another meeting with the king was arranged for 14 June at Mile End. This time, Richard spoke to the rebels. They demanded an end to serfdom, the system that kept some peasants tied to the land they worked and the person who owned it. To their surprise, Richard agreed.

After the meeting, rebels entered the Tower of London and seized the Archbishop of Canterbury and the Treasurer, two leading members of the government, and executed them. As violence continued in the city, another meeting was arranged for 15 June at Smithfield. During a scuffle, the rebel leader Wat Tyler was stabbed by the Mayor of London and killed. King Richard rode forward and managed to pacify the people, who began to disband and return home.

LISTEN TO THE
PODCAST

The Peasants' Revolt

Parliament would almost immediately undo Richard's agreement to the abolition of serfdom, angering the people and frustrating the young king. The government was quick to paint the revolt as a mindless act of violence, but it had causes stretching back to the social inequality exacerbated by the Black Death. Trouble continued around the country for months but was ultimately brought to an end. England had come close to a genuine revolution, but those with too much to lose had ensured it did not happen.

The Deposition of Richard II

Richard II became increasingly unpopular with his barons, who felt he lavished too much money and power on a small group of his favourites. In 1386, when the king was 19, a session of Parliament sat that is remembered as the Wonderful Parliament. It sought to remove Richard's favourites and establish a Commission of Government made up of fourteen barons with the power to rule the kingdom. Richard initially refused to engage with the session, until his uncle Thomas of Woodstock showed him a copy of the statute by which Edward II had been deposed.

The Battle of Radcot Bridge in Oxfordshire in December 1387 saw an army loyal to Richard crushed by his opponents, followed by another parliament in February 1388, known as Merciless Parliament. Thomas of Woodstock, along with the earls of Arundel, Warwick, Nottingham and Derby (the latter was Richard's cousin, Henry Bolingbroke) became known as the Lords Appellant for their introduction of the Appeal of Treason, which accused most of Richard's household and favourites of being traitors.

Richard tried to reassert his authority in the 1390s but was frustrated by his enemies. During this period, Richard's court developed a reputation for finery. The first English cookbook appeared. Richard himself is widely credited with inventing the cloth handkerchief, which courtiers noted the king used to wipe his nose. He commissioned the first surviving portrait of a king of England, which is today on display in Westminster Abbey, and in 1393 he commissioned a new hammerbeam roof at Westminster Hall, which was considered an architectural masterpiece and remains intact today. All of this only temporarily distracted the king from his desire to regain power.

By 1397, Richard felt able to strike back at his foes. The Earl of Warwick was arrested and imprisoned. Richard's uncle Thomas was also arrested and sent to Calais, where he died in custody amid rumours that Richard ordered his death. The earls of Nottingham and Derby accused each other of treason and were set to fight a duel when Richard sentenced them to exile instead. When John of Gaunt, Duke of Lancaster, Richard's wealthiest uncle, died in 1399, his son Henry Bolingbroke, Earl of Derby had his exile extended as the king tried to take Lancaster's lands into royal hands. When Richard visited Ireland later that year, Henry landed in England to claim his dukedom, only to find that he was being enthusiastically encouraged to replace Richard on the throne. The king's interference in questions of inheritance had made the barons of England nervous and keen to seek an alternative.

When Richard landed back in Wales, he was confronted at Flint Castle and taken into custody. One chronicler, Froissart, wrote that Richard's faithful greyhound Math left the king's side and made a fuss of Henry in a sign of what was to come. Taken back to London to appear before parliament, Richard was required to abdicate in favour of his cousin Henry, who became King Henry IV, the first Lancastrian monarch.

──────── **THE AGINCOURT CAMPAIGN** ────────

The reign of Henry IV was dogged by unrest and rebellion. Owain Glyndŵr asserted the independence of Wales. He was joined in revolt by the Percy family of the Earl of Northumberland, who felt they had not received the rewards they had been promised on Henry's accession. Further unrest came from the adherents of the Mortimer family of the Earl of March. The Earl of March at the time of Richard II's deposition was the seven-year-old Edmund Mortimer. Edmund was descended from Edward III's second son in a female line. Some believed that his claim to the throne was stronger than that of Henry IV, who was descended from the third son of Edward III in a male line. This question would remain unanswered for more than half a century but would not go away.

At the Battle of Shrewsbury in 1403, Henry IV defeated an alliance that sought to depose him and split England into three. Owain Glyndŵr would take Wales, the Percy family would become kings of the north, and the Mortimer family would rule the south of England. During the battle Henry's oldest son, 16-year-old Prince Henry, was struck in the face by an arrow. He survived, but it took several days to remove the arrow, and it left a scar that is the most likely reason all surviving portraiture of him as Henry V is in profile. Henry IV would survive these challenges but remained uneasy upon his throne until his death in 1413, aged 45.

On his accession, Henry V saw foreign war as the best way to heal, or at least distract from, the disunity at home. He almost immediately resurrected the English claim to the throne of France, which was then occupied by Charles VI, who struggled with mental illness throughout his life. By 1415

Henry had made his arrangements, and was preparing to leave for France when news of a plot reached his ears. Several men planned to assassinate Henry and his brothers and replace them with Edmund Mortimer, who was now a grown man. The leaders of the plot were arrested and executed. News of the plan had been brought to Henry by Edmund Mortimer himself.

Once he reached France, Henry was successful in taking the town of Harfleur. As he marched his army, depleted by the need to leave garrisons and by illness, towards Calais, a huge French army shadowed him. They met at the Battle of Agincourt on 25 October 1415, when a small English force relying heavily on archers defeated a much larger but poorly led French army. Agincourt mirrored the achievements of Edward III's reign at Crécy and Poitiers and the losses inflicted on France made it vulnerable to continued assault from England.

THE BABY KING

When the Duke of Burgundy was assassinated in 1419 by the heir to the French throne, Burgundy entered an alliance with England against France. Charles VI of France was forced to negotiate and agreed to the Treaty of Troyes with Henry V in May 1420. The treaty made Henry heir to the French throne and regent during Charles VI's life. Henry married Charles's daughter Catherine and the couple had a son, named Henry, in December 1421. Henry V returned to France but died on 31 August 1422, having possibly contracted dysentery. He left his son to inherit the crown at the age of just nine months.

LISTEN TO THE
PODCAST

The Battle of Agincourt

Over the decades that followed, the English effort in France continued, but faltered as money, men and leadership became increasingly sparse. In England, the minority government that ran the kingdom while Henry VI was too young allowed the emergence of factions. Henry's uncle Humphrey, Duke of Gloucester (Henry V's youngest brother), championed continuing the war in France to deliver his brother's vision. Others, led by the king's great-uncle Cardinal Henry Beaufort, Bishop of Winchester, favoured peace with France that would allow trade to flourish.

In 1429 Henry VI was crowned King of England at Westminster Abbey aged seven. Two years later, Henry was crowned King of France at Notre-Dame in Paris. He remains the only person in history to be crowned King of England in England and King of France in France. As Henry grew older, it became clear that his personality was nothing like that of his father. Henry VI was quiet, pious, and convinced that peace was the right way forward for England. Factions continued to split his court and tensions between Humphrey, Duke of Gloucester and Cardinal Beaufort intensified even as it became clearer that the king favoured the peace party of the cardinal.

Henry married in 1445. His bride was a niece of the Queen of France who brought no dowry or political advantage. Instead, as part of the arrangement, Henry agreed to hand over swathes of land in France to Charles VII, who had benefited from the emergence of Joan of Arc to be crowned king. Henry kept the deal secret in England for as long as possible but eventually had to begin the handover of land, which proved deeply unpopular. He became suspicious of his uncle Humphrey, and had him arrested in 1447 for plotting to kill him. Humphrey died in custody a few days later, on 23 February 1447, among claims that he was poisoned. Cardinal Beaufort died two months later, ending their bitter feud but moving the dispute into a new generation. Failures in France and unresolved tensions at home were a recipe for civil war.

A case can be made for 23 February 1447 being the real starting date of the Wars of the Roses.

——— THE WARS OF THE ROSES ACT ONE ———

In 1450, a popular uprising known as Cade's Rebellion held London for several days and was only ended by a battle on London Bridge that saw the crossing burned. In 1452, Henry VI's most powerful subject, Richard, Duke of York tried to impose himself on the king, citing favourites and bad counsel as the cause of the kingdom's problems. York was tricked, arrested, and forced to swear an oath at St Paul's Cathedral that he would never again raise an army against Henry. At the Battle of Castillon in France on 17 July 1453, English forces were roundly defeated in what would become the last battle of the Hundred Years' War. The resurgent French, using artillery to counter English archery, drove the invaders from all but Calais.

'The Wars of the Roses is the name that has stuck, though it wasn't coined in its final form until it appeared in Sir Walter Scott's novel, *Anne of Geierstein*, published in 1829. The name is based on the premise that the House of Lancaster was represented by a red rose and the House of York by a white one.'

Matthew Lewis, historian and podcast host

Success in France had made men rich. Defeat there made them restless. The problems with factionalism in England intensified. Henry fell ill, perhaps after hearing the news of the loss at Castillon. He became catatonic, and eventually the government rejected claims to a regency by his wife, Margaret of Anjou, and appointed York as Lord Protector. When Henry recovered on Christmas Day 1454, he swiftly dismissed York and reappointed his favourites to key posts.

When York and his allies, predominantly the Neville family of his wife, were summoned to a Great Council meeting in the Midlands in 1455, they feared facing the same fate as Humphrey, Duke of Gloucester. They raised an army and intercepted Henry at St Albans. Negotiations to avoid a fight failed and York's forces attacked the town, broke in and defeated the royal army. Henry himself was wounded by an arrow in the neck during the fighting. On returning to London, York was briefly appointed Protector again before being pushed aside once more.

Tensions simmered in the years that followed. Henry tried to bring the two sides to terms, holding a Love Day, a parade through the streets of London, to signify that peace had been secured. It fooled no one but Henry. Those who had lost family at St Albans wanted vengeance, and York still felt wrongly excluded from power. In 1459, York began to gather his forces at Ludlow in the Welsh Marches. His brother-in-law Richard Neville, the Earl of Salisbury, was faced by a royal army as he moved south but won the Battle of Blore Heath. Salisbury's son the Earl of Warwick brought part of the Calais

LISTEN TO THE
PODCAST

The Wars of the Roses

garrison with him. The Yorkists left Ludlow in October, heading for London, but heard news of a huge royal army approaching. They retreated and dug defensive positions in Ludlow.

Ludlow Castle

Ludlow Castle was one of the first castles in England to be rebuilt in stone, having been originally constructed in wood soon after the Norman Conquest. Located in the Welsh Marches, Ludlow was a powerful fortress that controlled the surrounding land. It belonged to a series of regionally significant families, and passed to Roger Mortimer in 1410 by marriage. He became a national figure after the deposition of Edward II. In 1425, with the death of the last Mortimer male heir, Ludlow passed to his nephew the Duke of York. Its significance, and wealth drawn from the wool trade, grew in the second half of the 15th century as the House of York became kings of England.

Henry's army arrived and the Yorkist lords fled from Ludlow in the night. York went to Ireland, and Salisbury and Warwick went to Calais with York's oldest son, Edward. In 1460, those in Calais invaded England, took London, and on 10 July faced Henry's army at the Battle of Northampton. The king was defeated and taken captive. It took many weeks for York to return but, when he did, he laid claim to the throne of England. York was descended in the male line from the fourth son of Edward III, whereas Henry's line was from that king's third son. However, York's mother was a Mortimer, a descendant of Edward III's second son, which reopened the question of where the best claim lay. In 1460, Parliament decided it rested with York, but declined to depose Henry VI. The Act of Accord made York and his children heirs to Henry's throne. It was a compromise that suited nobody.

——— THE WARS OF THE ROSES ACT TWO ———

Margaret of Anjou would not tolerate the disinheriting of her son. After raising an army in Scotland, she crossed into northern England. As she moved south, York took an army north, reaching Sandal Castle in Yorkshire. The two sides met at the Battle of Wakefield on 30 December 1460. York and his second son were killed. Salisbury was executed the next day, and the three heads were put on display on Micklegate Bar, one of the gates into the city of York. Continuing south, Margaret's force defeated the Earl of Warwick at the Second Battle of St Albans, while, on the Welsh border, York's heir Edward won the Battle of Mortimer's Cross to stop reinforcements from Wales joining Margaret.

The queen's army was refused entry into London, and withdrew. When Edward and Warwick arrived in the capital, they were welcomed and Edward was asked to take the throne in place of Henry. He accepted, but refused to undergo a coronation while an enemy army remained in the field. Edward gathered an army, marched north and faced the queen's forces at the Battle of Towton on Palm Sunday, 29 March 1461. Contemporaries described up to 29,000 casualties, a number that was almost certainly exaggerated, yet it probably was the bloodiest battle to take place on English soil. Edward was crowned King Edward IV, on his return to London, becoming the first Yorkist king.

Over the years that followed, Edward's relationship with his cousin Warwick soured. By the late 1460s revolts were breaking out and there was suspicion that Warwick lay behind the trouble. In 1469, the earl fled to France with Edward's brother George, intending to depose the king and place George, who was married to Warwick's daughter, on the throne. The plans changed quickly when Warwick secured French support to restore Henry VI, who had remained in custody in the Tower of London. Warwick invaded in 1470 and drove a poorly prepared Edward from England into exile in Burgundy. As he waited for Margaret and her son to cross from France, Warwick began what is known as the Readeption, the restoration of the deposed Henry VI.

Before Margaret could arrive, Edward, with Burgundian support, landed in Yorkshire. He claimed to only want the return of the dukedom of York, but once he reached the Midlands he shed this pretence. His youngest brother Richard had remained with him and was a key part of bringing George back into the fold. Edward reached London unopposed and set about re-establishing his rule. Warwick moved towards the capital with an army, and Edward marched out to meet him. They collided in early-morning fog at the Battle of Barnet on 14 April 1471. Warwick was killed as Edward secured another victory. On the same day, Margaret and her son, now 17, landed in the southwest. Edward set out with a fresh army and engaged them at the Battle of Tewkesbury on 4 May. The king won yet again, and Henry VI's only son was killed. When Edward returned to London, the death of Henry VI was announced amid rumours that Edward had his rival murdered.

More than a decade of settled security followed, during which Edward invaded France in 1475 and was bought off with a large payment and regular income from the French king. George tested his brother one too many times and was executed for treason in 1478. Edward IV died unexpectedly in April 1483 at the age of 40. His oldest son was proclaimed Edward V at the age of 12, but he would never undergo a coronation. During the summer, a story emerged that Edward IV's marriage had been bigamous. Hotly debated ever since, it was accepted as proven in 1483 and Edward V, along with his siblings, was declared illegitimate and incapable of being king. Instead, the last remaining brother of Edward IV became King Richard III. He faced a revolt in October 1483, and a lingering threat from an exile across the Channel named Henry Tudor. A defining conflict in English history was on the horizon.

The Globe Theatre on Bankside, London

PART THREE

TUDORS, STUARTS AND GEORGIANS

Camber Castle near Rye, East Sussex, constructed as part of
Henry VIII's coastal defence strategy

Chapter 7

The Two Tudor Henrys

──── **THE BATTLE OF BOSWORTH FIELD** ────

O n 7 August 1485, Henry Tudor landed at Mill Bay in Pembrokeshire with a small army. He was 28 and had been in exile in Brittany and then France for half of those years. As the last potential rival to Richard III's throne, he had been a magnet for dissidents. Born at Pembroke Castle in 1457, Henry hoped to harness more support from his native Wales. It was slow to come as he marched north along the coast, then turned east towards England.

He had royal blood in his veins. Henry's father, Edmund Tudor, had died before Henry's birth. Edmund was a half-brother of Henry VI through their shared mother. Edmund's wife was Lady Margaret Beaufort, who was just 13 years old when her son was born. Margaret was a great-great-granddaughter of Edward III, through John of Gaunt, a heritage shared with the Lancastrian kings but through an illegitimate line.

Henry had harnessed the opposition to Richard III's king-ship and solidified his position by promising to marry Edward IV's oldest daughter, Elizabeth. In 1485, he was given French men and ships with which to attempt an invasion. He entered Shrewsbury and marched along Watling Street, the Roman road that led to London. Richard III was in the Midlands, expecting an attack but unsure where Henry might strike. He marched out from Leicester to intercept Henry's army and prevent it reaching the capital.

The armies met at the Battle of Bosworth on 22 August 1485. The encounter was complicated by the presence of a third force, commanded by the Stanley family. Thomas, Lord Stanley was a key member of Richard III's government, but also Henry Tudor's stepfather. No one knew who he would side with as the battle began. Richard led a cavalry charge at Henry's position, but it was repulsed. Sir William Stanley, Thomas's brother, took the opportunity to enter the fray and cut down Richard and his household knights. In the aftermath, William recovered the crown Richard had been wearing and presented it to Henry. Three hundred and thirty-one years of Plantagenet rule had ended. The Tudor dynasty had come to the throne. The question was whether Henry could hold onto it.

THE FIRST TUDOR KING

Henry VII is sometimes written off a dour administrator with a penchant for micromanagement, particularly in his later

LISTEN TO THE
PODCAST

The Rise of
Henry VII

years. But his eye for detail led to the replenishment of the depleted treasury after years of instability. He imposed heavy fines on nobles, and diminished their power through the strengthening of the royal council and his own authority. There were still violent domestic clashes during his reign, including several attempts by pretenders to claim that they were the missing Princes in the

Tower. One pretender, Perkin Warbeck, made several land-ings, claiming he was the second son of Edward IV, an unwanted distraction for Henry.

Henry VII saw off these threats, and his 23-year reign (August 1485 – April 1509) would be the longest since Edward III. He was a patron of exploration, sponsoring the Genoese John Cabot's voyage across the Atlantic in 1496. He recog-nised the power of the united Spanish kingdom, and trod carefully on foreign policy, seeking diplomatic alliances and arranging strategic marriages for his children. His first son Arthur was married to Catherine of Aragon, the daughter of the powerful Spanish monarchs Ferdinand and Isabella, in 1501. His eldest daughter Margaret married the King of Scotland, James IV, in 1503, in accordance with the 'Treaty of Perpetual Peace' between England and Scotland. This union would produce the Stuart heirs to succeed to the throne once the Tudor line had died out.

Arthur and Catherine's marriage would be short-lived. After just six months, the couple came down with a mysterious 'sweating sickness'. Catherine survived, but Arthur died in April 1502 and she was left a widow. She found herself trapped in England for the next seven years while her father and Henry VII squabbled over her huge dowry. It was eventually agreed that she would marry the new heir to the throne – Henry VII's second son, who was also named Henry.

HENRY VIII

Henry VII died in April 1509. His son married Catherine of Aragon on 11 June, and the pair were jointly crowned two weeks later. The coronation marked the start of the reign of perhaps England's most famous monarch, Henry VIII, and he could not be more different from his cautious father: a charismatic, spendthrift, chivalrous Renaissance man, with a passion for martial glory and unafraid of making radical domestic changes.

The foremost change was his break from the Catholic Church, the launch of the English Reformation. This giant public policy revolution stemmed from the very personal matter of the king and queen being unable to bear a son and heir. Henry's hunt for an heir, and marital bliss, would see him wed six wives over his 38-year reign – another notable for its longevity. 'Divorced, beheaded and died. Divorced, beheaded, survived', the rhyme goes, and the story of Henry VIII's reign can be told through these relationships.

Catherine of Aragon

Raised at one of the most formidable courts of Europe, Catherine was a confident, intelligent and fiercely loyal queen. Her mother, Isabella, had plotted military campaigns alongside her father, and Catherine had inherited her iron-clad sense of duty.

Henry's early reign was marked by a new war against France. Western European politics in the first half of the 16th century was dominated by the Italian Wars, primarily between France and the Holy Roman Empire, but also Spain and occasionally England. Henry joined the side of the anti-French Holy League, created by Pope Julius II and assisted by Ferdinand of Aragon, Catherine's father. He formally declared war in April 1512 and invaded in June 1513. Siding with France in their 'Auld Alliance', Scotland then invaded England.

Queen Catherine oversaw the decisive defeat of Scottish forces at the Battle of Flodden on 9 September 1513, where Scottish king James IV was killed in battle. Catherine sent Henry a piece of his bloodied coat as a trophy. She wrote that she wished to send James's actual body, 'but our Englishmen's hearts would not suffer it.'

Henry returned from France that October after some success at the so-called Battle of the Spurs and the Siege of Tournai. However, these were a long way from emulating the seismic victories of his hero, Henry V and his treasury was sorely depleted. He decided not to continue his campaigns the next year.

In 1510 Henry had arrested and executed two of his father's most unpopular ministers, in what would become a habit of dealing with political disputes for the new king. Catherine had given birth to a stillborn girl in January 1510. On New Year's Day 1511 she gave birth to a son, but the boy would only live 52 days. The couple then had two stillborn sons in 1513 and 1515, but in 1516 Catherine gave birth to Mary, their only child who would survive into adulthood. Catherine's last known pregnancy came in 1518, but again the child, a girl, was stillborn.

The tragic failure to produce a healthy heir during the 1510s strained their marriage, and the young king's eye certainly strayed away from it. The number of the King's mistresses is disputed. He certainly had an affair from 1514 with Elizabeth Blount, who gave birth to an illegitimate son – also named Henry – in 1519.

──────── **THE REFORMATION IN EUROPE** ────────

The military conflict in Europe was ended by the Treaty of London, negotiated by Cardinal Wolsey of England, in 1518, without a decisive result. By then a religious fracture was starting to transform politics in Europe – England.

The selling of indulgences had become a well-known method for the Catholic Church to raise money during the Middle Ages. They allowed a purchaser to reduce their time in Catholic purgatory, the afterlife waystation where souls would be cleansed before moving on to heaven. In 1515, Pope Leo X issued new indulgences through the papal bull Sacrosanctis, the revenue from which would contribute to the building of St Peter's Basilica in Rome. In the Holy Roman Empire, a Dominican fundraising friar, Johann Tetzel, had a slogan attributed to him that wouldn't look out of place in a 20th-century advertising campaign: 'As soon as the coin into the box rings, a soul from purgatory to heaven springs.' Whether or not he said that exactly is not clear, but serious believers were shocked by the campaign's tastelessness. When a friar came knocking around Wittenberg selling indulgences to its peasants, a theology professor at its university, Martin Luther, snapped. He laid out his fury against Rome in a tract known as the Ninety-five Theses, with the popular story being that he nailed it to the door of All Saints' Church in Wittenberg.

'Why does the Pope, whose wealth today is greater than the wealth of the richest Crassus, build the basilica of St Peter with the money of poor believers rather than with his own money?'

Martin Luther

The Ninety-five Theses spread like wildfire through the Holy Roman Empire. Aided by Johannes Gutenberg's newly invented printing press, they also reached France, England and Italy by 1519. Those who agreed with the Theses started to be called 'Lutherans'.

Through the Holy League Henry VIII had been closely aligned with the papacy and staunchly defended it against Luther's teachings. In 1521 he published *The Defence of the Seven Sacraments*, and Leo X rewarded him with the title of *Fidei Defensor* (Defender of the Faith) that October. Diplomatically, Henry had also been on the charm offensive, meeting with King Francis I of France in June 1520 at the 'Field of the Cloth of Gold' near Calais. While this was an extravagant showcase of the two monarchs' wealth, it achieved little diplomatically; they would be at war once again the following year, as Henry sided with Charles V – the Holy Roman Emperor – who was the most powerful man in Europe, and Catherine of Aragon's nephew.

Anne Boleyn

Henry had an extramarital affair with Mary Boleyn, one of Catherine's ladies-in-waiting, from around 1522, and it has been speculated that she gave birth to two of his children, although they were never recognised as such by Henry. The king had grown impatient with the lack of a male heir from his marriage.

This was still a shaky time for the Tudors, with the dynastic chaos of the Wars of the Roses still within living memory. Thus a male heir would strengthen Henry's position. Henry's affair with Mary appears to have come to an end around 1526, and the king's gaze turned to her sister, Anne, who was known for her quick wit, fashion sense and charisma. This set into motion a chain of events that would not only lead to the end of Henry and Catherine's marriage, but also kick-start the English Reformation.

HEVER CASTLE

Dating back to the 13th century, Hever Castle was the family home of the Boleyn family. Thomas Boleyn inherited Hever in 1505 and, along with his wife, Lady Elizabeth Howard, raised Anne and her siblings there. Anne lived at the castle until 1513, and it also played a role in her courtship with Henry VIII, who visited frequently. Later, it passed to Henry VIII's fourth wife, Anne of Cleves, as part of their annulment settlement. Restored in 1903 by William Waldorf Astor, today Hever Castle showcases Tudor-era elegance with rooms featuring Anne Boleyn's personal items and Tudor portraiture.

The King's Great Matter

When the beguiling Anne refused to become only the king's mistress, as her sister before her had been, Henry determined to end his marriage to Catherine. This was known from 1527 as the 'King's Great Matter'. He argued that his marriage had been invalid because of Catherine's previous marriage to his brother, and this was why they had been cursed with no living sons. The devout Catherine rejected this, saying that her first marriage had never been consummated.

Without Catherine's consent, Henry had to ask Pope Clement VII for an annulment, but the Pope was a prisoner of Catherine's nephew, the Holy Roman Emperor who had seized Rome. Clement sent a letter to Henry in January 1531 forbidding him to remarry. In response, the king simply assumed supremacy over religious matters and gave himself permission.

Henry's senior minister, Cardinal Wolsey, had failed to negotiate the King's Great Matter. He was stripped of his power. He died in 1530, on his way to London to face a treason charge, and the strongest bulwark against an English split with Rome was removed. Anne Boleyn had lived in France, until 1522, and it is thought that she brought some Lutheran ideas home with her, which in turn influenced the king.

Henry banished Catherine from the court in July 1531, cruelly forbidding her to see their daughter, Mary. In a letter to Henry she damningly referred to Anne as 'the scandal of Christendom and a disgrace to you', and in her eyes she remained the Queen of England.

Henry passed a number of legislative acts between 1532 and 1534 that divorced England from Rome, including the 'Act of Supremacy', which declared him the 'Supreme Head' of the Church of England. He had also secretly married Anne Boleyn in January 1533, had his marriage to Catherine officially annulled the following May, and then had the noticeably pregnant Anne crowned Queen of England in June 1533. Catherine had been married to the king for 24 years, more than all his later wives combined. She had also been a popular queen, and was mourned when she died three years after the annulment, at 50 years old.

In September 1533, Anne gave birth to the long-awaited royal baby, but to Henry's disappointment it was a girl. That girl would grow up to become one of England's greatest monarchs, in Elizabeth I – but to Henry, she was just another daughter. After Elizabeth, Anne suffered two miscarriages. Like Catherine, she seemed unable to bear Henry a son.

Tudor Childbirth

Childbirth in the 16th century was hazardous, even for royalty. One in twenty women in Tudor England died in childbirth. But it wasn't just dangerous for the mothers. It is reported that only two out of every five babies born would live to adulthood. Many women lost babies before and after coming to term, and for queens of England this wasn't just a personal tragedy, but also a potential political crisis.

If a queen couldn't provide a male heir, it was her fault in the eyes of the state. In Catherine of Aragon's case, Henry started to believe he had been cursed for marrying his brother's wife, as stated in the Bible.

'. . . if a man shall take his brother's wife . . . they shall be childless'

Book of Leviticus (20:21)

There are some scientific theories as to why both Catherine and Anne Boleyn suffered so many failed pregnancies. Henry himself, unwittingly, may have been the cause. Of all the legitimate pregnancies attributed to the king and his first three wives, 70% resulted in miscarriage or stillbirth. This is compared to only 10% found in the noblemen closely associated with him.

Some studies suggest that Henry was positive for the Kell blood group; if Catherine and Anne were Kell negative, this may explain their multiple miscarriages and stillbirths.

There are other suggestions that diet was a contributing factor. The devoutly religious Catherine was known to fast regularly while pregnant, which may have inadvertently harmed her unborn children. Similarly, as time went on the stress of struggling to provide a male heir would have taken its toll.

Anne's Downfall

By 1536 Anne was pregnant again, and on 8 January news of Catherine of Aragon's death reached her and the king. They were reportedly overjoyed, and both wore yellow in celebration. Yet as one of Anne's rivals fell another emerged. At some point that month, the king set his eyes on Jane Seymour; in classic Henry style, she was one of Anne's ladies-in-waiting. Anne was fiercely jealous and more unaccepting of Henry's cheating than her predecessor. On one occasion that month she noticed Jane gazing into a locket given to her by Henry, and ripped it from her neck so hard she drew blood.

While Anne's fury grew, on 24 January Henry suffered a serious jousting accident and was knocked unconscious for two hours. Some historians have suggested that he may have suffered brain damage which had an impact on his already tumultuous moods. Five days later, possibly due to stress, Anne miscarried a son. The scathing Spanish ambassador, Eustace Chapuys, wrote, 'She has miscarried her saviour.'

Indeed, Henry's patience had worn thin. Some think her downfall was organised by Henry's right-hand man – Thomas Cromwell – to destroy a rival's influence, others believe it was set up by the king to quickly do away with Anne and have a son by Jane.

> 'He pursued her death with the same kind of vigour that he pursued to marry her . . .
>
> 'I don't think that he thought she was guilty of having multiple affairs with five different men that went on for 27 months but no one noticed somehow. But I do think that he felt that she had betrayed him and that she was deserving of that ultimate punishment.'
>
> **Natalie Grueninger, historian**

Anne went from Queen of England to traitor facing execution in the space of three weeks. On May Day 1536 she was arrested and taken to the Tower of London. The charges against her, now widely understood to be false, included high treason and adultery with five different men, including incest with her brother George.

After a show trial, Anne was found guilty, as were the other five accused. When the morning of 19 May arrived, however, she was apparently light-hearted. Discussing the skill of her specially hired swordsman with Tower constable William Kingston, she joked, 'I heard say the executioner was very good, and I have a little neck', wrapping her hands around it with laughter. Eyewitness accounts from the execution say that she held herself with courage, and delivered a speech that brought the audience to tears.

LISTEN TO THE
PODCAST

Anne Boleyn

TOWER GREEN

Tower Green, within the Tower of London, was the execution site for those with high status or royal standing during the Tudor era. The 'privilege' of being executed inside the Tower was reserved for those with significant rank or strong popular support, to shield them from public spectacle, scrutiny or assistance. Tower Green witnessed ten executions. Thomas More, once Henry VIII's Lord High Chancellor, lost his head there in 1535 due to his opposition to the Reformation and Henry's marriage to Anne Boleyn. One of his successor's Thomas Cromwell suffered a similar fate five years later. Two or three Queens of England met their end on that spot: Anne Boleyn (1536), Catherine Howard (1542) and the disputed 'Nine Days' Queen' Lady Jane Grey (1554). Today, Tower Green features a memorial sculpture to those condemned to death.

Jane Seymour

After the tempestuous Anne, Jane Seymour provided a calming presence for Henry and is commonly thought to have been his favourite wife. Jane was not as educated as either of her predecessors, but her gentle personality reportedly lent itself to peacemaking efforts at court – presumably in high demand, given that she was married to Henry just ten days after Anne had been beheaded.

Her reign coincided with the beginning of the dissolution of the monasteries. One of Henry's first actions after the 1534 Act of Supremacy was to tax the clergy, and he introduced a new 10% income tax on church lands. Money that would have previously gone to Rome was now flowing into the English treasury. His adviser Thomas Cromwell had meanwhile commissioned a survey to measure religious wealth in England. This *Valor Ecclesiasticus* was started in 1535, and is one of the most important historical documents of Tudor England.

Henry gave Royal Assent to the Suppression of Religious Houses Act in April 1536, and smaller monasteries began to be dissolved. While the Act complained of the apparently 'manifest sin, vicious, carnal and abominable living is daily used and committed among the little and small abbeys', this was really a way for the treasury to grab the wealth of monastic estates, by insisting that monastic reform was impossible:

'. . . that many continual visitations hath been heretofore had, by the space of two hundred years and more, for an honest and charitable reformation of such unthrifty, carnal, and abominable living, yet nevertheless little or none amendment is hitherto had, but their vicious living shamelessly increases and augments.'

Preamble of the Suppression of Religious Houses Act

Henry firmed up his rule by properly incorporating Wales into England. English became the official language and English law was implemented, while Welsh men could have representation in Parliament. The first Laws in Wales Act was given Royal Assent on the same day as the Suppression of Religious Houses Act, and the latter would also apply to Wales.

'That his said Country or Dominion of *Wales* shall be, stand

and continue for ever from henceforth incorporated, united and annexed to and with this his Realm of *England*.'

The Laws in Wales Act 1535

So while he'd broken with Continental Europe, Henry sought to unify the territories held by the English Crown. But in northern England trouble was brewing, and in October 1536 people in Yorkshire broke into open revolt.

The cause of the revolt was not purely the confiscation of Church and monastic property. Henry's heartless divorce from the popular Catherine and his ruthless execution of Anne Boleyn, for treason no less, had done much to undermine his rule. Skyrocketing food prices resulting from a bad harvest in 1535 had also added to the discontent. These combined religious, political and economic grievances resulted in what was the most dangerous rebellion in Tudor England. By December 1536 this 'Pilgrimage of Grace' had gained almost 40,000 supporters and spread throughout the northern counties. While solutions to the grievances were negotiated by the Duke of Norfolk and Earl of Shrewsbury, Henry had not given his authorisation. In the following spring, after another failed uprising in Cumbria and Westmoreland, the rebels were brutally suppressed, their leaders arrested and put on trial. Beginning in late May, several hundred people were executed for their involvement. In 1540, emboldened by the crushing of the uprising, Henry extended his dissolution of the monasteries to the major religious houses.

Just as his kingdom appeared unstable, Henry's domestic situation seemed finally settled. Jane Seymour is credited with reconciling him with his first daughter, Mary. As the now illegitimate daughter of Catherine of Aragon and Henry, she had been cast out of the line of succession and sent to live with her infant half-sister Elizabeth's household at Hatfield Palace in Hertfordshire.

Queen Jane also gave birth to Henry's long-awaited son and heir in October 1537. He would grow up to be Edward VI, but Jane wouldn't live to see this. After developing post-natal complications, she died less than two weeks after his birth, aged 29. Jane was the only one of Henry's wives to be given a queen's funeral, at which Mary acted as chief mourner. She was buried at St George's Chapel at Windsor Castle, where Henry himself would choose to be buried after his death in January 1547.

Anne of Cleves

With Jane's tragic passing, the throne beside Henry was – for the first time in decades – left empty. Chief minister Thomas Cromwell was dispatched in search of a new Queen of England. He successfully lobbied for Anne of Cleves, but it would not be a success. Indeed, this would be the shortest of all six marriages, with Anne ruling as queen only from January to July of 1540.

Anne was a German princess, whose union with Henry was really one of political expediency. Her brother William was Duke of Jülich-Cleves-Berg, and bore the rather promising epithet 'The Rich'. Her brother-in-law, John Frederick, Elector of Saxony, was also the head of the Schmalkaldic League, a powerful Protestant military alliance. Henry thought he'd be able to tap into this resource by marrying Anne, but it was no love match, and he had the marriage annulled after six months, citing its lack of consummation.

Henry blamed this on Anne's appearance, and in the 19th

century she was derided as the 'Flanders Mare'. The annulment could well have been more political than meets the eye.

> 'What I think went wrong for Anne's marriage to Henry was that Anne's brother was sneaking behind Henry's back and not telling him his plans.'
>
> **Heather R. Darsie, historian and author**

Henry allegedly called her some pretty foul things in their annulment proceedings, but seperation rarely brings out our better angels. The pair actually ended up being close friends. Anne became an honorary member of the royal family, known as 'the King's Beloved Sister'. Her generous settlement included Richmond Palace as well as Hever Castle, the childhood home of Anne Boleyn.

The man who arranged their doomed marriage did not fare so well, however. Henry's most trusted adviser of the last decade, Thomas Cromwell, was executed without trial on 28 July 1540, the same day that Henry married his next wife.

Anne, unlike the man who had championed her match, lived for nearly another two decades. She died in 1557 after, very unexpectedly, seeing both Edward and then Mary crowned.

Catherine Howard

Like Anne of Cleves before her, Catherine Howard would also have a very short marriage to Henry, but hers had a far less amicable termination. Instead, it matched the drama

LISTEN TO THE
PODCAST

Anne of Cleves

of his marriage to Anne Boleyn, who had been her first cousin. Thomas Howard, Duke of Norfolk, was uncle to both.

Catherine's life had been turbulent even before her marriage to Henry. As one of the many wards of her father's stepmother, the Dowager Duchess of Norfolk, she appears to have been in a sexual relationship with her music teacher, Henry Mannox, when she was as young as 13. Later, Catherine also became embroiled with the Dowager Duchess's secretary Francis Dereham.

After the Dowager Duchess found out, Catherine was sent to court to serve as a lady-in-waiting to Anne of Cleves. This position had been secured for her by her uncle, the Duke of Norfolk, who saw an opportunity in Henry's lack of interest in Anne.

The pair were married in July 1540. By this time, Henry was 49, bloated and in pain from an ulcer on his leg that would not heal. Catherine, on the other hand, was around 17. In the spring of the following year, Catherine seems to have resumed an affair with a courtier of Henry's named Thomas Culpeper. She and Culpeper had had a romance before Henry had set his sights on her.

After they had reunited, their meetings were organised by Jane Boleyn, Lady Rochford – the widow of Anne Boleyn's brother George and close friend of the queen. The relationship was uncovered in autumn 1541. The Archbishop of Canterbury, Thomas Cranmer, learned of her previous relationship with Dereham, and her affair with Culpeper was exposed when a love letter written by the queen was found in his room.

Cranmer launched an investigation into Catherine's alleged affairs and she was detained and questioned by the Archbishop himself in November 1541. Terrified and clumsily retracting and retelling her version of events, the young Catherine unwittingly doomed herself in these interviews. Both Culpeper and Dereham were executed for high treason that December.

Catherine received no formal trial. On 13 February 1542, she was executed for high treason, aged around 19. On her doomed route by barge to the Tower of London, she would have passed under the impaled heads of her lovers, Culpeper and Dereham, as she went under London Bridge. Lady Rochford was also executed, and both were buried in unmarked graves at the Tower's parish chapel alongside their family members, Anne and George Boleyn.

> 'Yes it was extreme foolishness, but also it says more about where the Henrician state was from 1541 to 1542, that something that foolish was transmogrified into something that monstrous.'
>
> **Gareth Russell, historian**

CRIME AND PUNISHMENT IN TUDOR ENGLAND

The volume of public executions, often politically motivated and without trial, was a stain on Henry VIII's reign. He may well be the most blood-soaked monarch in English history; one estimate is that more than 50,000 people were executed during his 36-year reign. Given that the population of mid 16th-century England was only around three million, that vast figure could be an exaggeration, but we do have the evidence for just how dangerous it was to be one of Henry's chief ministers or wives. The great changes brought about by his English Reformation, his paranoia about

LISTEN TO THE
PODCAST

Catherine Howard

the loyalty of followers forced to choose between their faith and their sovereign, led to a reign of terror. Even close and politically powerful advisers like Thomas More and Thomas Cromwell ended their careers on the executioner's block, and Cardinal Wolsey was on his way there too.

Henry never felt greatly constrained by law. In the case of Catherine Howard, a new law was passed that made it treasonous not to disclose premarital sexual relations to the monarch, and another made it treasonous to incite a person to engage in adultery as the Queen Consort. Jane Boleyn suffered a serious mental breakdown and was deemed insane, a state that usually protected someone from execution. Henry reversed that too, performing a number of legal acrobatics to ensure that everyone involved would be served the most severe punishment possible – death.

HAMPTON COURT PALACE

Hampton Court Palace was originally built in 1515 as a luxurious private residence for Cardinal Wolsey, but passed into Henry VIII's possession in 1529, and became one of his favoured residences. Expanded to accommodate courtiers and Anne Boleyn, the palace witnessed key events in Henry's life including the break with Rome, the birth of Edward VI, Jane Seymour's death and Henry's divorce from Anne of Cleves. Catherine Howard was accused of adultery and confined there before her execution in 1542. Visitors have reported seeing a ghostly 'Screaming Lady', believed to be Catherine, running down the 'Haunted Gallery' in distress, pleading for mercy. The palace was extensively rebuilt and expanded by King William III and Queen Mary in 1689 with architect Sir Christopher Wren.

─────── HENRY'S FOREIGN CAMPAIGNS ───────

Henry used the 1540s, the last decade of his life, to cement his legacy and dynasty.

In 1542 he passed the Crown of Ireland Act, creating the title of 'King of Ireland' for monarchs of England and their successors – a significant milestone in the conquest of Ireland. That year he also passed the second Laws in Wales Act, further unifying the legal, political and administrative systems of Wales with England. Alongside the earlier Act, these are often referred to as the Acts of Union.

In 1543 Henry made an alliance with Charles V, Holy Roman Emperor, to take on the Franco-Scottish axis. The following summer, 1544, he invaded France with 36,000 soldiers – the largest army sent overseas by an English ruler for another 150 years. He captured Boulogne in 1544, annexed territory around the town and even leased it to English settlers. The sea war with France saw the Isle of Wight raided and the indecisive Battle of the Solent ended with the loss of Henry's flagship the *Mary Rose* in July 1545. Mindful of his father's cross-Channel invasion, Henry was keen to secure England's coastal waters, and he formally founded the 'Navy Royal', the precursor to the Royal Navy, in 1546.

CAMBER CASTLE

Now isolated and largely in ruins, Camber Castle was constructed between 1512 and 1514 under Henry VIII's coastal defence strategy. Positioned near Rye as it is, it controlled port access and monitored the English Channel.

THE STORY OF ENGLAND

It underwent extensive rebuilding in 1539 and 1542–43, due to rising tensions with France. This transformed it into a large, concentric artillery fort, with a central keep and circular bastions, designed to deflect cannon fire and withstand a siege. By the late 16th century, silting of the harbours and military advancements rendered the castle obsolete. Closed in 1637 by Charles I and dismantled during the Civil War, it remains an unusual example of an unmodified Henrician fort and is Grade I listed.

Catherine Parr

The 1540s also saw Henry's final marriage, to Catherine Parr. This was despite her already being in love with Thomas Seymour – Jane Seymour's brother. Catherine, having caught King Henry's eye, considered it her duty to marry him instead. They wed in July 1543, one year and four months after Catherine Howard was beheaded. Parr had been married twice before, being titled Lady Burgh and then Lady Latimer, and she was to marry again around six months after Henry died, making her the most married English queen in history.

This is not Catherine's only claim to fame: she was a prolific writer, and is often credited as the first woman to publish work in her own name, with her *Prayers or Meditations* in 1545. This was very successful among English readers in the 16th century, helping to develop the new Church of England, and it's likely that some of her work was written in collaboration with Henry.

But she wasn't always in Henry's good graces. Though raised a Catholic, in adulthood Catherine harboured a number of reformist religious views, as seen in her writing.

Henry soon grew agitated by her insistence on debating religion with him; and, as usual, there were some ambitious characters waiting in the wings to unseat her.

Anti-Protestant officials such as Stephen Gardiner and Lord Wriothesley attempted to turn the king against Catherine, and an arrest warrant was eventually drawn up. A soldier was actually sent out to arrest her as she was out walking with the king, and was sent away – she succeeded in saving her own neck by artfully reconciling with Henry. Perhaps luckily for Catherine Henry did not live long enough to tire of her. He died in 1547 after less than four years of marriage.

During her queenship, Catherine also established very close relationships with the king's children. Elizabeth formed a particularly close relationship with her stepmother.

After Henry VIII died in 1547, his final queen, Catherine, was left £7,000 to support herself. She married Thomas Seymour, now uncle to the new king, and Lady Elizabeth moved into their household. While there, Seymour developed an inappropriate interest in the young Elizabeth and she eventually left their household to live elsewhere. It was rumoured that Seymour even wanted to marry Elizabeth, a claim that was used against him in a later treason trial. He was found guilty, and yet another noble went to the block.

The Great Hall, the only surviving part of Winchester Castle

Chapter 8

Crisis and Golden Age

───────────── **THE BOY KING** ─────────────

H enry VIII ruled for 38 drama-filled years on the throne. This complex, huge character was succeeded by his nine-year-old son Edward. As an eldest son, he was the only Tudor monarch groomed to reign, and it was assumed he would become as commanding a figure as his father had been. Yet he would never reach maturity and would spend his entire rule under a regency council. As had so often happened during the minorities of earlier medieval kings, powerful men loomed around Edward VI, hoping to further their own ends.

Before his death, Henry VIII had planned for a council of 16 to assist his son, but this was not enacted. Edward's uncle, the Earl of Somerset, was named Lord Protector until Edward came of age. This made him ruler in all but name. It also ignited a vicious struggle for power among frustrated factions of the nobility.

'At the end of January 1547 . . . there was a feeling that a single, powerful individual was needed to run the show.'

Stephen Alford, University of Leeds

Edward was the first monarch in English history to be raised as a Protestant and, even at his young age, he had a keen interest in religious reform. Capitalising on his Protestant upbringing, figures like Somerset and Archbishop Thomas Cranmer redoubled their efforts to embed Protestantism in England. In 1549 they issued an English Prayer Book, accompanied by an Act of Uniformity mandating its use.

This triggered the Catholic-led Prayer Book Rebellion in southwest England, and the separate Kett's Rebellion, which was more of an agrarian dispute in the face of poor harvests and the enclosure of common ground. Both revolts attracted significant numbers, but were bloodily suppressed, with the deaths of thousands. These tumultuous events led to Somerset's downfall, paving the way for John Dudley, Duke of Northumberland, to assume power. Dudley, in a swift and calculated move, orchestrated the removal and execution of his predecessor in 1552. Edward himself declared that his uncle's crimes included:

LISTEN TO THE
PODCAST

Edward VI

'. . . ambition, vainglory, entering into rash wars in mine youth, negligent looking on Newhaven, enriching himself of my treasure, following his own opinion, and doing all by his own authority, etc.'

The Chronicle and Political Papers of King Edward VI

By June 1553 it became apparent that Edward was dying, probably of tuberculosis, and a plan for his succession was set in motion. Not wishing to rewind the progress of Protestantism,

Edward's advisers encouraged him to exclude his half-sisters Mary and Elizabeth from the line of succession. Edward himself appears to have pursued this plan with passion, both on the grounds of his religious beliefs and also on the question of his sisters' legitimacy.

'All those accounts we have of Edward's final months and weeks do suggest that the king himself was putting fair amounts of pressure on his advisers to sign up to the "Devise" to ensure that it had legal status.'

Stephen Alford, University of Leeds

In his own hand, he penned an extraordinary statute, My Devise for the Succession, which diverted the royal line to the children and grandchildren of Henry VIII's younger sister (also named Mary). Edward's 16-year-old cousin, the reliably Protestant Lady Jane Grey, would become his heir. Jane's husband was Lord Guildford Dudley – the Duke of Northumberland's son. Jane on the throne would strengthen Northumberland's position. But Northumberland had reached too high. When Edward died in 1553 aged 15, Jane Grey succeeded; but she would be queen for just nine days.

BLOODY MARY

Mary Tudor had never recanted the Catholic faith she had inherited from her mother. She was also Henry's oldest surviving child. She had thousands of followers backing her claim, both for her faith and the family tree.

Mary wasted no time in making her claim; she headed to Framlingham Castle in Suffolk to raise support against Lady

Jane Grey. From Framlingham she wrote to the Privy Council, who soon realised the grave error they had made, and support for Northumberland and Lady Jane Grey collapsed. Mary was proclaimed Queen of England on 19 July 1553 from behind Framlingham's walls.

Mary reached London on 8 August, accompanied by her half-sister Elizabeth. Northumberland and Jane Grey were held in the Tower of London; Northumberland would be beheaded later that month. As Lady Jane Grey's short reign is widely disputed, Mary is considered the first annointed female ruler of England. Her Catholicism led her to attempt to reverse the English Reformation, burning hundreds of Protestants in the process, which earned her the epithet 'Bloody Mary'.

Mary was 37 when she was crowned. This was old to be wed and have children by the standards of the time, yet she searched for a marriage to secure her own Catholic dynasty. Trouble arose in early 1554 from Mary's desire to marry the Catholic Philip II of Spain. Protestant conspirators aimed to take London by force in Wyatt's Rebellion, but the city was too well defended. Lady Jane Grey's father had joined the rebellion, and, Jane having already been sentenced to death for her alleged usurpation, she was executed along with her father and husband that February.

Mary and Philip's marriage went ahead that July, despite the match being hugely unpopular. Together they waged an unsuccessful war on France, in January 1558 losing Calais – England's last possession on the Continent. It would never be recovered. That same year Mary suffered a false pregnancy, perhaps brought about by her intense desire to have a child and prevent her Protestant sister Elizabeth from succeeding her. Though the entire court believed Mary was going to give birth, a baby never materialised and the queen was left distraught. Soon after, Philip abandoned her to return to Spain, causing her further misery. She died in 1558 aged 42, possibly of uterine cancer, and her dream of returning England to Catholicism died with her.

GLORIANA

Elizabeth was a deeply unlikely sovereign. A girl, a third child, she had been declared illegitimate, subjected to imprisonment and plotting to deny her the throne, yet in November 1558 at the age of 25 she was declared queen. Her upbringing had been extremely testing. But these difficulties appeared to have shaped Elizabeth's character and given her remarkable political shrewdness. Over the course of her 45-year reign she guided England through a period of profound transformation.

From the earliest days of her reign, the question of Elizabeth's marriage was a matter of paramount importance, both domestically and internationally. An unmarried woman ruling England without a consort by her side was unprecedented, and her courtiers and advisers grappled with the implications of her remaining single. Nevertheless, Elizabeth had other ideas. In her very first speech to Parliament, she declared:

'I am already bound unto a husband, which is the kingdom of England, and that may suffice you.'

Perhaps her determination never to marry stemmed from her upbringing. She would have been too young to remember much of the circumstances of her mother's execution, but when Elizabeth was eight years old her third stepmother Catherine Howard was beheaded, leaving a deep and unsettling mark on the young princess. Even at that point, she is said to have declared to her household, 'I will never marry'. Evidence also suggests that the inappropriate advances of Thomas Seymour when she was a teenager, instilled in her a deep-seated suspicion of the men around her. It may also have fostered a sense of the need to protect her autonomy and her body – the very embodiment of the Crown itself after she became queen.

Despite numerous suitors vying for her hand from across Europe, including King Philip II of Spain, King Eric XIV of Sweden and Francois, Duke of Anjou, Elizabeth deftly wielded these potential alliances to her political advantage. She would often defer decisions, frustrating courtiers by her constant delaying, but that helped to avoid climactic moments of crisis through her decades on the throne. She mastered the art of diplomatic manoeuvring, skilfully concealing her true intentions and emotions behind an inscrutable veil.

Instead of marriage, she meticulously crafted the persona of the 'pale, divine Virgin Queen', surrounded by adoring courtiers and immortalised in the art and propaganda of the era.

Nowhere is the cult of Elizabeth more vividly shown than at Kenilworth Castle, in the heart of Warwickshire. Now a ruin, this architectural marvel began its life as a Norman keep before being transformed into an extraordinary castle by Robert Dudley in the 16th century. Elizabeth gave Dudley the castle in 1563, and – after throwing her one of the most extravagant parties in history at Kenilworth – it appears he hoped she might also give him her hand in marriage.

The Closest Suitor

Born in 1532, Robert Dudley, 1st Earl of Leicester, was a strikingly handsome and incredibly wealthy English nobleman. His brother was the husband of Lady Jane Grey, and so once Mary triumphed, he was imprisoned in the Tower of London at the same time as the young Elizabeth, with whom he had been childhood friends. He avoided the block, was released and eventually pardoned by Mary.

On 18 November 1558, the morning after Elizabeth's accession to the throne, Dudley was given the important position of Master of the Horse, and played a central role at her coronation. From the earliest years of Elizabeth's reign, she and Dudley were extremely close, and their relationship was the cause of much speculation and gossip in Tudor society. In April 1559, Philip II of Spain was informed:

'Lord Robert has come so much into favour that he does whatever he likes with affairs and it is even said that her majesty visits him in his chamber day and night.'

While there's no hard evidence of a romantic relationship between the two, they were certainly deeply attached to each other. Dudley took Elizabeth on picnics in St James's Park and showered her and her household with gifts. They even built up something of a secret code in their correspondence, and Dudley used an emoji-like symbol when he signed off his letters; he would write two Os, with little pupils and eyebrows over them. Elizabeth would call him 'her eyes'.

But there were many obstacles to a love match. Dudley was married and in 1560 his wife, Amy Robsart, died in mysterious circumstances. More importantly, Elizabeth, as queen, simply did not want to submit to a husband. That didn't stop him from trying, and her final trip to Kenilworth has been described as one of the most expensive marriage proposals in history.

In the Tudor era, it was customary for the monarch to tour the country and stay at the houses of the nobility, with all expenses paid for by their host. This led to some large home-owners demolishing parts of their property to avoid the cost of royal visits – but not Dudley, who did the complete opposite.

During her summer progress of 1575, Elizabeth spent a glorious 19 days at Kenilworth Castle. It was unprecedented for her to spend so long in any one place during a summer, but Dudley had transformed the place especially for her and her stay was essentially a three-week party. Some of the more opulent entertainments included:

- Elaborate pageants, including one with an 18-foot mermaid floating in the lake.
- Firework displays that featured 'fiery darts and thunderbolts which shake the earth and toss the waters below'.
- The revealing of two elaborate portraits of Elizabeth and Dudley.
- Hunting on the estate and walking through the ornate gardens.
- A play written on the spot by playwright George Gascon when wet weather rained off his original play.
- Pamphlets printed, describing everything that happened over the whole 19 days.

The cost of this stay was rumoured to be £1,000 a day and Dudley (who earned around £5,000 a year) had been preparing for it for years.

During their friendship Elizabeth visited Kenilworth four times, and each time Dudley fixed it up a little more, spending around the vast sum of £60,000 in all. He built her an apartment building, four storeys high, one with private access to her chambers through a connected door. In the gardens he built an aviary encrusted with gems, filled with exotic birds. The iconography is unsubtle: there are lots of references to love and images of their initials entwined. This was one of the all-time great marriage plays: an incredible expenditure to show off his prestige, power, wealth and commitment.

In pulling out all the stops, Dudley wanted to establish himself at least as Elizabeth's unquestionable favourite. But he never married her, and the money he spent on entertaining Elizabeth plunged him and his heirs into debt. He more or less stayed in favour, however, except for a couple of blips.

'He failed to marry Elizabeth, but we're still talking about him, so he succeeds in some ways. I think that was part of the plan, was that 500 years from now we're still talking about it.'

Joanne Paul, University of Sussex

Three years after Kenilworth, Dudley secretly married Elizabeth's younger, prettier cousin, Lettice Knollys. When that was revealed, he was in big trouble. Elizabeth never spoke to Lettice again, but Dudley eventually managed to worm his way back into favour. When he died in 1588, she mourned him. She labelled their final correspondence 'his last letter' in her own hand, and kept it by her bedside until her own death. Dudley had been a rock in Elizabeth's turbulent life, a companion, confidant, friend, perhaps even a lover, to the woman who was forging the role of female sovereign.

The Shakespearean Theatre

During Elizabeth's reign, the theatrical scene in England flourished, bolstered by the queen's own fondness for plays and spectacles. The emergence of professional acting troupes was fostered through sponsorship from the queen, aristocrats and other affluent patrons who could afford such lavish entertainments, and they were often invited to perform at court.

Since the English Reformation, plays no longer adhered to religious convention or revolved around Catholic holidays. Playwrights were granted the freedom to explore diverse narratives, characters and settings, which captivated Tudor audiences. Among these playwrights, none attained greater renown than William Shakespeare.

The greatest English dramatist ever to have lived, Shakespeare captivated contemporary audiences, and posterity, with tales of love, tragedy, high politics, colonialism, war and slapstick. Seeking opportunities beyond his hometown of Stratford-upon-Avon, Shakespeare ventured to London during the late 1580s or early 1590s. This move marked the beginning of a transformative period in his life, where he immersed himself in the world of theatre, first as an actor, then as a playwright and part-owner of his own company. No English writer has been more influential.

LISTEN TO THE
PODCAST

Tudor Feuds,
Explorers and Fanatics

The Globe Theatre was constructed in 1599, utilising timber salvaged from another venue established by actor Richard Burbage's father in Shoreditch. The theatre boasted a capacity of up to 3,000 spectators and debuted with a performance by the Lord Chamberlain's Men, presenting either *Henry V* in the summer of 1599 or *Julius Caesar* in September. Ownership of the theatre was shared between Richard Burbage, Shakespeare and other actors from their company. The original theatre burned down on 29 June 1613, during a performance of *Henry VIII*, but was reconstructed the following year. It was demolished during the English Civil War to make way for residential buildings. Located just 230 metres from where the original theatre stood, a modern reconstruction of the Globe opened in 1997. As its predecessor may have also done, it opened with a performance of *Henry V*, and continues to put on productions of Shakespeare's best-known plays over 400 years later.

Shakespeare's repertoire famously includes numerous history plays, which dovetailed neatly with the political objectives of the ruling Tudor dynasty. These works emphasised the perils of civil strife while exalting the Tudor dynasty's founders, depicting their adversaries as malevolent despots. Richard III, as the final ruler of the House of York, is immortalised as a deformed, merciless antagonist, Henry VII was hailed as a paragon of virtue.

Shakespeare helped to give England a sense of itself. Divinely blessed, exceptional, set apart from a continent ruled over by capricious despots. Shakespeare's *Henry V* seems to have been written around 1599, just before the invasion of Ireland by Elizabeth's dashing favourite, the Earl of Essex.

The contemporary world lurks between the lines of his histories.

A MARITIME POWER

The successes of Elizabeth's England were not restricted to the stage. After a century of uprisings, Elizabeth's reign was notable for relative domestic tranquillity. A northern rebellion and several plots were put down with a severity that reminds us that she was indeed her father's daughter. She embraced the strategic transformation that had emerged since the discovery of the New World. Her father had dreamt of resurrecting the Plantagenet empire in France; under Elizabeth seafarers set out to carve out empire in the wider world. Indeed her adviser and astrologer John Dee coined the phrase 'British Empire' over which Elizabeth would rule as Arthur reborn.

England became a maritime power, trading posts were established, and the first attempts were made to send out settler colonies. The men tasked with exploring became the founding fathers of empire, John Hawkins, Francis Drake, Martin Frobisher and Walter Raleigh. They were pioneers, adventurers and traders, but they were also conquerors, plunderers, slavers and pirates. They were known collectively as the Elizabethan Sea Dogs.

Explorers used new sailing technology to push north into the Arctic, west to the Americas and south to the African coast and Asia beyond. Just before her reign Hugh Willoughby and Richard Chancellor attempted to find a Northeast Passage to the Far East, pushing along the frozen coast of Russia. Chancellor sailed into the White Sea and set up a trading route to the Muscovites. Willoughby froze to death in the Arctic ice in 1554, trying to reach the Far East. Later ventures aimed to forge a sea route west round, or possibly through, the Americas to reach China. John Hawkins led the way to the west, the first to take English hulls into the Spanish Main.

The 1494 Treaty of Tordesillas between Spain and Portugal had divided the Americas into two. The Spanish claimed all the territory to the west of the Cape Verde Islands, essentially the whole of the Americas, apart from the coast of Brazil, which was given to the Portuguese. Everyone else, including England, were interlopers.

Hawkins's intentions were to break into the lucrative American trade: sail south to Africa, force enslaved Africans in shackles in the hold and then head for the Caribbean or 'Spanish Main' to sell the slaves and buy cargoes of sugar. He pioneered what became known as Triangular Trade. His trading voyages with the Spanish colonies in 1562 and 1564, were technically illegal, but Hawkins's supply of slaves and bribes led the Spanish colonial authorities to turn a blind eye. But in September 1568 Hawkins was caught by a larger Spanish fleet at what is now Veracruz, on the Mexican Caribbean coast. Initially, the commanders agreed a truce that would allow both fleets to use the anchorage. However, the Spanish never intended to follow its terms, and attacked the English ships. Hundreds of English sailors were captured. Their fates were grim, imprisonment, enslavement or execution. Only two English vessels escaped, one sailed by Hawkins, the other by his cousin and protégé Francis Drake, whose hatred for the Spanish was stoked, and who would take an epic revenge on the Spanish throughout a career as Elizabeth's most famous Sea Dog.

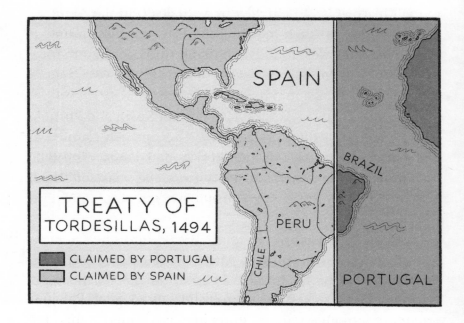

TREATY OF
TORDESILLAS, 1494

CLAIMED BY PORTUGAL
CLAIMED BY SPAIN

SPAIN

BRAZIL

PERU

CHILE

PORTUGAL

With Elizabeth I's backing, from 1577 to 1580 Drake led an expedition to circumnavigate the world, becoming the first Englishman to do so, plundering Spanish shipping and ports as he went. Hawkins would become Treasurer of the Navy in 1577, and modernised and expanded it as all-out war with Spain loomed.

THE GOLDEN HIND

The *Golden Hind*, originally named the *Pelican*, was Sir Francis Drake's ship during his circumnavigation of the world. He renamed the ship during the voyage, in honour of his main patron, Sir Christopher Hatton, whose crest featured a golden hind (female deer).

The voyage took place during rising tensions between England and Spain, which culminated in the undeclared Anglo-Spanish War in 1585. Drake's expedition aimed to disrupt Spanish shipping and capture treasures from Spanish colonies, and the *Golden Hind* returned laden with Spanish plunder, cementing Drake's reputation as a navigator and privateer. Moored at Deptford, it became the first 'museum ship', but disintegrated around 1650. Today, a full-sized, seaworthy reconstruction of the *Golden Hind* is located on the River Thames's south bank.

The Americas

Two other Sea Dogs, Martin Frobisher and Walter Raleigh, were more famous for their efforts in North America than for attacking Spanish possessions in the south. Frobisher had an early career as a privateer, plundering Portuguese and French ships along the coast of Africa and the Atlantic. In 1577 he embarked on one of three voyages to discover the Northwest Passage, but was unsuccessful. His second and third trips were funded by speculators lured by the promise of gold. They lost their money as he returned to England with hundreds of tons of pyrite (fool's gold), which was worthless. Yet he would go on to work closely with Drake and would play his part when Spain moved to crush the upstart English.

Walter Raleigh was a mariner with a vision. He was more focused on settlement. After a savage apprenticeship in the conquest of Ireland, he aimed to establish English colonies that could be used as trading posts and entrepôts in North and Central America. The territory of 'Virginia', named for the 'Virgin Queen' Elizabeth, was founded by settlements backed by Raleigh, although he never went to North America himself. He was the driving force behind the 'lost colony' of Roanoke, founded in 1585, which had disappeared without a trace by 1590.

The Spanish Armada

All this illegal English trading, piracy and settling in the Spanish Americas enraged Spain. A cold war was deepened by the religious divide between the two nations. England supported its fellow protestants in the Netherlands as they fought to throw off Spanish domination, and the final straw was Elizabeth's execution of her catholic cousin and heir, Mary Queen of Scots. In May 1588 King Philip II of Spain, ruler of an empire that spanned the globe, ordered a huge fleet – some 150 ships carrying 18,000 men – to set sail for the English Channel, gather a Spanish army in Flanders and invade England.

Fuelled by the support of the Pope and other Catholic allies, Philip II saw this Armada as the ultimate solution to England's defiant Protestant queen and her meddling Sea Dogs. In response a pack of them, Drake, Hawkins, Frobisher and others came together to harass the Spanish Armada all the way from Cornwall to Kent. As it anchored at Calais waiting for the Spanish army to embark they launched a fireship attack, scattered the Spanish ships and threw themselves at it during a great battle off the coast of the Spanish Netherlands at

LISTEN TO THE
PODCAST

The Spanish Armada

Gravelines on 8 August. Hawkins had prepared the English fleet well. It had small yet powerful battleships, armed with cannon, which transformed the way naval warfare was fought. The Spanish ships were larger and less manoeuvrable: they were floating castles which aimed to grapple their enemy and storm aboard. The English kept their distance and fired volley after volley of iron shot. The Armada lost five ships at Gravelines, but was nearly driven aground before it was rescued by a wind shift and pushed into the North Sea.

The next day, Elizabeth delivered a stirring speech to her troops at Tilbury that has echoed down the centuries as one of the best in English history:

> 'I know I have the body of a weak and feeble woman; but I have the heart and stomach of a king, and of a king of England too, and think foul scorn that Parma or Spain, or any prince of Europe, should dare to invade the borders of my realm.'
>
> **Elizabeth I, The Tilbury Speech**

But the English army would not be needed. The Armada was forced north round Scotland and then Ireland. Bad weather would finish the job started by English cannon. High winds drove dozens of ships ashore on the west coasts of Ireland and Scotland.

England was emerging as a naval power. But Britannia did not rule the waves quite yet. A counter 'English Armada' led by Drake left England the following April, but suffered a similar fate to the Spanish. Further Spanish fleets were sent in 1596, 1597 and 1601, but the weather continued to frustrate the ambitions of the world's most powerful man.

The Rise of Mercantilism

At sea trade and war were crewmates. Sailors were warriors and merchants. Portuguese, Dutch and English traders scrambled to create fortified enclaves down the African coast and on the fringes of the Indian Ocean that could supply fresh food and water to merchant ships. The prize was the import of novel, delicious commodities. Spices like pepper, nutmeg and cinnamon had been traded in small quantities in England since Roman times, but with much better access to overseas markets led to them becoming much more common.

> 'The English might've made their money in the Middle Ages on wool and mutton, but now you had spices coming from the East, things like nutmeg and pepper. They were almost like a kind of powdered gold because for the space they took up in a barrel, you could get an awful lot of money for them.'
>
> **Angus Konstam, historian**

Englishmen also dreamt of precious metals. The mines of Potosí, in modern-day Bolivia, provided so much silver from 1545 on that it led to severe inflation in Western Europe by the end of the century – although many Spanish traders grew immensely wealthy in the process. Hearing this and other more fanciful tales about the untapped wealth of the Americas, Walter Raleigh became obsessed with El Dorado – a mythical jungle city made of gold. He had famously brought tobacco and potatoes back from North America in 1586, and made smoking fashionable at the royal court, now he sought incalculable wealth. He led two expeditions in 1595 and 1617 in search of El Dorado, but returned unsuccessful.

A Golden Age?

What remains of Winchester Castle amounts to a medieval hall, which is now surrounded by administrative buildings. At one end of the Great Hall the huge (and alleged) Arthurian Round Table has been hung on the wall, itself a piece of propaganda with a Tudor rose planted in its centre. This Great Hall served as a courtroom for Sir Walter Raleigh's trial for treason after he was implicated in the Main Plot against James I in November 1603. Found guilty and sentenced to death, he was held in the Tower of London until 1617, then granted release on the condition that a new expedition would return with treasure. Raleigh's son was killed by Spanish sailors and the altercation cost Raleigh's head. He was executed on 29 October 1618 at the ripe old age (for the time) of 66.

The Sea Dogs were always a change of wind direction, a stray cannonball, or a policy change in London away from disaster. Theirs was a world shaped by royal favour and seizing the tide at the flood. They tasted triumph and catastrophe. With Raleigh executed, Drake died on raid into the Spanish Main in which he had stumbled from defeat to defeat. They were celebrated as pioneers of both English naval strength, and maritime commerce. They carried the English flag, language and goods to a multitude of ports all over the world. But they were also thugs. They made money from enslaving other humans. They were hard men of conquest and colonisation. It may have been a 'Golden Era' but only for those close enough to bask in its uneven glow.

Elizabeth's legacy was not as glorious as her apologists would have us believe. Her bloody, expensive, seemingly endless war in Ireland is a stain on her reputation. Munster was racked by famine, scorched earth warfare and atrocities over decades of violence that left as much as a third of its population killed. In the 1590s the crisis was reached as Catholic rebels led by the Earl of Tyrone came close to driving the English out of Ireland. At vast expense the English government clung on, and moved Protestant communities to Ulster to settle confiscated land. An ambitious demographic move with lasting consequences.

History though has been kind to Elizabeth. In a Europe torn apart by religious differences, war and discoveries, England was stable. On her death on 25 March 1603, Elizabeth left a new idea of England and its role in the world as a maritime, trading, fledgling empire. The East India Company was born which would develop the world's biggest commercial company of the following century. England's, and later Britain's, rise to global hegemony is rooted in the reign of Elizabeth. When the queen's successor, James VI of Scotland, now James I of England, made the long journey from Edinburgh down to London to claim the throne, the England he observed was a land of plenty. The England Elizabeth I bequeathed him was prosperous and rich in possibilities but, as he was to discover, it was also divided, febrile and restive.

Corfe Castle, Dorset, captured in 1645 after a long siege

Chapter 9

The English Revolutions

I n the 17th century England was a basket case. The 'land of revolutions', quipped the French. A foreign, Scottish dynasty took the throne; there were at least two revolutions, multiple uprisings, and a series of civil wars and invasions. The monarchy was abolished, a king beheaded, and there was a military dictatorship. The monarch returned, but his brother and successor were driven into exile following a massive foreign invasion led by his son-in-law. There was a whirlwind of violence and political upheaval. In the aftermath of the Reformation a stable religious settlement remained elusive, and the balance of power between Parliament and the hereditary divine right of kings was contested.

The Hapless Stuarts

The Stuart family were somewhat hapless. Only once in over a century did the succession pass in an orderly manner from father to son. That son however ended up on trial and losing his head, while his son made a humiliating escape to France. The later Stuarts failed to produce the required heirs of the right religious persuasion, and after 111 years their distant cousins of the House of Hanover were invited to take over. But despite this chaos, England would enter the 18th century well placed: a constitutional monarchy and fast-growing mercantile economy that supported global ambitions. The ugly duckling of Europe since the mid-15th century was growing into a powerful swan.

Queen Elizabeth I had refused to name an heir for fear of being undermined. When she died there was the possibility of civil war, but James VI of Scotland was her nearest relative, descended from Henry VIII's sister, Margaret Tudor, and he was invited to be King James I of England.

'The potential for civil war was very real and greatly feared ... one of the most dramatic episodes really is the last few weeks and months of Elizabeth's life where of course this great Tudor queen, who we put on a bit of a pedestal today, had failed in the main task of monarchy, which was to preserve the succession, and she had wilfully and persistently refused to marry and name an heir, so she really had left England totally in the lurch.'
Anna Whitelock, City, University of London

James was 36 years old, and had been King of Scotland since 1567, initially as a minor and gaining full control of government in 1583. He styled himself as King of Great Britain and Ireland, and based himself in England: he returned to Scotland only once in his life. While he pushed for closer union from the start of his reign, England and Scotland would remain a 'composite kingdom' of personal union, rather than a political one. Britain would get a combined flag, the 'Union Jack', in 1606 (Jack deriving from 'Jacobus' – the Latin version of 'James'), but Scotland maintained its own parliament, laws and customs.

The golden glow of Elizabeth's England can blind us to the serious economic and religious problems facing the country. The population had grown rapidly during the Tudor period, from 2.2 million at its beginning to close to 4.1 million by the time James I was crowned. But alongside this growth came an income squeeze – food prices rose 800% between 1500 and 1640, while wages increased just 300%. This was set against a backdrop of falling global temperatures known as 'the Little Ice Age'; the Great Frost froze over the Thames for six weeks in 1608, and repeatedly harsher winters led to a collapse in food supply. England experienced famine in 1601–2, and another more serious catastrophe unfolded between 1622 and 1624, towards the end of James I's reign, when it's estimated that around 5% of the population of Lancashire died in what was the nation's last major famine.

RELIGIOUS CHALLENGES

Henry VIII's break with Rome to create a new independent Church had been his solution to a very specific problem, but it had enormous and far-reaching consequences. It splintered the religious and political landscape. Most accepted Protestantism as a new way of life, but a minority clung to Catholicism and faced persecution. As often happens in times of turmoil, extreme groups on the fringes of both sides began to emerge. Some of the specific religious groups and terms are below.

- **Calvinism** – mainstream Protestantism, which was roughly interchangeable with Anglicanism, those who followed the Church of England. Also known as Reformed Christianity.

- **Puritans** – a subgroup of more orthodox Calvinists felt the English Reformation had not gone far enough, and wanted to rid the Church of England of remaining Catholic practices.
- **Presbyterianism** – a form of council-led Calvinist church government that was practised particularly in Scotland. No one group or person had more influence over another in church matters – thus (similar to Puritanism) they rejected the idea of bishops.
- **Episcopal** – a form of church governance managed by bishops. The Church of England remained Episcopal, leading to conflict with Puritans and Presbyterians alike.
- **Recusants** – Catholics who refused to submit to the Church of England and continued to practise in private. Due to its close trading links to majority-Catholic Ireland, the north-west of England had the highest proportion of recusant Catholics.

In early 17th-century England, Catholics were very much in the minority. James I's arrival on the English throne did little to allay fears of persecution, and some turned to militancy. The infamous Gunpowder Plot of November 1605 saw Sir Robert Catesby lead a Catholic attempt to blow up the Houses of Parliament and assassinate the new king, with the intention of replacing him with a Catholic monarch. The plot was foiled by an anonymous letter sent to a courtier. Guards searched Westminster Palace on the evening of 5 November and found Guy Fawkes, another conspirator, guarding 36 barrels of gunpowder. On 27 January 1606, the eight surviving conspirators were found guilty of treason and sentenced to be hanged, drawn and quartered. An Act of Parliament designated 5 November as a day of thanksgiving. The tradition of gathering, building bonfires and partying endures to this day.

Despite the grisly demise of the plotters, James actually loosened the laws against Catholicism. Under Elizabeth I, the people of England had been required by law to attend her Protestant communion and recognise her as head of the Church, or potentially face execution. Under James I, as long as other denominations kept their views to themselves and didn't cause trouble they were mostly tolerated. But both Catholicism and Puritanism were seen as threats to the authority of the monarchy and the Church of England, and religious discrimination would continue.

One way that religious groups could escape persecution was to emigrate across the Atlantic. The first permanent English colony in the New World, aptly named Jamestown, was founded in 1607. In 1620 a ship of Pilgrims (who weren't quite Puritans, but similar) emigrated from Plymouth aboard the *Mayflower*. Some 150,000 would follow them west to America in the first half of the 17th century, and the first eight American colonies would be founded along the eastern seaboard.

At the behest of petitioning Puritans, James I arranged the Hampton Court Conference of 1604, but refused to rearrange the episcopal form of Church government. 'No bishop, no king,' he said when pressed on the issue. A new translation of the Bible – the King James Version – was commissioned at the conference, and is seen as a foundational text of English literature.

With Parliament too, James was often uncompromising. He dissolved it for seven years from 1614. He was a prolific writer, and his works *The True Law of Free Monarchies* and *Basilikon Doron* argued for the divine rights of kings – something that would rub off strongly on his son Charles I. James was a keen patron of other writers. Shakespeare's players became The King's Men. John Donne and Francis Bacon enjoyed royal favour. The theatre remained a key part of court life. In foreign policy, he sought to extricate England from expensive foreign wars, or avoid them altogether, as a self-styled *Rex Pacificus* (Peacemaker King), while also rebuilding the nation's finances. In 1604 he signed a peace treaty with Spain, ending a near-20-year conflict and the threat of invasion. He likewise rebuffed requests to join the Protestant Alliance in Europe at the outbreak of the Thirty Years' War in 1618.

SOMERSET HOUSE, THE STRAND, LONDON

Built in 1547 for Edward Seymour (Duke of Somerset), Somerset House soon came under Crown ownership, and Elizabeth I resided there during Queen Mary I's reign. James I signed the Treaty of London (1604) with Spain here, and throughout the 17th century it housed royal consorts, including Charles I's wife Queen Henrietta Maria. During the Civil War, Parliament repurposed parts for army headquarters and used it to host Oliver Cromwell's lying-in-state. Substantial rebuilding occurred following the Restoration, including an impressive riverfront, yet, despite further renovations by Sir Christopher Wren in 1685, after the Glorious Revolution Somerset House fell into decline. Starting in 1775, the building was redesigned in a neoclassical style, and began housing government and naval offices, cultural societies, and later the Inland Revenue. Today, Somerset House is known for its art galleries and cultural events.

The epithet 'the wisest fool in Christendom' has been affixed to James I, possibly due to diplomacy or his often lecturing and tactless communication style. Yet his avoidance of foreign war and insistence on taking the 'middle path' in the face of dangerous religious division provided much-needed political stability. It could not be said that he was loved by his English subjects; there was bigotry about his Scottishness, and his favouritism created jealousies. That partiality seemed to extend to romantic affairs with several men; his lover George Villiers became the Duke of Buckingham in 1623, the first non-royal duke since 1483. Buckingham would survive James's death and maintain his importance into the early reign of Charles I.

CHARLES I

It was Buckingham's swashbuckling expeditions against Spain and France that would exacerbate antagonisms between Charles I, Parliament and the people. Buckingham was responsible for two fiascos; an expedition to relieve French Protestants in La Rochelle ended in defeat, and his attempt to emulate the mighty Francis Drake by raiding the Spanish coast descended into a drunken farce as sailors died of disease and poor logistics saw them succumb to scurvy and starvation. Buckingham also arranged a controversial marriage for his royal master, to Henrietta Maria, the Catholic daughter of Henry IV of France.

Military failure, government funds squandered, a Catholic French queen – these were not popular. Charles was not the man to heal these divisions. He had inherited his father's strong beliefs in the divine right of kings, and was high-handed when it came to relations with Parliament. In his first four years as King of England, he dissolved Parliament three times, only recalling it when he ran out of money. But Parliament had little appetite to back Buckingham's adventures, and rather than vote for more funds they tried to impeach the over-mighty duke.

Creative Taxation

England's treasury was empty, but it was one of the least-taxed nations in Europe. The Stuarts were paying the price of Elizabeth I's policy of selling land to pay her bills, which meant they had less Crown revenue and struggled to secure loans. Charles I had his advisers root through statute books to find any archaic legislation that could help his cause. Among his methods were:

- **The Distraint of Knighthood** – previously unused for a century, requiring men earning over £40 a year from land to present themselves at Charles's coronation to be knighted. Wealthy men who did not attend were fined.
- **Forced loans** – landowners were forced to lend the king money in 1627 to pay for the French war. Refusing to pay could mean imprisonment without trial.
- **Martial law** – an indirect method that forced citizens to feed and house sailors and soldiers, meaning the people bore the cost of supporting the military in their own homes.

Parliament responded by forcing Charles to assent to the Petition of Right of 1628, clarifying individual protections against the Crown. Its passing in June led to widespread public celebrations, but its enforcement would not last. Buckingham was assassinated shortly after, although not at the behest of Parliament. The king was devastated by the loss of his closest ally, and conflict with the Commons in March 1629 led to Charles once again dissolving it. It was the beginning of 11 years of 'personal rule' whereby Charles used royal prerogative, without Parliamentary consent, to raise money.

'One of the big problems that the Crown has in this period is that the value of their tax base is going down in real terms because of inflation. They find it difficult to increase the amount of tax that they're collecting in line with the real value of what they need. And that means that they have to then go to Parliament and say, can we have some more money, please? And Parliament basically says, no, unless you give us these kinds of concessions and that repeated process of negotiation becomes very, very fractured.'

Jonathan Healey, University of Oxford

From 1634, Charles increased a feudal levy called 'ship money'. This medieval legislation had been used by Plantagenet kings to bolster naval funding in times of war, and could be raised by royal prerogative without Parliamentary approval. But Charles used it in peacetime, and extended its collection from coastal areas to inland counties. Opposition grew during the 1630s and in 1637 MP John Hampden was prosecuted for non-payment. Judges found against Hampden were a close 7 to 5, suggesting a split in the judiciary.

Religious Crisis

Not content with driving through semi-legal revenue-raising measures, Charles plunged headlong into religious controversy. He appointed William Laud as Archbishop of Canterbury in 1633. Laud was a 'High Church' Anglican who seemed to border on being Catholic and enraged Puritans with his attempts to bring back ritual and practices from the Catholic Church. His introduction of a Scottish Book of Common Prayer was met with riots in Edinburgh in July 1637, the start of violence that would soon spill out across the three kingdoms. In April 1638 Scots signed the National Covenant and voted to expel bishops. The king interpreted this as an act of rebellion, and planned to subjugate his Scottish subjects by force. Charles reluctantly recalled Parliament, after its 11-year absence, in April 1640 in an effort to raise money, but refused to meet Parliamentary demands to resolve all their grievances. He dissolved it within a month. The Scottish Covenanters invaded the north of England in the autumn of 1640, and occupied Newcastle. They demanded £850 a day until they left England, and Charles was forced to recall Parliament again in November.

Parliaments

The period 1640 to 1660 saw enormous turbulence and two of the most famous Parliaments in English history:
- **Short Parliament** – beginning in April 1640, this Parliament lasted only three weeks before Charles dissolved it.
- **Long Parliament** – beginning in November 1640, this Parliament ensured it could not be dissolved without its own

consent, which technically didn't happen until 1660. Within this were various army purges, leading to the 'Rump' (1648) and the 'Barebones' (1653) Parliaments.

The new Parliament acted quickly to end any return to personal rule. It had the king's close adviser, Thomas Wentworth, Earl of Strafford, executed for treason in May 1641. Archbishop Laud was impeached the same month. Bit by bit, Charles's prerogatives were whittled away. Non-parliamentary taxes, such as ship money, were declared illegal. A treaty with the Scots was reached in July, and they left Newcastle a month later. But by the summer of 1641 the majority of the House of Commons were convinced that Charles was so untrustworthy that they should take a much greater role in governing the kingdom.

Parliament had become increasingly dominated by Puritans, who found themselves frustrated by bishops in the House of Lords. They moved to dismantle the Church hierarchy, from which it was only a short hop to questioning the monarchy itself. Charles saw his Catholic Irish subjects as a source of support against increasingly hardline Protestants. Charles's attempts to raise loyal Catholic troops further alienated his English antagonists, who threatened retaliation. This, in turn, pushed Catholic army officers in Ireland, fearing a wave of Protestant repression, to rebel. Irish Catholics had long resented the presence of the Ulster Plantations in the north, and they now moved to disarm Protestants before they could move against them. In late 1641

LISTEN TO THE
PODCAST

17th Century
Revolutionary England

sectarian violence led to massacre, and some 4,000 Protestants were killed, with thousands more being expelled. The Catholic rebels produced a forged warrant to say they were acting on the king's behalf.

The deepening crisis led Parliament to narrowly pass the Grand Remonstrance, a list of 200 demands for reform. Charles refused to agree to the terms, and on 4 January 1642 he stormed the House of Commons, accompanied by armed soldiers, in an attempt to arrest five MPs who were believed to be ringleaders of the resistance. But the five members had been warned ahead of his arrival and had escaped down the River Thames.

Both Parliament and the City of London refused Charles's demands to hand over the five members and revolutionary violence tore through the city. It was clear that the king had lost control of his capital, and on 10 January he fled. Tensions rose over the following months as Parliament passed an Act enabling it to raise its own army. In June, it approved a list of propositions that sought a larger share of power. Charles rejected this too; a political, peaceful settlement was getting ever more unlikely. The king turned to force as he raised the royal standard at Nottingham on 22 August 1642. The age of civil wars had begun. The battles that ensued were among the most brutal to have taken place on English soil. Towns, villages and families were torn apart when forced to choose between the Parliamentarians and Charles I's Royalists.

──────── **THE FIRST ENGLISH CIVIL WAR** ────────

Historians now recognise the Civil Wars as the bloodiest conflict per capita in recorded British history. The conflict had its roots in relations between the Stuarts' three kingdoms, England, Scotland and Ireland, so 'The Wars of the Three Kingdoms' might be a better label than 'English Civil War'. There were three spasms of violence in England, all with important Scottish involvement. The bloodiest was fought from 1642 to 1646, but a second bout came in 1648, and there was an Anglo-Scottish war from 1650 to 1652. The Parliamentarians would also invade Ireland in 1649, and complete a savage reconquest by 1653. There were more than 600 battles and sieges, which, added to massacres, dislocation, famine and low-level violence, resulted in the loss of around 4% of the population of England and Wales, and considerably more in Scotland and Ireland.

The first major battle of the conflict, the Battle of Edgehill, was fought in Warwickshire on 23 October 1642. Any expectations that the conflict might be fleeting were quickly dispelled. The battle was bloody but inconclusive, and it set the tone for the next two years of war. Neither side would land a decisive blow. After Edgehill, Parliament was just strong enough to prevent Charles from entering London. He established his headquarters in Oxford over the winter.

By the spring of 1643 the nation was being mobilised. As many as 10% of adult males would eventually be called to arms for the Parliamentarians, who came to be known as the 'Roundheads', and the Royalists, who were dubbed the 'Cavaliers'. Both labels were initially used by the opposition as terms of derision, before being widely accepted as the Civil Wars rolled on.

Over the summer of 1643, the Cavaliers briefly gained the upper hand. Victory on 30 June at the Battle of Adwalton Moor, near Bradford, saw the king's forces take control of northern England. Just two weeks later, they had also gained the southwest after defeating Parliamentarians at Roundway Down in Wiltshire. But Parliament had a major advantage in a prolonged struggle – control of London. With a population of half a million, the capital was larger than the next 50 English towns combined. It was also the heart of English trade and finance and was easier to defend than a great swathe of countryside.

Scotland too would prove invaluable to the Parliamentarians. After the military setbacks of that summer, Parliament allied with the Scots on condition that Scottish-style Presbyterianism would be adopted in England. This 'Solemn League and Covenant' was agreed in September 1643, and that same month saw a Parliamentary victory at the Battle of Newbury. Scottish forces invaded England in early 1644, besieging York, and Parliament won a decisive victory at Marston Moor, the largest battle of the English Civil Wars, on 2 July. Northern England fell into the hands of Parliament.

There were plenty of twists and turns to come, however. Over late August and September, the Royalists captured some 5,000 Roundhead infantry at the Battle of Lostwithiel, which won them back control over southwest England. In December 1644 a Parliamentarian Lieutenant General and MP for Cambridge, Oliver Cromwell, gave a fiery speech in which he argued that the war would never be won unless Parliament's military strength was overhauled. Reforms followed; most importantly, Parliament forged a new, professional, military force: the New Model Army.

> 'Cromwell suffers from no doubts whatsoever, because being a born-again military Puritan fits in so much with the rest of his character, it fits in with his exceptional tendency to see the world as divided into the goodies and the baddies, and the baddies as deserving of no mercy whatsoever, especially if they take up arms.'
>
> **Ronald Hutton, University of Bristol**

These reforms propelled Parliament to victories the following year. In the process, Oliver Cromwell emerged as a central figure. A brilliant strategist and deadly tactician, his grasp of cavalry was brilliant. In two key battles in summer 1645, at Naseby and then Langport, the New Model Army under Cromwell and his colleague Thomas Fairfax crushed the Royalists. The king's forces started to desert, due to lack of pay and the looming spectre of defeat. Soon resistance was largely limited to garrisons desperately holding out in sieges. Charles fled north and surrendered to a Scottish force near Newark in Nottinghamshire on 5 May 1646. Wallingford, the last English Royalist stronghold, fell in July. Harlech in Wales held out until the following March.

LISTEN TO THE
PODCAST

The Rise of
Oliver Cromwell

CORFE CASTLE

In one of the more celebrated sieges, Corfe Castle in Dorset held out until it was captured in spring 1645. A medieval royal castle, it had held King John's crown jewels, as well as Edward II during his imprisonment. Its imposing position on top of a hill and its thick walls had made it extremely difficult to capture, and it survived one siege in 1643. On Parliament's orders it was 'slighted' (demolished) in March 1645. The extensive ruins serve as a reminder of the Civil War's cultural vandalism, although there were clearly valid military reasons at the time for the slighting. Many other beautiful castles were destroyed, while Roundhead soldiers ransacked religious sites like Winchester Cathedral and Oliver Cromwell even melted down the Tudor crown jewels.

Killing a King

After nine months of negotiations, the Scots eventually released the king to Parliament in exchange for £400,000 (£47 million in today's money) and withdrew from England. At this stage Charles was still regarded as an indispensable figure and necessary component of any constitutional settlement. He was shuffled between a series of locations before being held under house arrest at Hampton Court Palace, a gilded cage from which he managed to escape in November 1647. He made his way to the Isle of Wight, but Parliament caught up with him, and he was held in Carisbrooke Castle.

Towards the end of the war, groups of rural farmers had banded together as 'Clubmen', intending to drive soldiers from either side out of their area. The people were tired of war. To pay for it, Parliament had imposed heavy taxes and confiscated the lands of gentry on the Royalist side. Parliament could do little to alleviate terrible harvests and plague outbreaks, which only intensified demands to reach a settlement or Restoration. Against this grim backdrop, in June 1647 the Puritan-led Parliament also introduced one of their most infamous pieces of legislation – the Ordinance for Abolishing of Festivals. Christmas was cancelled, leading to riots in major towns. To many people Charles's tyranny of the 1630s had simply been replaced by the tyranny of Parliament.

The army took control, marching into London in August 1647 to purge Parliament of those who sought to disband it and reach a settlement with the king. Parliament had also failed to meet the implementation of Presbyterianism to the expectations of the Scots. In December, the king showed his duplicitousness and signed a secret deal known as The Engagement, which promised to impose Presbyterianism in England if Scottish forces helped to restore him to power. He succeeded in engineering a Scottish invasion in 1648. Several pro-Royalist uprisings also broke out across England and Wales. It was a Second Civil War.

For the most part the Parliamentarian forces comfortably suppressed this poorly coordinated insurgency, and the fighting only lasted six months. Nonetheless, there were several significant clashes, notably the Battle of Maidstone that June, which saw Fairfax defeat Kentish Royalists, and the Battle of Preston in August, a showdown between Cromwell's New Model Army and a troop of Scottish Covenanters led by the Duke of Hamilton.

There was also a substantial revolt in South Wales that began as a dispute over unpaid military wages before escalating into a full-blown Royalist rebellion that dragged on for four months, until Cromwell's forces finally besieged the insurgents' stronghold in Pembroke.

Despite their victory, the army and Parliament were still split over whether to reinstate Charles or remove him. The army decided on the latter, and purged the House of Commons for the second time on 6 December 1648. Some 45 MPs were imprisoned and over half prevented from taking their seats. Only a minority of the remaining MPs would participate in the 'Rump Parliament'. Over the next two months, it moved to try Charles for treason, an unprecedented charge for a king to face. He was accused of pursuing 'a wicked design to erect and uphold in himself an unlimited and tyrannical power to rule according to his will, and to overthrow the rights and liberties of the people therein represented.'

At the conclusion of a three-day trial in January 1649, Charles was declared guilty and sentenced to death by execution. His death warrant was signed by 59 men, one of them being Oliver Cromwell. The judgement read:

'For all which treasons and crimes this court doth adjudge that he, the said Charles Stuart, as a tyrant, traitor, murderer, and public enemy to the good people of this nation, shall be put to death by the severing of his head from his body.'

—— THE KING IS DEAD. THE WAR GOES ON ——

On the evening of 29 January 1649, Charles said goodbye to three of his children. He told the two youngest not to cry and to obey their elder brother, Charles. Upon his imminent death, Charles I believed, his son would become the lawful, divinely ordained ruler of England, Scotland and Ireland.

Anxious not to shiver from the cold, as it might be mistaken for fearful quaking, Charles requested a second shirt before being led to his execution. As he stepped forward onto the scaffold that had been built outside the Banqueting House on Whitehall, he looked out over the crowds and made a short speech that was lost in the wind.

At the centre of the platform Charles was confronted by the instruments of his demise: a quartering block and a razor-sharp axe. Two men in masks stood to attention. The king lowered his neck to the block. After a brief pause, he stretched out his hand to indicate that he was ready. The executioner severed his head with one clean blow.

England no longer had a monarch. It was the start of an 11-year period of 'Republican' rule, often referred to as the Commonwealth. As far as the Royalists were concerned, though, Charles I's eldest son, also named Charles, became the rightful king the minute his father's head fell into the basket. Even if his status as King of England remained contentious throughout the Commonwealth, the Scottish Parliament proclaimed him king on 5 February 1649, a few days after his father's execution.

With England now securely in Parliament's grip, Oliver Cromwell was dispatched to Ireland. A Catholic Confederation had taken control during the chaotic years of the Civil Wars, and had allied with those who wished to see Charles II restored to the throne. In retribution for the 1641 rebellion, the New Model Army invaded and employed the most brutal methods to subjugate the island. The town of Drogheda was put to the sword in September 1649 on Cromwell's orders. More atrocities followed at the sack of Wexford in October. By May 1650, with much of eastern Ireland subdued, Charles II abandoned his Irish followers, pivoting dramatically to a policy of working with the Scottish. Cromwell in response left Ireland to take command of English forces for an invasion of Scotland.

In league with the Scottish Covenanters, Charles II was raising an army to invade England. But on 22 July 1650 the New Model Army moved first, forcing a Scottish retreat to Edinburgh. That September Cromwell led a surprise attack at Dunbar, taking at least 6,000 Scottish prisoners, and the following July he largely ended Scottish resistance to the north. Refusing to surrender, and believing the English population would rally to his cause, Charles II then invaded England. Few Englishmen rallied to the Royalist banner, and the badly outnumbered Cavalier army was defeated at the Battle of Worcester on 3 September 1651.

Boscobel House and the Royal Oak

Charles II was one of the few Royalists to escape from Worcester. Anxious to avoid a fate like his father's, he fled north to Shropshire and took refuge at a remote hunting lodge named Boscobel House. When Cromwell's search parties arrived, he spent a miserably wet day in the branches of a large oak tree. After six more adventurous weeks on the run, he eventually made his way to Shoreham-on-Sea in Sussex, where he boarded a ship to France.

Charles II's narrow escape was an impressive feat of derring-do that would do no harm to his reputation, but in the practical world of hard power Parliament was once again utterly dominant. Their opponent had been trounced in battle and forced out of the country in ignominy. The Battle of Worcester was the final major engagement of the Wars of the Three Kingdoms and the Third English Civil War. Scotland would be absorbed into the Commonwealth, with its Parliament abolished. A settlement followed in Ireland in 1642, leading to the confiscation of Catholic lands and a series of punitive laws. Thousands of Irish people were sent to the New World as forced labourers. Ireland would not forget Cromwell's nor English brutality.

———— THE COMMONWEALTH ————

Parliament's rule was strict. Along with the banning of Christian festivals, pubs were closed, theatres were shut, sports were banned. Excessive swearing could land you in prison. Taxes were high to fund a vast military complex.

The revolution began to eat its own. Furious at the Rump Parliament for being ineffectual, on 20 April 1653 Cromwell stormed the Commons with armed guards to deliver a lacerating speech that has echoed down the ages.

> 'It is high time for me to put an end to your sitting in this place, which you have dishonoured by your contempt of all virtue, and defiled by your practice of every vice. Ye are a factious crew, and enemies to all good government . . . Is there a single virtue now remaining among you? Is there one vice you do not process? . . . So! Take away that shining bauble there, and lock up the doors. In the name of God, go!'
>
> **Oliver Cromwell**

Cromwell dismissed the Rump and created a new 'Nominated Assembly' of 144 unelected MPs, which popularly became known as the 'Barebones Parliament'. They achieved little more than the 'factious' Rump, and that December Cromwell took power as 'Lord Protector' – king in all but name. Little more than a year later an ill-fated Royalist uprising pushed England and Wales further into the hands of the army. Cromwell divided the nation into ten regions where Major-Generals would administer and maintain security. They acted as virtual dictators within their areas, heavy-handed and making clumsy attempts to implement moral reform.

Cromwell was even offered the kingship in 1657, but refused it. Part of his reasoning may have been that the royal role would put him under more legal restraint than that of Lord Protector. Ultimately Britain under Cromwell was Britain under control of the Puritan army with a supreme leader – a theocratic dictatorship. Parliament had fought the civil wars on the basis that the king could not be above the law, but Cromwell was. He would tax by decree and imprison without trial, yet he firmly believed his actions were in the name of God – just like Charles I before him.

The Commonwealth was glued together by Cromwell's conviction and the strength of his personality. When he died in 1658, Britain's 'Republican' experiment disintegrated. His son Richard was briefly his heir as Lord Protector, but he had neither the support nor the stomach for it. After just eight months, a powerful clique in the army assembled the Rump, which voted to dissolve itself and end the Protectorate.

'[The Commonwealth] was the worst of both worlds . . . it was like a corrupted monarchy. It had promised so much but at the end of the day, Cromwell kind of stole the king's clothes, and so the fact that his son was going to succeed him . . . it was actually "so what's the difference?". If we'd had a more genuine experiment in what it would be to be a republic, and that remained true more to its principles, or at least some of the principles that many people believed that were born in that time of the civil wars, then perhaps it would have had a greater chance of success and the restoration of the monarchy not be so relatively easy.'

Anna Whitelock, City, University of London

Charles II was invited to return from exile and become king under a revived monarchy; it was a Restoration. After landing in May 1660, he basked in the widespread celebrations that accompanied his homecoming. Printers were quick to celebrate their new monarch. His heroic adventures were emphasised. It's no coincidence that so many Restoration-era pubs were named the Royal Oak.

THE RESTORATION

Charles did his best to pretend that the Commonwealth had never happened. The Restoration proclaimed that Charles II had been king since the death of his father in 1649. Acts of Parliament from the reign of Charles I remained in force, while those of the Commonwealth were voided. Some Crown and Church lands confiscated and sold off by Parliament were returned, and many Royalist leaders who had been forced into exile made their way home. Other changes were tacitly accepted in a careful spirit of compromise.

Charles acted magnanimously, and had been careful not to seek too much retribution. From his Dutch exile in the city of Breda, he made a series of pledges, known as the Declaration of Breda which provided a general pardon for crimes committed during the English Civil Wars, with the exception of those directly involved in the killing of his father. He gave these promises legal force with the Indemnity and Oblivion Act in April 1660.

There was relief and some euphoria at first. Pubs and theatres were reopened, while the much-missed Christian festivals were restored. There were developments in the field of science too. Charles was a patron of the Royal Society, founded in November 1660 as a national academy of science. He also founded the Royal Greenwich Observatory in 1675. This new scientific community fostered the conditions for Isaac Newton to produce his great work *Principia* in 1687, shortly after the king's death.

THEATRE ROYAL, DRURY LANE

During the Restoration, Thomas Killigrew and Sir William Davenant received royal patents from King Charles II to establish two theatres, one being the Theatre Royal in London's Drury Lane. Four different theatres in total have occupied the site, which remains the world's oldest theatre site in continuous use – and has a reputation as one of the most haunted too. Built by Sir Christopher Wren in 1663, the original theatre was known as 'Theatre Royal in Bridges Street'. It flourished under Charles II's reign, showcasing plays by eminent Restoration playwrights and gaining royal favour. Prominent actors performed there, including Nell Gwyn, Charles II's long-time mistress. After it was destroyed by fire in 1672, a second theatre opened in 1674, followed by a new, updated theatre in 1794. The current Grade I listed theatre, opened in 1812, is owned by composer Andrew Lloyd Webber.

But the honeymoon did not last. London and the country at large suffered its last great plague outbreak in 1665–6; it likely killed 100,000 people. Then the capital was devastated by the Great Fire of London in early September 1666. The Second Anglo-Dutch War of 1655–67 ended in humiliation when Dutch ships sailed up the River Medway and annihilated the Royal Navy; they towed the flagship the *Royal Charles* back to the Netherlands as fires raged through Chatham Dockyard.

Charles himself also built up a reputation as a 'Merry Monarch'. He had spent some of his exile in the opulent settings of Louis XIV's French court, and is credited with popularising both champagne drinking and yachting in England. He also popularised not repaying his loans. Over the course of his reign Charles had a legion of mistresses and 17 acknowledged illegitimate offspring. Charles married the Portuguese Catherine of Braganza in 1662, an unpopular choice given her Catholicism. It was a loveless marriage, with Charles even insisting that various mistresses serve the queen at court, like Barbara Palmer, who bore him five children and was a Lady of the Bedchamber. The distraught queen suffered three miscarriages and the royal couple produced no legitimate heirs. Charles's younger brother was the Catholic James Duke of York. He was not a popular choice. Parliamentary opposition stirred again.

Plots

In 1678 a crisis was sparked by an implausible 'Popish Plot'. Outlandish claims swirled. Queen Catherine was said to be planning to poison the king and bring Catholic James to the throne. Anti-Catholic hysteria in both England and Scotland, never hard to inflame, hit new heights. James was implicated through conspiratorial letters found in the study of his secretary.

Parliament attempted to remove James and any other Catholic from the royal succession, which Charles refused to agree to. He shared his father's belief in divine right: God made kings, not Parliament. He dispensed with Parliament as much as he could and ruled without them, relying on secret funding from Catholic France. This 'Exclusion Crisis' gave birth to the first political party, the Earl of Shaftesbury's 'Whigs', who pushed for the exclusion of James. Another faction, known as 'Tories', were largely supportive of the king and his opposition to an Exclusion Bill. Having won some concessions, the Whigs in Parliament backed down. James's succession was assured, although acceptance of it wouldn't last.

Charles II died of a stroke in 1685, having made a deathbed conversion to Catholicism. Throughout his reign he had sought to balance his three kingdoms, riven with religious and political divisions. Where possible he had tried to reduce the burden on religious minorities. In 1673 he had attempted to repeal statutes against Nonconformists. Fierce Parliamentary opposition forced him to assent to the Test Acts, which forbade practising Catholics and dissenting Protestants from holding public office. Personal charm, a canny grasp of people and religious flexibility allowed him to maintain his rule over a fractious realm.

AN ILL-FATED REIGN

James II had little of the political astuteness that had allowed his big brother to survive his greatest challenges. He was a headstrong military commander, who opened his first Parliament with a veiled threat:

'. . . the best way to engage me to meet you often is always to use me well'.

It seemed a decent legacy. People remembered the civil wars and had little appetite for a repeat. He could work with the many Tories in Parliament. Trade was booming and Parliament assigned all revenue raised from taxes on that trade to James for as long as he lived. There were challenges. He was forced to put down a rebellion led by Charles's eldest illegitimate son, James Scott, the Duke of Monmouth. An overwhelming Royalist victory at Sedgemoor was followed by a heavy-handed execution of more than 300, including Monmouth, who was James's nephew. James grew the army, and filled many top positions with Catholics.

It did not take him long to fall out with almost everyone. Whigs were enraged by his sympathy for Catholics, Tories were estranged by his attempts to relieve the burden on dissenting Protestants. In the face of cross-party opposition, James dissolved this 'Loyal Parliament' and opted to rule without it. He caused further consternation with his Declaration of Indulgences in 1687, which lifted the penal laws against these other religious groups by royal prerogative, which was met by widespread opposition by Anglican clergymen.

———— THE GLORIOUS REVOLUTION ————

James was already 54 in 1688 and his second marriage was child-less. It was expected that his Protestant daughter Mary, and her Dutch husband, William of Orange, would succeed him. But on 10 June his second wife Mary of Modena, a Catholic, gave birth to a son – James Edward Stuart. This was the final straw for disgruntled politicians across the party divide. Catholicism meant foreign-ness and tyranny. The child meant a Catholic succession. Members of the political elite asked William and Mary to intervene. Most notably, the 'Immortal Seven', a group of powerful magnates, sent their formal invitation on 30 June:

> '. . . the people are so generally dissatisfied with the present conduct of the government, in relation to their religion, liberties and properties (all which have been greatly invaded), and they are in such expectation of their prospects being daily worse, that your Highness may be assured, there are nineteen parts of twenty of the people throughout the kingdom, who are desirous of a change . . .'
>
> **Invitation to William by the 'Immortal Seven'**

William had been amassing his forces since April. A vast navy, more than twice the size of the Spanish Armada and carrying 40,000 men, set sail on 1 November. The stage was set for a bloody repeat of the civil wars, but it did not materialise. In the face of invasion, James II appears to have suffered a mental collapse and his army deserted him, leaving William's army to march uncontested into London.

The last successful invasion of England was unquestionably a foreign one. William's army was made up largely of Dutch and Continental troops. But William himself was in the Stuart line of succession. He was a grandson of Charles I through his mother Mary, and his wife and cousin, another Mary, was the daughter of James II. To sweeten the prospect of a foreign king he was made to accept the throne, for the only time in English history, as a joint sovereign, with his wife Mary.

They were crowned as King and Queen of England, Ireland and Scotland in April 1689. James had fled to France. He had thrown his Great Seal into the River Thames, so Parliament was able to claim that he had abdicated rather than been defeated and driven into exile. The price of his crown was that William was forced to agree to a sweeping programme of reform: a new Bill of Rights, guaranteed regular meetings of Parliament, restrictions of standing armies, and more freedoms for Protestant dissenters through the Toleration Act. Catholics, meanwhile, saw little improvement in their legal status, and they would be entirely excluded from the succession. Quickly these reforms came to be hailed as a 'Glorious Revolution'. The battles of the 17th century between king and Parliament had been largely settled. The sovereign was not above the law. They owed obligations to their subjects, and ruled only with their consent.

The Iron Bridge in Shropshire, constructed in 1779

Chapter 10

Industrial and French Revolutions

T he Industrial Revolution was one of the most important
events in human history, and it began in Britain. It was
driven by the mechanisation of the textile industry, but would
eventually transform almost every aspect of life, from transport to agriculture. New inventions, such as the steam engine,
and the development of the factory process would make Britain
the workshop of the world. The causes of the revolution are a
hot topic of debate among historians. England and Scotland
had gone through great political strife in the 17th century, but
despite that maritime trade and an entrepreneurial culture had
developed. The relative domestic stability of the 18th century,
easy access to credit and investment and a functional legal
system provided the necessary environment for rapid growth.
Different parts of England and Scotland claim to be the precise
birthplace of the Industrial Revolution, but we're going to
focus here on the remarkable story of the English West
Midlands.

———— COAL, COKE AND IRONBRIDGE ————

Traversing the River Severn to the south of Telford, Shropshire,
is the world's first large iron-made bridge, constructed in 1779

and now the centrepiece of the historic village of Ironbridge. It was constructed by floating ten 70-foot, 38-tonne ribs cast in iron upriver, then throwing them 55 feet into the air to form five great arches. This soaring metal skeleton supported a 100-foot-long roadway, linking the two sides of the gorge, and the hillsides became a vast coal mine.

In nearby Coalbrookdale in 1709, Abraham Darby used coke instead of charcoal to smelt iron in his blast furnaces for the first time. This was a big step forward. Coal was used for firing ceramics, refining salt and making bricks, glass and soap, but its sulphurous impurities meant it wasn't suitable for smelting iron. Coke was a purer fuel than coal. Made by smothering smoking coal in peat turf, it was lighter, cheaper to use, and burned much hotter. With coke, inexpensive cast iron became readily available. Darby's goals were fairly modest: he established a profitable business making cooking pots. But he was helping to set the stage for the Industrial Revolution. His grandson, Abraham Darby III, would build the Iron Bridge. And for the refreshment of those at the coalface, coke also proved convenient in the brewing of pale ale.

The particular geology of the Severn Gorge helps explain why Ironbridge became a wellspring of the Industrial Revolution. Certain coals were better for coking, while another coal, used in steam engines, was called steam coal. Britain had an abundance of easy-access coal, and Ironbridge contained a wide range of it, plus different clays, limestone and iron ore. The glacial gorge also made mining easier, bringing valuable minerals close to the surface.

While today the gorge rings with birdsong, a few centuries back it would have resembled J.R.R. Tolkein's Mordor, drenched in smoke. Photographs from the late 19th century depict an area that has been devastated, with few trees, little under-growth, and spoil heaps everywhere. When they were exploit-ing the resources beneath the ground, nobody cared much about what they did with the refuse. In the century since the industry of Ironbridge petered out, nature has once again taken over the gorge.

Going Iron-Mad

Another ironmaster to leave a mark in Coalbrookdale was John Wilkinson, a sponsor of the famous Iron Bridge. He invented a precision boring machine that helped make cannon barrels – arguably the first machine tool – and piston cylinders used in early steam engines pioneered by James Watt. So fascinated was John Wilkinson by the potential of iron, which made him his fortune, that he acquired the nickname 'Iron-Mad'. He built the first iron boat in 1787 and later had several iron coffins made, plus an iron obelisk to mark his grave in the Cumbrian village of Lindale-in-Cartmel. Coalbrookdale isn't the only place with a claim to being the birthplace of the Industrial Revolution, but its contribution is undeniable.

'We call ourselves *one* of the birthplaces of the Industrial Revolution. The seminal thing is Abraham Darby smelting iron . . . But it's also the development of things like mould tech-nology. John Wilkinson is in the area as well, and he's classed as the father of machine tools. So you've got the combination of a lot of iron production and technology developing at an amaz-ing rate.'

Kate Cadman, Ironbridge Gorge Museum Trust

——————— THE TEXTILE REVOLUTION ———————

Textile manufacturing drove the Industrial Revolution in England. It was largely located in south Lancashire and around the Pennines. The weaving of silk, wool and linen fabrics became much easier to do at scale, but it was the king, cotton, that eclipsed them all.

Britain's cotton industry in the late 1700s was ripe for reinvention. It was a 'cottage' industry, with workers weaving products, by hand, from home. This could lead to difficulties in maintaining quality and transporting goods, while workers were difficult to mobilise at short notice. Britain's higher wages also meant it was difficult to compete with high-quality but cheap Indian products.

Merchants and inventors investigated how to increase the productivity of their labour. They sought new technology that would lower costs. In 1733, John Kay's flying shuttle was among the first of these inventions. It was a small wooden tool that let weavers 'fly' a weft thread from one side of a loom to the other, halving the weavers necessary for the task. By the mid-1700s it had been widely adopted.

Further innovations transformed the industry. Kay's flying shuttle increased production speeds, and demand grew for more spinners to keep the looms working. The next big step was James Hargreaves's invention of the spinning jenny. Created in 1764, it could spin many spindles at a time by rotating a wheel, while a bar could be moved by the same operator to adjust the thread. It tripled the speed of a spinner, a rate that would improve

LISTEN TO THE
PODCAST

Industrial Revolution

more. Within 20 years, 20,000 of these spinning jennies were in use in Britain.

Richard Arkwright's water frame was another step forward; it used falling water to drive continuous spinning. This 1769 machine needed much more energy, which shifted production from homes to factories, as they could be sited by rivers. The flow of water turned huge paddle wheels, which in turn drove spinning shafts along the length of the factory. In 1779 Samuel Crompton's spinning mule combined the jenny with the water frame to create stronger and finer yarn. The mule became the most common spinning machine from 1790 and it would eventually be powered by the defining technology of the age: the steam engine. The mule was still being used for fine yarns into the late 20th century.

Textile Innovations

Invention	Inventor	Year
Flying Shuttle	John Kay	1733
Spinning Jenny	James Hargreaves	1764
Water Frame	Richard Arkwright	1769
Spinning Mule	Samuel Crompton	1779
Power Loom	Edmund Cartwright	1785

Thanks to this generation of technological transformation, the manufacturers of northwest England gradually came to dominate the manufacturing of cotton. In 1790, operators of a hundred-spindle mule could spin the same amount of raw cotton in 1,000 hours as spinners in India could do in 50,000. The water frame reduced this to 300 hours, and an upgraded version of Crompton's mule halved that again. Within a few decades, British-made yarn and cloth was being sold in India itself.

CROMFORD MILL

Richard Arkwright is often credited with inventing the modern factory, having constructed the Cromford Mill in 1771. Arkwright's cotton mill at Cromford in Derbyshire was one of the first factories built specifically to house machinery, rather than just to assemble workers in one building. It was also the first water-powered cotton spinning mill and initially employed 200 workers. Cromford Mill ran day and night with two 12-hour shifts.

To begin with, factories would have resembled warehouses, but by around 1804, with the addition of steam power and chimneys, writers such as William Blake were writing of the 'dark Satanic mills' appearing across the north of England.

'The north has the right climate – it's wet, which is perfect for textiles – it has access to the Atlantic market via the port of Liverpool, and it has the perfect environment, including things like coal, which is really accessible, and major rivers to fuel water works. And of course it had the population, which had grown significantly thanks to industrialisation over the course of the 18th century.'

William Ashworth, University of Liverpool

────────── **THE STEAM ENGINE** ──────────

Early steam engines were relatively simple, capable of producing a few horsepower while using a lot of fuel. But the fact that steam power's promise outran its performance for decades did not stop steam power becoming an object of faith. When Thomas Newcomen's atmospheric engine was invented in 1712, it only became profitable in England because there were so many mines to pump water from. The contraption used coal to generate steam in a cylinder. When the steam cooled, it condensed into liquid. This formed a partial vacuum that allowed atmospheric pressure to push down on a piston, then up, then down. The result was a steam engine that could operate machinery.

LISTEN TO THE
PODCAST

Steam Power

HORSEPOWER AND WATTS

Horsepower was the measurement of power coined by Scottish steam engineer James Watt. It relates to power equivalent to a number of horses that a steam engine could generate. The 'Watt' is a later unit of electrical power created in the late 19th century, named after the engineer.

James Watt made crucial improvements to the steam engine in the 1770s. Watt and his business partner Matthew Boulton installed around 400 of their Boulton & Watt stationary steam engines between 1775 and 1800. These were used for pumping water and driving machinery. Meanwhile, by 1800 over a thousand Newcomen engines had been installed in Britain. Cornishman Richard Trevithick developed the high-pressure steam engine around the turn of the 19th century, and with that the power produced increased exponentially, reaching the equivalent of tens of thousands of human beings working. Now there was the power capacity to have moving steam engines, and the locomotive was born. Trevithick first built a road-based locomotive, the Puffing Devil, in 1801, but soon train haulage would transform British industry. The first locomotive-hauled railway journey took place in Merthyr Tydfil in February 1804, marking the start of a transport revolution.

The Land of Long Chimneys

Steam power would lead to the expansion of factories, and with them came greater demand for industrial labourers. Agricultural workers, or those finding themselves displaced by the new technologies, were drawn to the expanding cities throughout northern England. These urban areas often found their own particular specialism complemented by another.

City	Main Industry
Manchester	Cotton
Leeds	Wool
Newcastle-upon-Tyne	Shipbuilding
Durham	Coal mining
Stoke-on-Trent	Ceramics
Sheffield	Steel
Derby	Locomotives

Cotton

Northern England in particular was packed with factories. In 1837, the cotton manufacturer Thomas Ashton, who ran a mill in Hyde, near Manchester, called it 'The land of long chimneys'. Manchester was nicknamed 'Cottonopolis' around the same time.

But cotton couldn't easily be grown in Britain, and northwest England's insatiable demand was straining its traditional supply. Peace with the newly formed United States of America in 1784 opened up trade, which added to imports from the West Indies. In both of those regions cotton was picked by enslaved workers. The northwestern port of Liverpool became a fulcrum for this industry. Its ships played a leading part in the trade in human beings. Ships from Liverpool could take manufactured goods from nearby Manchester and the rest of the northwest to Africa, where they would be traded for enslaved people, who would be taken to the West Indies and the southern United States to grow sugar and cotton; then these commodities were brought back into northwest England.

LIVERPOOL DOCKS

Opened in 1715, Liverpool's 'Old Dock' was the world's first enclosed commercial wet dock. Accommodating up to 100 ships, it facilitated the import of raw cotton from the Americas and export of finished textiles, establishing Liverpool as a central hub for the 18th-century cotton trade. As trade grew, newer docks replaced the Old Dock. The

Royal Albert Dock complex, opened in 1846, introduced Britain's first non-combustible warehouse system, enabling direct ship-to-warehouse loading. The docks also pioneered the world's first hydraulic cranes in 1848. Liverpool dominated 19th-century global trade, handling 9% of the world's total. Having been damaged by World War Two air raids, the docks closed in 1972, but reopened in 1984 after redevelopment. Liverpool's waterfront became a UNESCO World Heritage Site in 2004, but was delisted in 2021 due to concerns over development plans and deterioration of the historic site.

──── SLAVERY'S PEAK AND ABOLITION ────

Cotton manufacture was intertwined with the international slave trade, which peaked in the 1780s. Alongside profits, though, an awareness of the horrors of the trade grew, and an abolitionist movement emerged. Famous campaigners, some of them formerly enslaved people, began to speak out against the brutality and inhumanity of the system. Georgian confectioners started purchasing sugar from the East India Company that advertised itself as not made by slaves, to try to distance themselves from the bloodstained sugar of its rivals. It became a badge of honour to use East India sugar – ironic given its ruthless colonisation of South Asia. The autobiography of the formerly enslaved Olaudah Equiano, reprinted over and over, became one of the most influential and powerful condemnations of the time. Another voice was Charles Ignatius Sancho, the first black African man known to have voted in Britain, who became a well-connected man of letters.

'It's almost as if he's [Sancho] calling to the empathy of the nation that he's adopted in to say, think for ten seconds what it would be like if this were you. And that to me is a very beautiful and simple way to try to get people to connect with the issues that you have around you as a black person or as anybody who's isolated, oppressed, or in any way persecuted for who they are.'

Paterson Joseph, author, actor and activist

The road to freedom was long and arduous for abolitionists. Campaigners like Thomas Clarkson and William Wilberforce toured Britain and Europe, relaying in visceral detail the horrors of the slave trade. Eventually, with tireless lobbying inside Westminster, Wilberforce had a breakthrough – the Slave Trade Act was passed in 1807. By then British and colonial ships had forcibly transported some 3.4 million Africans across the Atlantic to be sold into slavery in the Americas. 500,000 had died in the Middle Passage. The Slave Trade Act made it illegal for any British ship or subject to trade enslaved people. But like all change, it was slow, and plantation slavery in the British colonies continued. Full emancipation wasn't achieved until 1838, after Queen Victoria came to the throne.

Even then, no freed slave was compensated. Even though the slave trade had technically been abolished in the British Empire in 1807, companies were still profiting from slave labour in other countries. Ports like Liverpool continued to receive shipments of slave-harvested cotton from the United States until 1865.

Entrepreneurs and Workers

Some of the entrepreneurs of the Industrial Revolution had close links to the slave trade. Samuel Greg (1758–1834), the founder of Quarry Bank Mill in Cheshire (at one point the largest textile mill in the country), enlarged his family fortune with a sugar plantation in Dominica, where he held hundreds of enslaved Africans. But, contrastingly, some industrialists were abolitionists. Josiah Wedgwood, whose Staffordshire pottery company produced affordable decorated earthenware and stoneware, created anti-slavery medallions that became an icon of the abolitionist movement. These depicted an enslaved worker, bound in chains and kneeling, with the words, 'Am I not a man and a brother?' encircling him. First released in 1787, they were worn as pendants and used on hairpins, and became a fashion statement that furthered the abolitionary cause.

But despite their very different attitudes towards slavery, Greg and Wedgwood both looked after their workers. Greg developed a 'model village' to house workers at Styal near Quarry Bank Mill. At Etruria, Wedgwood's complex in Stoke-on-Trent, there were 76 houses for some 300 employees, and amenities included bakehouses and even a bowling green. While progressive, these innovations were still business decisions; a healthier workforce would be more reliable, while the provision of housing near the factories would improve attendance.

Both of these entrepreneurs also relied on child labour, which was very common. When housing was provided, entire families could be employed at a mill and its community. Some industrialists were also subsidised to keep children out of workhouses, but some cotton mill owners exploited this. Over half of Greg's workforce from 1790 were children and many of them were subsidised. Those housed at Quarry Bank Mill did get reasonable lodgings, food and a light education, and did not have to endure corporal punishment.

Other children were not so fortunate. Regulation of child labour was non-existent before the 1833 Factory Act, which banned children under nine from factory work and set maximum hours for other age groups. The Sadler Report, an important precursor to the act, interviewed people who had been employed as children, forced to work from 5 a.m. to 8 p.m. and beaten for tardiness.

'I generally was beaten when I happened to be too late; and when I got up in the morning the apprehension of that was so great, that I used to run, and cry all the way as I went to the mill.'

Matthew Crabtree, interviewee in the Sadler Report

Campaigners for better factory conditions would often compare the treatment of mill-workers with that of enslaved people. If this was far from the case with the artisan workers at Wedgwood's Etruria estate, it was more appropriate in larger industrial cities where workers were effectively owned by the enterprise. Many were locked into a lifetime of indebtedness to an employer and, if a worker caused trouble and lost their job, they faced destitution.

The production process was now ruled by the factory owner. A major change from the pre-industrial economy was that people began to work to the clock. Working hours for people employed in cottage industries or agriculture had been determined either by themselves, whether the task at hand was done, or indeed by the weather or daylight. Machines operating around the clock, powered by water or steam, needed tending constantly. The only pauses were those ordered by the owner.

Winners and Losers

Changes in the economy were initially gradual. In the cotton industry, spinning and finishing saw mechanisation in the 1780s, but weaving still needed to be done by hand. Indeed, even by 1820 10% of the male population were still employed as handloom weavers. Mechanisation of other parts of the process had driven down the cost of cotton yarn, increasing demand for weaving and thus wages. But when high pressure steam was used to power looms, handloom weavers quickly saw their incomes collapse. The effect was either poverty or men forced into other sectors, which depressed wages.

The inventor's gain was thus often the worker's pain. Industrialists were incentivised towards mechanisation by high labour costs; unemployed workers enjoyed no safety net. There was terrible urban poverty. The incidence of infants dying before their fifth birthday was in some cities at the beginning of the 19th century as high as three in five, driving the average life expectancy (from birth) for working city dwellers down to the low thirties. The entrepreneurs, meanwhile, were part of a swelling middle class that, from around 10% of the population in 1800, by 1850 had grown to some 25%. Some of these entrepreneurs were propelled into riches previously reserved for the landed gentry. Richard Arkwright, the inventor of the water frame, was originally apprenticed as a Preston barber, yet by the time of his death was earning £20,000 – worth nearly £2.5 million in today's money. Another extraordinary social climber was Elkanah Armitage, born in 1794. Having begun as a spinner's helper at the age of eight, he later owned mills employing over 600 people. He went on to become a politician and was knighted by Queen Victoria.

UNREST AND CRISIS

Workers facing falling wages often took to organised protest. In Spitalfields, London, a centre of the silk-weaving industry, income drops exacerbated by immigration led in the late 1760s to regular riots. As the Industrial Revolution advanced, rioters also aimed their rage directly at machines. Ned Ludd, a semi-mythical character, was alleged to have broken two stocking frames in 1779. He became the Robin Hood-esque figurehead of the Luddite movement, which was responsible for a spate of machine smashing in Nottingham in the 1810s. The government responded harshly with the punishment of being transported to Australia, or even death.

Machines were not the only target of mob anger. The Gordon Riots broke out in London during June 1780, primarily in opposition to emancipatory measures for Catholics. The week-long riot was the most destructive in the capital's history, and before the army was called in several hundred people were killed. Alongside anti-Catholicism were a range of social and economic grievances, many driven by the war in America. When defeat came in that conflict, Prime Minister Lord North's government collapsed, causing such chaos that Britain would go on to have five prime ministers in two years:

Prime Minister	Party	Term Start	Term End
Lord North	Tory	1770	1782
Marquess of Rockingham	Whig	27 March 1782	1 July 1782
Earl of Shelburne	Whig	4 July 1782	2 April 1783
Duke of Portland	Whig	2 April 1783	19 December 1783
William Pitt the Younger	Tory	19 December 1783	14 March 1801

Thus 1782 was the first 'Year of Three Prime Ministers'. This unnerving state of affairs would recur thrice in the 19th century – and again, to great consternation, in 2022. The crisis clearly took a severe toll on George III, who even drafted an abdication letter in 1782. The king's interference in the House of Lords in December 1783 also led some in Parliament to talk about his actions as 'subversive of the constitution of the country.' William Pitt (the younger son of a previous prime minister, William Pitt 'the Elder') became the youngest prime minister in British history at the age of 24. Pitt was supported by the king, but less so in the Commons; he narrowly won a no-confidence vote just two months into office. But both Prime Minister Pitt and George III survived and went on to have long tenures, during which they both gained widespread popular support.

But George III was not well. It is probable that he suffered from bipolar disorder, which became more acute during the late 1780s. By the autumn of 1788 he was suffering a serious breakdown, and plans were drawn up for his eldest son, George, Prince of Wales, to act as regent. There was no legal precedent for such a move, and the king could not give assent due to his incapacitation. William Pitt opposed it, believing that the new Prince Regent would likely remove him from office. Dramatically, as the Regency Bill went before Parliament in February 1789, the king recovered, and the crisis was averted.

———————— THE FRENCH REVOLUTION ————————

Just six months later, French revolutionaries stormed the Bastille in Paris. A new National Assembly abolished feudal privileges and issued the Declaration of the Rights of Man in August 1789, based on the principle that 'men are born and remain free and equal in rights.' The French Revolution was viewed from Britain with a blend of curiosity and consternation. With the Gordon Riots and the American Revolution fresh in the mind of those at Westminster, there was palpable fear that republicanism could spread across the Channel. There was certainly widespread sympathy for the revolutionaries, but a combination of genuine attachment to the constitution, patriotism and government repression meant there was no armed insurrection.

The French Revolution divided intellectuals. The Whig MP and philosopher Edmund Burke, who had been supportive of the American Revolution, defended traditional institutions and predicted chaos and tyranny through his pamphlet *Reflections on the Revolution*, published in November 1790. In response, Burke's one-time friend Thomas Paine published *The Rights of Man*.

Paine was born in England in 1737, but emigrated to America with the help of Benjamin Franklin in 1774. His pamphlet *Common Sense* was a viral sensation for American patriots during the American Revolution. *The Rights of Man* was a much longer treatise, but similarly successful, although this time his target was Britain. Paine argued that people had a right to overthrow a government that did not respect their fundamental liberties and rights. He was also critical of hereditary succession, commenting that George III's incapacity was an example of why monarchies were fundamentally flawed. It sold one million copies, a stunning number, and many more would have heard it read aloud in ale- and coffee houses. It found a willing audience among political reformers, religious dissenters and workers. But Pitt's government viewed it as a revolutionary tract, and Paine fled to France in September 1792 to avoid trouble. He was found guilty of seditious libel that December, and sentenced to death, but he never returned to England to face his judgement.

Other European monarchies were bitterly opposed to revolution in France. In August 1791 the Holy Roman Emperor Leopold II, the brother of French queen Marie Antoinette, made the Declaration of Pillnitz in support of the French monarchy. Prussia added its voice too. By April 1792, revolutionary France was facing economic meltdown, and fear of foreign intervention to restore the *ancien régime* led it to declare war on Austria. The monarchies of Europe, including Britain, were drawn into what became known as the War of the First Coalition.

War made France increasingly radical. An insurrection in Paris in June saw the powerless royal family swept entirely from office and imprisoned. The First Republic was declared in September 1792, and that same month the enthusiastic citizen soldiers of the French Army repelled the advancing Prussian army at Valmy.

French King Louis XVI was executed for treason in January 1793. The new constitution of the French Republic was suspended that summer, and a year-long Reign of Terror was unleashed. Sixteen thousand people were executed. Facing military setbacks, in August 1793 France announced the *levée en masse*, mass conscription for men aged 18 to 25, which swelled the ranks of its armies. During 1794 this force had considerable success defeating coalition forces outside of France's borders.

Britain maintained its long-term strategy of providing naval power with subsidies to its European allies, but it was largely a failure. British support for French royalists at the Siege of Toulon in the second half of 1793 was ended by a talented young artillery commander, Napoleon Bonaparte. In the Low Countries the following year British troops could not stop a decisive coalition defeat. In the war at sea, the British Channel Fleet under Lord Howe won a victory on the 'Glorious First of June' of 1794, but its attempts to wrest full control of the West Indies were a disaster. Out of 89,000 officers and men sent across the Atlantic between 1793 and 1801, a staggering 70% became casualties, largely due to disease. By 1797 subsidising Britain's allies had become unsustainable, and the Bank of England was forced to suspend cash payments. Coalition members were exhausted, revolutionary France was dominant. Most agreed to peace terms. Britain, however, would fight on alone.

The Irish Rebellion

Inspired by the French Revolution, the Society of United Irishmen had been formed in 1791 with the goal of independence from Britain under an Irish republic. The Society was outlawed in 1794 and forced underground, but its leadership under Wolfe Tone forged close links with France. With British forces committed elsewhere, France intended to land an expeditionary force in Ireland during the winter of 1796–7 to support a United Irishmen uprising. But, as with so many other invasions of Britain and Ireland, the plan was scuppered by terrible weather. Over 2,000 Frenchmen drowned with hardly a British cannon fired, and the only French troops to land in Ireland quickly became prisoners of war. One separate detachment of over 1,000 men landed at Fishguard, Pembrokeshire, on 22 February 1797, but surrendered within two days. This was technically the last invasion of mainland Britain.

Undeterred by the failure of major French support, the United Irishmen launched a rebellion in May 1798. Some 50,000 rose up in their cause, but the risings were uncoordinated. By August British troops had largely suppressed the revolt, and while the French landed another expeditionary force it failed to meet rebel forces and surrendered in a matter of weeks. A second French expedition was defeated off the coast of Donegal in October, and Wolfe Tone was captured. He was sentenced to be hanged, but on 19 November 1798 cut his throat with a penknife and died, becoming a martyr of Irish nationalism. The exact number of casualties of the Irish Rebellion is disputed, but with at least 10,000 Irish deaths it was the greatest struggle in Ireland since the Jacobite War ended in 1691. In response, the Irish Parliament was abolished and Ireland brought into the newly created United Kingdom of Great Britain and Ireland with effect from 1 January 1801. Ireland would be represented by 100 MPs at Westminster, although Catholics remained barred from voting or representation.

NAPOLEON

In France the monarchy had been abolished and the king and queen executed. On 10 November 1799 Napoleon Bonaparte, who had gone on to enjoy a stellar military career after Toulon, led a *coup d'état* and established himself as First Consul. British successes continued to come at sea. In August 1798 Admiral Nelson annihilated a French fleet at the Battle of the Nile. This encouraged other European allies to rejoin the war against France and a Second Coalition was assembled. Britain made major gains in Egypt, India and the West Indies during 1801, but on the Continent the Coalition was once again frustrated, at great cost. A brief period of peace after the short-lived Treaty of Amiens in March 1802 was followed by the resumption of hostilities. Napoleon became convinced that he had to knock out Britain, and direct invasion was the way to do it. A huge expanse of French territory in North America was sold to the United States. This French North American empire was called Louisiana but it stretched far beyond the borders of the modern state of Louisiana, incorporating some or all of 15 present US states. This helped to fund Napoleon's powerful Grande Armée, which awaited its opportunity on the Channel coast of northern France.

THE DROP REDOUBT AND MARTELLO TOWERS

As the threat of a French invasion loomed from 1803, Britain constructed a vast network of coastal defences. Extensive enhancements were made to fortify Dover's Western Heights between 1804 and 1814, making it one of the great artillery fortresses of Europe. These included the

Drop Redoubt (one of two forts), and batteries and barracks for a large garrison. Access to the harbour was facilitated by the 'Grand Shaft', a 140-foot-deep cylinder containing three staircases for rapid troop movement. Additionally, a chain of 103 Martello towers (circular brick towers, armed with rooftop cannons) was constructed between 1805 and 1812 following the coastline from Seaford in East Sussex all the way round to Aldeburgh in Suffolk, to defend vulnerable areas. While 45 Martello Towers remain, many are in ruins or have been repurposed, and only nine are in their original condition.

The Napoleonic Wars

The Napoleonic War of 1803–1815 would be the climax of the long series of Anglo-French wars of this period, and the greatest in scale and cost. Napoleon would never invade Britain but, having crowned himself Emperor of the French on 2 December 1804, he smashed Britain's allies on the Continent within the next couple of years. Austria and Russia were forced to come to terms after their decisive defeat at Austerlitz, exactly a year after Napoleon's coronation. William Pitt, then in his second term as prime minister, understood the scale of this defeat and died, a broken man, the following month. Prussia was crushed in October 1806. Napoleon's armies had achieved a domination in Europe not seen since the Roman Empire. But Napoleon had a problem – Britain was still ascendant at sea. While Britain remained hostile, the Royal Navy could blockade French ports, disrupt maritime trade and send aid to any of Napoleon's enemies.

On 18 October 1805 a combined French and Spanish fleet left the Port of Cadiz. Three days later they encountered 27 waiting British ships of the line under the command of Admiral Nelson off Cape Trafalgar. Knowing that his men were far better drilled, Nelson plunged his outnumbered ships into the Franco-Spanish line, cutting it in three. He was shot by a French sniper in combat, but before he died he knew victory was total. The Royal Navy destroyed one ship and captured another 23 out of a total of 33. The British fleet lost no ships of its own. Any hope of invading Britain was now extinguished.

Napoleon's Unravelling

Unable to subdue Britain, Napoleon aimed to squeeze it economically until the British government came to terms. From November 1806 he enacted a large-scale embargo known as the Continental System, which would prevent European states from trading with Britain. It was unenforceable and unpopular and would lead to his unravelling.

Britain's long-term ally Portugal refused to join the Continental System, leading to a French invasion of the Iberian Peninsula. Spain, France's former ally, resisted. The French found themselves deeply unpopular occupiers facing guerrilla warfare. Britain landed an army in Portugal under Arthur Wellesley. It was the start of the Peninsular War, which dragged on for nearly six years and became a terrible drain on French gold, prestige and manpower. Britain, with control of the sea, was able to supply allied forces much more easily than France, and a combination of guerrilla and conventional warfare wore down French forces. But further afield the Continental System was causing economic damage to those forced into it. And in

1811 Russia reopened trade with Britain, provoking Napoleon to make his most fatal mistake.

On 12 June 1812, Napoleon's massive invasion of more than 400,000 troops crossed the Vistula into Russia and stormed east. After the bloody Battle of Borodino, they reached Moscow that September, to find it largely unoccupied. Fires burned through the city, unchecked by the absent civic authorities and the capital was very soon reduced to a smouldering ruin. Unable to come to terms with the Russians, and facing winter without supplies in the remnant of a city without shelter, Napoleon was forced to return to Central Europe. But harrying Russian attacks, bitter cold and desertion utterly depleted the retreating army – possibly to as little as 10,000 of the vast force which originally crossed the Vistula. This, combined with a decisive British and allied victory at Salamanca on 22 July 1812, was a lethal blow to Napoleon's empire. The vast Battle of Leipzig, fought in October 1813, saw the destruction of the French Army east of the Rhine and the Coalition soon invaded France. Napoleon was forced to abdicate in April 1814, and went into exile on the tiny Mediterranean island of Elba. The Napoleonic Wars were over, for now.

Napoleon had been frustrated by implacable British opposition. While Coalition armies lost vast numbers on European battlefields, Britain could continue to offer to pay and equip yet more armies, while its blockade of French ports helped to destroy the French economy. The Continental System caused some damage to British trade, but what it lost from Europe it could make up from overseas. The greatest challenge came with the breakdown of American relations that led to the War of 1812. Britain was overstretched fighting the Americans and the French at the same time; the tensions were partially responsible for the assassination of Spencer Perceval, the only prime minister in British history to be murdered in office, in May 1812 when he was shot in the lobby of the House of Commons by an aggrieved merchant. But the Industrial Revolution was driving the British economy to vast growth, and gave Britain an edge in producing weapons of war. The national debt nearly trebled, to an eye-watering 200% of GDP, with the costs of funding the war, but the Treasury avoided default with tax rises, including the first income tax, and maintained the confidence of the bond market with prudent management.

Napoleon's Last Stand

There was one more extraordinary chapter to go. In February 1815 Napoleon dramatically returned from exile and quickly took Paris. The restored King Louis XVII fled and Napoleon was back in power. Rather than wait for the inevitable onslaught, Napoleon struck first, leading an army towards Brussels. He defeated the Prussian forces at the Battle of Ligny on 16 June and turned on an Anglo-Allied army under Arthur Wellesley, by now the Duke of Wellington. The Iron Duke, as he was nicknamed, blocked Napoleon's road north on a ridge near the village of Waterloo. For the whole of the 18th of June his allied army composed of British, Dutch and German troops held off the French Army.

Napoleon was past his prime and overconfident. He called Wellington a 'bad general' and said his own victory 'would be like eating breakfast.' In fact it was a savage attritional struggle; in the words of Wellington, 'the nearest-run thing you ever saw in your life.' Napoleon was defeated. Prussian forces arrived over the afternoon and the French Army, outnumbered and fighting in two directions, broke and fled. Taking no chances, the British sent Napoleon to see out his days on the Atlantic island of Saint Helena, with no prospect of return. He died a prisoner on 5 May 1821.

The Duke of Wellington was later asked who was the greatest military commander of all time. He replied: 'In this age, in past ages, in any age, Napoleon.'

The Battle of Thiepval Ridge, 1916

PART FOUR

PEACE AND WAR

The statue of Florence Nightingale at Waterloo Place, London

Chapter 11

'Pax Britannica'

On a cloudless summer's day in 1819 a huge crowd gathered at St Peter's Field, Manchester. It was warm, it was dry, home entertainment options were limited. Most importantly of all, the 60,000 Mancunians were angry, desperate and hungry. They had come to demonstrate for political reform and representation in a difficult economic period. Despite having a population of around 100,000, Manchester returned no MPs directly to Westminster, and the whole county of Lancashire sent just two. Local magistrates were scared that the crowd would riot, and had around 1,000 troops on standby to keep order.

One of the leading demonstrators, the well-known orator and activist Henry Hunt, arrived in the early afternoon to a rapturous reception. The jumpy magistrates ordered his arrest. Inexperienced cavalrymen from the Manchester and Salford Yeomanry charged into the crowd to get their man. They drew their sabres, hacking and slashing at the press of men, women and children. Magistrates then called upon the 15th Hussars to disperse the crowd, and they too rushed forward with sabres drawn. Eighteen people were killed in the chaos and hundreds more were injured. It was labelled the 'Peterloo Massacre', a shameful episode in which the tactics so celebrated at the

Battle of Waterloo just four years previously had now been deployed against the king's own subjects at home.

Napoleon's defeat at that titanic clash may have paved the way for decades of British global dominance, but the early years of this new 'Pax Britannica' ('British Peace') saw great challenges at home. An economic slump in the post-war years drove high levels of unemployment, while protectionist trade policies kept food prices high. A miserable 'Year Without Summer' in 1816, likely due to a massive volcanic eruption in the East Indies, only added to the desperation. In fast-growing industrial cities like Manchester, conditions for many were unbearable, and talk of revolution hung in the air.

THE END OF AN ERA

On 29 January 1820 George III died. In the final years of his life he had been incapacitated by mental ill health, and for the last decade his son had ruled as Prince Regent. But the prince was unpopular. He was often in the press for his affairs and misdemeanours, and his fabulously expensive tastes jarred with the grinding poverty of so many of his subjects. His coronation cost over 20 times more than his father's and he excluded his estranged yet popular wife, Caroline of Brunswick, from the occasion entirely. Over a reign of 59 years, the third longest of any British monarch, George III had presided over the Industrial Revolution, the defeat of France and great changes in the British Empire. His death was, in many ways, the end of an era.

By 1820 the influence of the monarch had waned. George III's illness had accelerated the transfer of power away from the crown. George IV was 57 when he came to the throne. A heavy drinker, obese and possibly addicted to laudanum, in the late 1820s he retreated from public life. His main political contribution was his public opposition to Catholic emancipation, for which calls had been growing across the Irish Sea. Irish lawyer Daniel O'Connell had drawn similar crowds to those on that fateful day at St Peter's Field through his Catholic Association. Like Henry Hunt, O'Connell was campaigning for political representation; the Irish Catholic majority at the time were unable to become MPs or hold military commissions or public office. The issue plunged the end of the decade into perpetual crisis.

1827 was another 'Year of Three Prime Ministers' and by January 1828 the veteran Duke of Wellington had been appointed. He was a lot less capable in Westminster than he had been at Waterloo and served only two short terms. He was a hardline, arch Tory, but even he came to accept that, without Catholic emancipation, Ireland was facing civil war. O'Connell won a by-election in County Clare, but would not take the anti-Catholic Oath of Supremacy. Despite the king's opposition, the Roman Catholic Relief Act was passed the next year, allowing men like O'Connell to take their seats in Parliament.

The Road to Reform

It was not only Ireland that was haunted by the spectre of insurrection. Cavalry charges could only stem the demands for reform for so long. When a Whig Reform Bill was defeated by the Tories in the House of Lords in October 1831 there was widespread unrest, with major riots in Nottingham, Derby and Bristol. Another bill was passed by the Commons in March 1832. On 7 May a vast demonstration known as the Meeting of the Unions gathered in Birmingham; 200,000 people, largely from the middle classes, showing their support for the bill. Despite this the Lords threw it out again that evening. Enraged Britons gave vent to their anger. It may well have been as close as Britain has ever got to popular revolution; troops occupied unruly towns, while political unions threatened mass non-payment of tax. One Anglican clergyman described a 'hand-shaking, bowel-disturbing passion of fear.' Prime Minister Earl Grey, who had already resigned once due to the rejection of the bills, resigned again. Wellington was recalled, but was unable to form a government. Grey returned and pleaded with King William IV to pack the Lords with Whig peers, which he agreed to. In the face of this threat, the House of Lords allowed the 'Great Reform Bill' to pass, largely through abstentions, and it received Royal Assent on 7 June 1832. There was a political sigh of relief across the country.

The Great Reform Act brought in sweeping electoral change. Ancient parliamentary boroughs which had become depopulated over the centuries had become known as 'rotten boroughs' with just a handful of electors. These few electors were easy to bribe or coerce which put enormous power into the hands of rich landowners. Many of these rotten boroughs were finally done away with and 67 new constituencies were created. The franchise was also extended to include more male property owners, but in effect the proportion of adult males eligible to vote increased from around 5–10% to about 20%. For many working-class campaigners this simply didn't go far enough, and Chartism, a mass, more working-class movement, would gain strength through the decade, carrying the torch of reform.

'What the Great Reform Act really did was to transfer control of the Commons from the Crown to the electorate, and that meant that prime ministers now had to look outwards to the public more than upwards to the Crown.

Robert Saunders, Queen Mary University of London

THE GREAT REFORMS

The Reform Act ushered in a range of 'progressive' reforms through the 1830s and 1840s.

- **Factory Act (1833)** – introduced restrictions on children working in factories, outlawing work for those under nine and introducing daily work hour limits for other age groups.
- **Slavery Abolition Act (1833)** – abolished slavery in most British colonies, leading to the freeing of 800,000 enslaved Africans, largely in the West Indies.
- **Poor Law Amendment Act (1834)** – effectively created a new government department for overseeing poor relief in workhouses.
- **Municipal Corporations Act (1835)** – introduced elected councils in boroughs and cities, aiming to increase accountability and efficiency in local government.
- **Mines and Collieries Act (1842)** – prohibited mining work for women and girls, as well as boys under 10.

LISTEN TO THE
PODCAST

British Prime Ministers

These Acts, so obviously necessary from the modern perspective, marked a change in how the government saw its own role;

previously Westminster had employed a very light touch in regulating industry. Even now, though, they were far from the foundations of the welfare state. The Poor Law amendment, for example, denied those in poverty food, clothing or money unless they entered workhouses, where conditions were miserable. The Slavery Abolition Act emancipated slaves, but it was the slave owners, not the formerly enslaved people, who were given compensation. Many of those newly freed men and women found themselves bound in servitude in unequal 'apprenticeships'.

SHAFTESBURY MEMORIAL FOUNTAIN

One campaigning reformer of the era was Anthony Ashley-Cooper, also known as Lord Shaftesbury and 'The Poor Man's Earl'. He was instrumental in the passing of the laws relating to child labour, and later championed reform of laws relating to mental health and education. His philanthropic work is commemorated by the winged statue known as Eros, in Piccadilly Circus, London, which was unveiled in 1893 and stands at the southwest of Shaftesbury Avenue. Contrary to popular belief, the statue is actually of Anteros – the Greek god of requited love.

Social reform had been driven by industrialisation and subsequent urbanisation. In 1801, around 20% of the British population lived in urban areas of more than 10,000 inhabitants. By 1851 this had risen to 40%, and it rose again to 75% by the end of the 19th century. Between 1801 and 1914, Britain's total population quadrupled. This growth led to two significant social problems. Firstly, the leap in the birth rate led to a vast increase in the number of children who needed far more from the government in terms of education and poor relief than previously. Second was that, in the absence of proper planning or sanitation, conditions in fast-growing cities were squalid. Those migrating from the countryside and imagining clean streets and the promise of wealth must have been aghast; endless slums and the stench from open sewers were the norm in working-class areas. Epidemics of cholera in 1832 and 1848–9 each killed over 50,000 people. This forced the 1848 Public Health Act, which aimed to improve basic sanitation in cities, but progress enacting the reform was slow.

In rural areas during the 1840s, conditions were also tough. The decade became known as the 'Hungry Forties'. To protect domestic farms, and the landed elite who owned them, 'Corn Laws' had kept corn prices artificially high since the end of the Napoleonic Wars, benefiting landowners at the expense of the poor.

Famine

Then in 1846 disaster struck – a devastating potato blight swept through northwest Europe, and nowhere was the suffering worse than in Ireland. The Irish peasantry relied heavily on potatoes; for around a third of its population they were the principal food source. The potato blight led to a 90% fall in the typical crop yield in 1846. The ensuing famine raged on for seven years and transformed the demographic balance of the British Isles; around one million Irish people died, and another million would emigrate. While most went to America, many

Irish immigrants settled in England, in cities like Liverpool and London. The population of Ireland was around eight million before the famine, and it has never recovered – it now stands at just over five million. The lacklustre British government response to the tragedy would spur Irish nationalists to renew their drive for independence.

The Irish Potato Famine forced Robert Peel, the Tory prime minister, to defy his party and repeal the Corn Laws in 1846. He split his party and was forced to resign. To free-market liberals the Corn Laws had depressed economic progress, as they were protectionist and forced working people to spend more money on food. Anti-repeal Tories like the young Benjamin Disraeli lamented but notably failed to reintroduce protectionism when they gained office in years to come. Britain had made its choice; free trade became a national mantra for generations.

——— THE TECHNOLOGICAL BIG BANG ———

The world was opening up. Steam power had revolutionised transport. Ships were finally freed from dependence on the wind, and on shore the railway network exploded. While the first steam locomotives had moved along the tracks in the first decade of the century, a milestone was George Stephenson's Locomotion No. 1 in 1825. It was the world's first steam locomotive to carry passengers on a public line – the Stockton and Darlington Railway in northeast England. It paved the way for the construction of the Liverpool and Manchester Railway, which opened in 1830. The first train was drawn by Stephenson's 'Rocket', which had won the 1829 Rainhill Trials to find the best locomotive.

Between 1826 and 1836, 378 miles of railway track opened in Britain. By 1848, Britain had a 5,000-mile railway network. Previously, the fastest way to get around the country was on turnpike roads by horse and carriage, or by boat via a river or canal. But railways made travel faster, more comfortable, and affordable. They also enabled the development of the postal system and newspaper distribution, while reducing freight costs and fuelling the growth of cities. Railway stations in Blackpool, Scarborough and Brighton opened during the 1840s, enabling seaside towns to become popular summer holiday destinations.

Pioneering engineer Isambard Kingdom Brunel designed and built several major railway lines, including the Great Western Railway in 1833. He also led the construction of the Thames Tunnel, the world's first tunnel beneath a navigable river, and later Bristol's Clifton Suspension Bridge, which opened in 1864. He turned his brilliant mind to shipping too; Brunel's steamship the SS *Great Western*, launched in 1837, was the first propeller-driven ocean-going iron ship.

SS GREAT BRITAIN

The SS *Great Britain*, launched in 1843, was another of Brunel's steamships. At 98 metres long, at the time of its launch it was the largest passenger vessel afloat. In 1845 it became the first iron-hulled, propeller-driven steam ocean liner to cross the Atlantic, completing the voyage in 14 days. After years of service and a salvage operation in 1970, the ship was restored, and is now a popular museum ship in Bristol.

The Great Exhibition

These technological leaps forward were celebrated at the Great Exhibition, which opened in May 1851. Hosted inside a huge iron-and-glass structure in London's Hyde Park dubbed the 'Crystal Palace', it was considered the first modern World's Fair – a festival showcasing the achievements of various nations. It attracted over six million visitors over five months, equivalent to a third of Britain's entire population at the time. Charles Darwin, Karl Marx, Charlotte Brontë and Charles Dickens all attended. Although the event contained exhibits from around the world, more than half of the 100,000 items on display came from Britain and its colonies alone.

Among the groundbreaking innovations featured at the Great Exhibition was the electric telegraph. Although the concept of using electrical signals for communication had already been explored by various inventors including the Englishmen William Fothergill Cooke and Charles Wheatstone, the first practical electrical telegraph had been developed by Samuel Morse and Alfred Vail in America in 1837. It was refined by British engineers and showcased at the exhibition, along with designs for a submarine cable from Dover to Calais by John and Jacob Brett. This cable was successfully laid across the Channel on 25 September 1851 and the feat announced just as the exhibition closed.

Subsequent developments, including the first transatlantic telegraph cable linking the UK and America in 1858, revolutionised communication, enabling almost instant long-distance messaging. It would transform trade and diplomacy, but it was perhaps in the world of journalism that the telegraph made its biggest impact. News now spread far faster than a galloping horse, and for the mass audience of newspaper readers the world had shrunk.

──────────── THE VICTORIAN AGE ────────────

Queen Victoria officially opened the Great Exhibition, while her husband, Prince Albert, was one of the main organisers of the event and led the closing ceremony. Victoria had ascended to the throne aged 18 on 20 June 1837, succeeding her uncle, King William IV. Born in 1819 at Kensington Palace, the daughter of Prince Edward (George III's fourth son) and Princess Victoria of Saxe-Coburg-Saalfeld, Victoria was initially fifth in line to the throne. After the deaths of her father and grandfather in 1820, she was raised under close supervision by her extremely protective mother and her 'comptroller', John Conroy. Their elaborate and strict system of rules for Victoria's upbringing – the Kensington System – aimed to render her weak-willed and dependent upon them, in the hope that they would one day be able to wield power through her.

KENSINGTON PALACE

Kensington Palace, the childhood home of Queen Victoria, has been a royal residence since the 17th century. It is currently the official London residence of the Prince and Princess of Wales and the State Rooms (managed by Historic Royal Palaces) are open to the public, displaying many paintings and other objects from the Royal Collection. The Palace's beautiful gardens also provide a serene retreat in the heart of London, with its Sunken Garden, including a statue of Princess Diana, arched arbour of Cradle Walk and wildflower meadow.

Victoria's isolation intensified when it became clear, when she was around 11 years old, that she was in line to become queen. Her three uncles ahead of her in the line of succession – George IV, Frederick Duke of York and William IV – all died with no surviving legitimate children. As you might expect, upon her ascension, Victoria liberated herself from her draconian domestic arrangements.

Following Victoria's coronation on 28 June 1838, rather than her mother and Conroy, both of whom she exiled to the remotest apartments in Buckingham Palace, she sought guidance from the Whig prime minister Lord Melbourne.

Victoria had been smitten with her cousin Prince Albert, the German Prince of Saxe-Coburg and Gotha, from the day they met in 1836, and on 10 February 1840 they married. Albert then became an important political adviser to her and a vital influence in the first half of her life. The pair would also become parents to a family tree large enough to place its members in many European royal courts, earning Queen Victoria the moniker of 'the Grandmother of Europe'.

THE EMPIRE AT ITS HEIGHT

Around 20 years into Victoria's reign, in the 1850s, Britain stood at the very pinnacle of its global power. Economic growth from the Industrial Revolution began to benefit the population at large, and standards of living began to dramatically increase. Britain accounted for nearly 20% of the entire world's manufacturing output, and was unmatched as the sole superpower.

The European monarchies had faced a wave of popular uprisings in 1848, they were more interested in survival than a strategic contest with Britain. Across the Atlantic, the United States was pursuing westward expansion, absorbing new states, and teetering on the edge of civil war over the question of slavery. To the east, Asia was not yet enjoying the competitive advantages of industrialisation; China was weakened by clashes with Britain and the vast opium imports that followed its defeat. The ailing empire was then torn apart by the vast, catastrophic Taiping Rebellion, which killed more people than World War One.

'What is happening at the time, the European revolutions, America's tied up in slavery, China's tearing itself to pieces as well, so Britain's really got very few rivals. It was a moment of modernity where Britain really got a clean field to impose its values in a hard, but more often than not in a soft kind of way, which it believes it's transmitting.'

Ben Wilson, historian

Britain's victory in the Napoleonic Wars had seen it make major gains in the Indian Ocean, the West Indies and South Africa. It had almost complete supremacy over the world's oceans, with the naval strength of at least the next three nations combined. British influence had extended into the Persian Gulf, through the destruction of the Qawasim fleet in 1820 and the enforcement of an anti-piracy treaty on all Arab rulers in the region. It was in Central Asia where the greatest challenges lay. From 1830 Britain had become embroiled in the 'Great Game', a jostling for power in the region with Russia. It feared its rival would sweep southward to threaten India. To protect India the British found themselves drawn further into the interior of the continent. It was hostile terrain. An invasion of Afghanistan in 1838 had ended in the entire expeditionary force being massacred.

The term 'Pax Britannica' often used for this period is something of a misnomer; Britain was involved in a vast number of wars around the world as its empire expanded. As well as the Afghanistan invasions, there were the Opium Wars and wars in New Zealand, India and West Africa.

But Britain avoided major conflict in Western Europe for nearly 100 years; it was not until March 1854 that it once again fought a European rival, as the cold war with Russia went hot. The so-called Crimean War was largely the result of Russia's ambitions to expand its influence at the expense of the declining Ottoman Empire. British attempts at mediation failed as Russia pushed into the Balkans. Britain and France aimed to shore up the Ottoman Empire and restrain the Russians. In 1853 they sent an amphibious force into the Black Sea to invade Crimea and strike at the headquarters of the Russian Black Sea Fleet.

——— THE CRIMEAN WAR ———

The Crimean War was never popular in Britain. Allied forces defeated the Russian army at the Battle of Alma in September 1854, and the siege of the Russian base at Sevastopol began. It dragged on for a miserable year. The war saw modern technology such as steamships and telegraphs put to use, often for the first time, but men were killed and maimed in shocking numbers, just as they always had been in war. Disease, freezing weather and a lack of medical care led to one-fifth of the British force losing their lives. Pioneering war correspondent William Howard Russell provided dispatches for *The Times*, reporting on the harrowing conditions soldiers faced on the front lines. Roger Fenton travelled to Balaclava as one of the first war photographers, and produced a famous image of the battle, *In the Valley of the Shadow of Death* – an ominous empty valley littered with cannonballs. Poet Laureate Alfred, Lord Tennyson offered a heroic spin by penning 'The Charge of the Light Brigade', about a battle that took place in a valley near the one photographed by Fenton and referenced it, but the poem famously told of the cavalry's unquestioning valour under incompetent command:

> *"Forward, the Light Brigade!"*
> *Was there a man dismayed?*
> *Not though the soldier knew*
> *Someone had blundered.*
> *Theirs not to make reply,*
> *Theirs not to reason why,*
> *Theirs but to do and die.*
> *Into the valley of Death*
> *Rode the six hundred.*

FLORENCE NIGHTINGALE
MEMORIAL AND MUSEUM

Nurse Florence Nightingale had already gained national fame for her work caring for sick and wounded soldiers near Constantinople before she travelled to the Crimean peninsula. There she managed a team of nurses and became a pioneer of using statistics in battlefield medicine, while her evening visits to the wards of wounded soldiers earned her the moniker 'The Lady of the Lamp'. She is remembered, with lamp in hand, at a memorial statue in St James's, London. A museum dedicated to her life and work is at the nearby St Thomas's Hospital, across Westminster Bridge.

A near-bankrupt Russia sued for peace in March 1856. The Anglo-French-Turkish alliance had won, guaranteeing the integrity of the Ottoman Empire and halting Russian expansion around the Black Sea; but the war had made the difficulties of fighting large-scale, far-flung conflicts clear. The British effort had also stretched its ability to police its colonies. Troops sent to fight in Crimea had come from India, potentially undermining the British presence in what was considered the jewel of its empire.

——— REBELLION IN BRITISH INDIA ———

Since Robert Clive's victory at the Battle of Plassey in 1756, the British East India Company had subjugated over two-thirds of the Indian subcontinent. The company annexed the Punjab in March 1849, and did the same in the central Nagpur region in December 1853. But the company's flagrant expansionism, economic exploitation and coercive policies were fuelling resentment among its Indian subjects. Indian troops serving in the Bengal Army were frustrated by discrimination, which meant lower pay than for Europeans, and were wary of the prospect of being made to serve overseas.

The catalyst for rebellion came with the introduction of the Pattern 1853 Enfield Rifle. In 1856, the East India Company ordered around 10,000 of these, and rumours spread that their paper-wrapped cartridges were greased with pig and cow fat, or a combination of the two. This offended the religious beliefs of both Hindu and Muslim soldiers, who had to bite the cartridges to load their rifles, and across India soldiers refused to take part in musketry drills. Discontent flared into outright mutiny in several camps, but it was at Meerut on 10 May 1857 that the first major incident broke out. With local support, Indian troops killed some of their officers and forced others to flee. The rebels quickly made for Delhi, where they encouraged the nominal Mughal emperor Bahadur Shah II to renounce his loyalty to the Company and declare himself Emperor of all India. He did so, and the revolt quickly spread across the northern provinces.

Known at the time as the Indian Mutiny, this rebellion against British rule became infamous for savage violence. The British media amplified the horrendous details of the massacres of British men, women and children carried out by Indian rebels. One at Cawnpore in June 1857 saw the death of around 120 British women and children, and the lurid accounts fired British soldiers' thirst for revenge. No quarter was given as the British carried out terrible and disproportionate reprisals. In his expedition to relieve Cawnpore, General James Neill ordered the hanging of anyone suspected of being a mutineer. Non-combatants were executed out of hand and houses burned. Yet his approach made him a hero of the British Empire, and his statue still stands in Ayr, Scotland. It is difficult to determine how many Indians died as a consequence, but estimates are that more than 100,000 Indians were killed over the 18-month rebellion, and likely many more died due to the effects of famine and disease.

There is no question about the depth of anti-British feeling in some parts of India, but not in all parts, and that saved

Britain's empire. The revolt lacked unity; there was at the time little concept of a shared Indian nationality. Many Indian troops remained loyal and served the British, while Hindu/Muslim and regional divisions further fragmented the rebellion. The revolt was brutally suppressed by July 1859, but Whitehall was not going to allow the East India Company to carry on running India. It was the end of two and a half centuries of public–private partnership in South Asia. The Government of India Act was passed in 1858, marking the birth of the British Raj.

> 'There is a culture shift with the Raj. Suddenly it's very English. So mixing with the locals is frowned upon very much ... English are just confined to the clubs, which are white only, no Indian ever allowed in there, except for serving staff ... With the Raj, it's a very strict rule from Westminster. You've got to follow the rules and segregation really increases.'
>
> **Shrabani Basu, historian**

The 1850s had been a bloody decade for Britain and its Empire and after the Crimean War its close relations with France had once again turned sour. An 1858 assassination attempt on French emperor Napoleon III by a group of revolutionaries, including Britons, raised fears of French retaliation against Britain. The prospect of an invasion by a man named Napoleon was back on the cards.

PALMERSTON'S FOLLIES

The 'French Scare' led the prime minister Lord Palmerston to commission an expensive building programme of defences on the English coastline. The first shot up near Portsmouth, with their main batteries facing towards the port to protect against land attack. The nickname 'follies' came from critics who dismissed them as costly ornamental buildings with little practical value. Fortifications were strengthened at Dover, Portchester and many other coastal sites. Fort Albert, built to protect the Needles Passage on the west side of the Isle of Wight, was completed in 1856.

LISTEN TO THE
PODCAST

The Raj and Indian Independence

The Indian uprising had also highlighted the haphazard nature of the British Empire. The East India Company had enriched itself, conquered territory and caused huge strategic headaches for London, while resisting direct government control. Elsewhere, the empire would expand in similarly opportunistic and even anarchic ways.

THE SCRAMBLE FOR AFRICA

There was no grand plan for the British Empire; indeed many academics and politicians believed it was in fact a drain on British resources. By the late 19th century, however, there was a powerful lobby in favour of further conquests; colonists who saw opportunities in farming, logging and prospecting allied to missionaries and others who were enthusiastic about proselytising British values around the world. A global 'civilising' mission came to justify the plunder of resources. A popular press fired up enthusiasm among new voters at home. British troops enjoyed even greater advantages than before. Steam-powered gunboats, rapid-firing rifles and artillery were used to subdue local resistance. Telegraphs and railways would improve communication and logistics. As the gaze of Europe fell on Africa, Britain had the wherewithal and the cause to join what would become the 'Scramble for Africa'.

Even by 1850, not a great deal was known about Africa in Europe. From what little information Europeans had, two consensuses emerged. One perceived Africa as somehow left behind, in need of their help in accelerating its progress towards a European notion of civilisation; the other valued the continent only for its enormous wealth in ores, metals, forests and wood, which could be taken back to Europe.

Britain had seized Cape Colony during the Napoleonic Wars, and added Natal in 1843. But aside from this southern tip of Africa, in 1860 there was not much 'red on the map'. There was the legacy of the slave trading posts along the west coast, with a presence in the Gold Coast (Ghana), Nigeria and Sierra Leone. But disease and difficult terrain had largely limited the Europeans to the coasts. In 1870, still only around 10% of Africa was under European control, but over the next 40 years a revolution in medicine, machines and competition in Europe all led to a transformation.

Quinine, an effective antimalarial, helped hold one deadly enemy at bay. It became an ingredient in tonic water, thus ensuring that gin and tonic became the staple for Brits in India. Life-saving, literally. Steam engines powered boats swiftly up fast flowing rivers and their crews were armed with ever more lethal firearms.

In Europe, the plates were shifting, powerful states rising

and ambitions unleashed. Italy had unified in 1861. Ten years later, the German Empire was forged in war against France. This new empire was proclaimed in captured Versailles, and celebrated its birth by seizing two rich provinces, Alsace and Lorraine, from their defeated enemy. These powers saw Africa as the quickest way to build an overseas empire.

Britain, focussed as ever on its Indian empire, took control of Egypt in 1882 to ensure safe use of the new canal through Suez. Rivals demanded compensation. France enlarged its conquests in northwest Africa, Germany in the east and south-west. The Congo was a huge expanse of central Africa that none of the great powers really wanted but they all insisted that none of the others should get. Eccentrically, it was given to King Leopold of Belgium to be run as a private fiefdom – with genocidal consequences.

Britain found itself drawn ever further into the interior, attracted by imperial adventurers and the desire to protect core interests in Egypt and the Cape or lured by gold. Concerns for Egypt drove the British to try to subdue Mahdist forces in Sudan. An eventual crushing victory at the Battle of Omdurman in 1898 led to the conquest of Sudan. Britain invaded Zululand in 1879, extending its territory in South Africa. British interests there were also threatened by the Boers, the descendants of Dutch settlers. The Second Boer War (1899–1902) was a large and costly conflict to enforce British supremacy across southern Africa. Sir John Seeley wrote in 1883 that Britain's bringing a giant swathe of the world under its sway had happened, 'in a fit of absence of mind.' It is true that there was little evidence of London setting the strategic goals of expansion. Instead traders, missionaries, land-hungry farmers all pushed the frontiers in different directions. When they ran into trouble they wrapped themselves in the union flag and, supported by howling tabloid headlines, insisted the honour of the empire was at stake. More often than not, a harassed Whitehall official would indeed order a column of red-coated infantry to march, and they expanded the red on the map with every step they took.

Queen Victoria died on 22 January 1901 at the age of 81. Over the course of her 63-year reign, the longest for any British monarch to that point, Britain and its empire had experienced monumental change. The population had exploded, and moved; a majority of Britons now lived in cities. Building on the Great Reform Act, further expansions to the electorate in 1867 and 1884 had widened it to over 5.5 million, albeit only to reasonably affluent men. Railways had revolutionised journeys between cities, while sanitation and electric lighting transformed them from within. Victoria had been crowned Empress of India in 1883, a piece of titular inflation with no change in her status as a constitutional monarch. By the end of her reign, her empire covered one-fifth of the globe's territory. The public lined the streets as Victoria's funeral carriage trundled through London in a great moment of national mourning. The new King Edward VII walked behind his mother's coffin. Next to him was his nephew, Victoria's oldest grandson, German Kaiser Wilhelm II.

───── THE ROAD TO WORLD WAR ONE ─────

The Scramble for Africa saw 90% of the continent brought under European control by the turn of the century. By 1914 there were only two sovereign African countries, Ethiopia and Liberia. With greatly expanded empires came long borders fizzing with the potential for friction. The great powers had assembled to settle their differences in Berlin over the winter of 1884–5, but it was not a lasting solution. The Fashoda Incident of 1898–9, an Anglo-French spat over territory in east Africa, led to a war scare. German rivalry with France also blew up into two Moroccan Crises in 1905 and 1911. In Europe, two opposing power blocs had emerged: the Triple Alliance of 1882, with Germany, Austria–Hungary and Italy finding that their interests aligned; and France and Russia, who had countered this to form their own alliance. Europe was divided into two camps – one at the centre, the other on the periphery. At the turn of the 20th century Britain was reluctant to choose either of them. Soon, though, it would have to pick a side.

The British had lost their monopoly on revolutionary technology. The Industrial Revolution had spread abroad. In 1880 Britain was responsible for a huge 23% of global manufacturing, but after that other nations caught up and Britain experienced relative decline. Soon Germany was ascendant on the Continent. The new nation was industrialising rapidly, unhindered by legacy technology, and an economic explosion saw it pip Britain in relative manufacturing output by 1914. Its unified population was also some 20 million larger than Britain's, while the German navy was being expanded with the intention of matching its North Sea neighbour. The construction of German super-battleships or 'dreadnoughts' sent the British press and political classes into paroxysms.

This was reflected by the growing trend of 'invasion literature' that gained popularity after the 1870–71 Prussian victory over France. Often serialised in newspapers, it began with

George Chesney's publication of *The Battle of Dorking* (1871), which imagined an unnamed yet German-speaking foe devastating England. A sense of foreboding drove sales of millions of similar titles over the next 50 years. Of these, H.G. Wells's *War of the Worlds* (1897) is well known for posing the potential invasion in extraterrestrial terms, but William Le Queux's popular *The Great War in England in 1897* (1894) made the fears mildly more realistic; in this novel Britain faces France and Russia's combined might, and with Germany's military assistance drives out the invading French, which leads to the further growth of the British Empire.

In fact Britain took the other path. In 1904 it agreed the Entente Cordiale with France, which resolved long-standing colonial disputes. Britain also resolved the 'Great Game' with Russia through a 1907 agreement. Britain was now in much closer alignment with the European powers allied around Germany's flanks – although it was not yet in any formal alliance. William Le Queux had in 1906 published another bestseller, *The Invasion of 1910*, which redefined the likely adversary as Germany. Le Queux emphasised the need to build up defence in the face of a growing German military, and it went on to sell a million copies.

Europe rushed headlong into catastrophe in the summer of 1914, through a toxic mix of colonial rivalry, competing nationalisms, spectacular naivety and terrible luck. World War One began at the very peak of European power, yet it precipitated Europe's downfall. The assassination of the Austro-Hungarian heir to the throne, Franz Ferdinand, triggered a series of alliances. Empires mobilised their militaries, itself seen as an act of war. Germany invaded Belgium to strike at France. Once their ancient enemy had been knocked out, they could concentrate on Russia in the east. Britain, not formally allied to anyone but a guarantor of Belgian independence, faced a decision. Stand aloof and let Germany grow ever stronger in Europe, with access to ever more Channel ports for its ships, or intervene to save Belgium, help France and contain Germany. It chose the latter. Few foresaw the devastation this decision would bring. From 4 August 1914, Britain was once again fighting in mainland Europe, but this time at an industrial scale and intensity.

Emmeline Pankhurst addressing a five-thousand-strong crowd

Chapter 12

The Great War

It's 1 July 1916. British trenches, near the upper reaches of the River Somme in France, are packed with anxious young soldiers. They stand, one man pressed tightly against the next, clutching rifles close to their chests. Some swig from flasks, many smoke cigarettes to take their mind off what is to come.

All of them are waiting for a break in the artillery barrage that's been hitting German positions opposite them for a week. No-man's-land has been torn by artillery fire into a moonscape of shattered trees and gaping shell craters. As the sun rises further from the horizon, the call comes down the line to fix bayonets.

Junior officers stare intently at their wristwatches, counting down the minutes until Zero Hour. At 07:30, shrill whistles pierce the silence up and down the line. The stillness transforms into activity as the first wave of troops clamber up ladders and march towards German lines.

Sergeants and corporals push more men forward towards the enemy. But it very quickly becomes clear that the artillery has failed to cause any significant damage. German defences, deep underground bunkers, have largely withstood the bombardment. Their barbed wire is intact.

As the British march forward, the defenders emerge shaken but unharmed. They pour a deadly stream of rifle and machine-gun fire into the advancing troops, grinding the British to a halt, inflicting horrendous casualties.

By the end of the first day of the Somme, some 57,000 British soldiers were dead, wounded or missing. It's remembered as the bloodiest day in the history of the British military and the hope for a quick, decisive breakthrough had been shattered. The Battle of the Somme would ultimately drag out over five long months of attritional warfare. There would be a staggering 420,000 British casualties and over half a million German casualties before its end.

THIEPVAL

The rural area of the Somme region today is dotted with nearly 350 British Commonwealth cemeteries where close to 150,000 soldiers were laid to rest. The imposing 50-metre-high red-brick memorial at Thiepval lists 72,337 missing British and South African servicemen who fought in the Somme region between 1915 and 1918 and who have no known grave.

BRITAIN AT THE OUTBREAK

THE ACCRINGTON PALS MEMORIAL

The town of Accrington had raised a battalion with other nearby east Lancashire towns such as Burnley, Blackburn and Chorley, and this became known as the 'Accrington Pals'. They first saw action on the first day of the Somme on the most northerly part of the assault. Of around 700 Accrington Pals who went over the top, 235 were killed and 350 wounded within 20 minutes. The Accrington Pals are remembered at the Sheffield Memorial Park, near the village of Serre-lès-Puisieux, as well as in their hometown.

If you had told a British official ten years earlier that, a decade later, a massive British army would be taking on the Germans in a huge conventional battle in northern France, they would have been speechless. For much of the 19th century, Britain had avoided the expensive European entanglements in which she'd been enmeshed for so much of the 18th century and focussed instead on her own global trade and empire. Britain's army was tiny, and its planners more familiar with the Transvaal than with Flanders.

Britain had entered the struggle against the German-led Central Powers in 1914 with what the German kaiser Wilhelm is said to have derided as a 'contemptible little army'. The navy was still twice the size of Germany's, which was its closest rival. But Britain's army was described as an imperial policing force. The campaigns against the Zulus in South Africa, or the Mahdis in Sudan, were very different from facing an industrialised European enemy. By 1914, the German Army had ten times the number of soldiers than Britain, and was much better prepared for Continental warfare. The initial British Expeditionary Force that landed in France in August 1914 consisted of six infantry divisions and a few brigades of cavalry. By the end of 1914, it had suffered over 90,000 casualties, a huge proportion of its strength at the start of hostilities.

In August 1914, the veteran campaigner Lord Kitchener was

appointed Minister for War. He foresaw a long struggle that required a mass volunteer army, and made a direct appeal to the public. One of his methods was to create 'Pals Battalions', whereby men could be certain that they would serve alongside their friends and colleagues. The first of these was raised from stockbrokers in the City of London on 21 August 1914. A few days later, another battalion was raised in Liverpool.

> 'This should be a battalion of pals, a battalion in which friends from the same office will fight shoulder to shoulder for the honour of Britain and the credit of Liverpool.'
>
> **Lord Derby**

In early September, Kitchener's famous call to arms – his pointing portrait above WANTS YOU – was published on the front cover of a popular magazine, and soon became an icon of wartime propaganda. In that month alone, over 450,000 men volunteered, many through local Pals Battalions, and by the year's end close to 1.2 million had done so.

Early Failures

A similar number of men joined up in 1915. It would take time, however, for that massive expansion to deliver results on the battlefield. German forces could not be made to budge on the Western Front in France and Belgium. In February 1915 Britain and its allies tried to force their way through to Istanbul, the capital of Turkey, hoping to knock the Ottoman Empire, a German ally, out of the war. The initial naval attack on the Dardanelles failed to destroy the Ottoman defences, and in April an amphibious landing of troops from Britain, Australia,

New Zealand and France on the Gallipoli Peninsula became mired in trench warfare similar to that of the Western Front. That spring also saw a severe shortage of artillery shells that led to a political crisis at home.

That autumn a British offensive on the Western Front, at Loos, was repelled at the cost of nearly 60,000 casualties. The BEF's commander-in-chief Sir John French was subsequently replaced with Douglas Haig. Attritional warfare around the Belgian town of Ypres was also causing huge numbers of casualties. These setbacks unsurprisingly dampened down enthusiasm. Although the first two years had brought in 2.5 million volunteers, the war machine needed more. In January 1916, the government passed the Military Service Act, bringing in conscription.

——— THE FIRST DAY OF THE SOMME ———

In early 1916 the French Army was fighting for its existence. In late February, Germany had launched a huge attack at Verdun that led to one of the most terrible battles in history. Pressure mounted from French High Command for a British-led offensive further north at the Somme. But there were deep flaws in the plan. The Germans occupied strong fortifications on the higher ground in the region, while the French put enormous pressure on the British to attack before the British Army was realistically capable of defeating the Germans. So, the British had to attack in a place where they hadn't really wanted to, at a time earlier than their choosing, and with fewer French troops than had been promised months before in the early planning stages.

LISTEN TO THE
PODCAST

The Somme

By the first day of the Somme, over 200,000 British and French troops had amassed near the front lines. Divisions of new army soldiers took their place between divisions of old army, professional soldiers, in the hope that this new force would gain strength and support from the more experienced veteran units on their flanks. A colossal week-long bombardment commenced on 24 June 1916, with British artillery firing some 1.5 million shells. General Rawlinson, commander of the Fourth Army, wrote that nothing could exist at the conclusion of the bombardment in the area covered by it, an idea widely repeated by the men. 'Not even a rat' was one of the optimistic phrases repeated in dugouts and bars at the time. Rawlinson was proved terribly wrong: the rats, the German infantry, their heavy guns ... most did in fact still exist. The attack was a disaster. After 140 days of bloodshed, the British and French forces had advanced just six miles, and the offensive halted in November as weather worsened.

Both sides were spent. It would all come down to which had the greater reserves. The exhausted German forces withdrew to the even more heavily fortified Hindenburg Line, and dug in for a defensive war on the Western Front in early 1917. The Allies simply prepared to try to keep pushing them back. A French assault at Aisne was repelled, sparking mutiny, while another British-led offensive at the Third Battle of Ypres, also known as Passchendaele, became bogged down in unseasonal August mud, at the cost of another 300,000 men.

These appalling losses were just some of the vast numbers who were killed and wounded around the Belgian city. Winston Churchill wrote that 'a more sacred place for the British race does not exist in all the world'. Despite the huge loss of life at the Somme, it was actually at the Ypres Salient in Flanders that

Rochester Castle guards the River Medway. In the 12th century, the huge keep was added and it is the tallest remaining example in Europe. The site of several sieges, it was taken by rebels during the Peasants' Revolt of 1381.

In December 1400, King Henry IV welcomed the Byzantine Emperor Manuel II Palaiologos to London. Manuel is the only Byzantine ruler to visit England, which he described in a letter home as 'a second civilised world'.

In 1381, the Peasants' Revolt saw tens of thousands of people from the countryside seek societal change. The rebels moved into London, burning the Savoy Palace and executing the Archbishop of Canterbury and the Treasurer.

Hever Castle in Kent is a stunning moated castle dating back to the 14th century. Geoffrey Boleyn purchased the castle in 1462; his great-granddaughter Anne Boleyn grew up there.

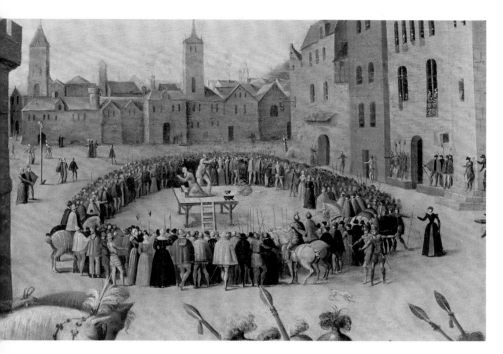

ecutions within the Tower of London were rare events. Only ten took place on Tower Green between 1483 and 1601, including the executions of three Tudor queens. Today, a monument commemorates those who were executed there.

Framlingham Castle in East Anglia dates back to the 12th century. In 1553, Edward VI's sister Mary was at Framlingham Castle when she learned that the Council had proclaimed her the new Queen of England after her brother had died.

Mary I is often considered the first queen regnant of England. As part of her successful quest to revert England to Catholicism, she executed many Protestants, earning her the nickname 'Bloody Mary'.

During her 45-year reign, Elizabeth I made England Protestant again, oversaw a period of vast expansion and saw off several threats to national security, including the Spanish Armada. Known as the Virgin Queen, she never married.

n 1771, Sir Richard Arkwright opened the world's first successful water-powered cotton spinning mill at Cromford Mills. Over the next two decades, several other warehouses and workshops cropped up nearby, as well as Cromford Village, which housed the growing workforce.

On 16 August 1819, around 60,000 people gathered in St Peter's Field, Manchester to demand reform of parliamentary representation. A cavalry charge was ordered to quell the protest, killing eighteen and injuring several hundred. This is known as the Peterloo Massacre.

Spanning the Avon Gorge in Bristol, the Clifton Suspension Bridge was designed by Isambard Kingdom Brunel. Work began in 1831 and was completed in 1864. The bridge is 214m long and sits around 76m above the River Avon.

The Thiepval Memorial was erected between 1928 and 1932 to commemorate those killed in the Somme who had no known grave. It records the names of 72,000 British and South African soldiers, 90% of whom died between July and November 1916.

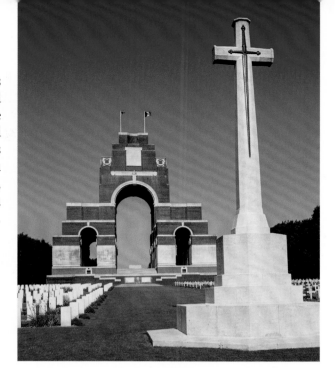

From 31 May 1938 onwards, the Cabinet War Rooms were installed in the basement of a building in Whitehall. Now a museum, the rooms have been preserved just as they were when the lights were turned off in 1945.

Imber on Salisbury Plain was requisitioned in 1943 for the American military to train in a European village setting, evicting the population of around 150 in the process. Tours of the village are offered on specific open days.

Purchased by the War Department in 1913, Orford Ness in Suffolk was a military test site. RADAR was developed here between 1935–7, and it was used to test atomic weapons during the Cold War.

Britain sustained its greatest number of casualties. Through the course of the four-year war, five battles involving British forces took the lives of around a quarter of a million men. Estimates for total casualties for both sides in this attritional chokepoint reach as high as one million. Britain was paying a high price for its defence of Belgian sovereignty.

YPRES

The Tyne Cot Cemetery, near Passchendaele, is the largest cemetery for Commonwealth forces in the world. Here there are marked graves for 11,965 fallen soldiers, 8,369 of whom are unnamed. The stone wall surrounding the cemetery contains the names of over 30,000 British and New Zealanders 'whose graves are known only to God'. Another memorial in Ypres, the Menin Gate, was unveiled in 1927, and its walls are engraved with 54,896 names of 'the armies of the British Empire who stood here from 1914 to 1918 and to those of the dead who have no known grave'. Every night at eight o'clock since 2 July 1928, only interrupted by German occupation of Belgium during World War Two, 'The Last Post' has been played here by buglers from the Ypres Last Post Association.

THE DECISIVE YEAR

By 1918, the stalemate had cracked. In the east, revolution had swept through Russia in November 1917, and its new communist government agreed punitive peace terms with Germany on 3 March 1918. The Austro-Hungarian Empire was on the brink of similar collapse and Germany was facing dire food and equipment shortages as a result of Allied naval blockades. Enraged by submarine attacks on its shipping in the Atlantic, the United States of America had also entered the war on the side of the Allies.

With the fall of Russia in the east, the Germans were able to concentrate one last major offensive in the west, hoping to win the war before America could make itself felt on the battlefield. This huge Spring Offensive began in late March 1918, with 74 German divisions attacking 23 miles of Allied lines defended by 26 British and 24 French divisions. The next few months would prove to be the biggest test for the Allies in the entire war, with the German Army advancing some 50 miles and inflicting over 800,000 Allied casualties. But Germany suffered similar losses, and advancing troops outran a creaking supply system. By summer the offensive had petered out. The Allies were bloodied, but undefeated. The German forces were exhausted. It was now the turn of the Allies.

The British Army in 1918 was probably the best army the nation has ever fielded. Despite the casualties suffered that spring, there were 1.25 million soldiers for a new offensive, many hardened by battle experience, aided by similar numbers of French and Americans. The British had served a savage apprenticeship. Their army was fine-tuned. Technology too had transformed war. The days of massive artillery bombardment followed by a human wave infantry assault, as at the Somme, were over. Artillery was now much more accurate, and the technique of providing creeping barrages for rapidly advancing men to take cover behind had been much improved. Aircraft could strafe and bomb enemy positions, while massed tanks could punch holes in enemy lines and crawl over their trenches. The tank was a British invention first deployed at the Somme in September 1916, but they had been too few in number and too unreliable to provide a breakthrough. Now these machines would be used en masse.

> 'The Allied soldiers understood that the nature of war was changing. They were being taught different formations in the attack. They could see how tanks and aircraft were working in unison. They were being led by officers who were skilled often now in wireless, flash spotting and sound ranging. So I think they were a much more confident group. I think they knew that they had tactical and military superiority over the enemy.'
>
> **Richard van Emden, historian**

At the Battle of Amiens, which roared into being on 8 August 1918, Britain deployed over 500 tanks, and the Royal Air Force and French equivalent supported with over 1,900 aircraft. This combined arms operation punched a hole in the German lines that advanced seven miles in its first day, leading to the surrender of some 20,000 German troops. The German warlord General Ludendorff would later call it, 'The black day of the German Army.' Further attacks at the Somme and Noyon later in August broke the German lines and the Allies fought on to the Hindenburg Line. By this point, German morale was waning. Huge casualties and supply shortages were leading to mass surrender. The Allies punched through the Hindenburg Line at the Second Battle of Cambrai on 8 October 1918. To match these battlefield defeats, Germany's allies were collapsing across the Balkans and Middle East. Revolution broke out in Germany itself. It could not go on.

─────────────── **THE COST OF WAR** ───────────────

On the 11th hour of the 11th day of the 11th month of 1918, an Armistice was signed between French and German delegations at Compiègne. The war was over. It had been a costly victory; the Allies had suffered over a million killed, wounded or captured during the Hundred Days Offensive that ended the war. In all, Europe had suffered around ten million combat deaths and the same number of deaths among civilians, and the collapse of empires ensured that there would be more violence in the months to come as new nations fought over the spoils.

It was the bloodiest war in British history, unsurpassed by even World War Two. Britain suffered 880,000 deaths, comprising 6% of the adult male population, leading to a notable gender imbalance in the 1921 Census, with 109 women for every 100 men. Barely a street had gone without losing a son, father or a husband, and almost every family was affected, or knew someone who was. The journalist Arthur Mee defined a 'Thankful Village' as one that had lost no men in the war and he estimated that there were only 32 such villages in England. From at least 1915, in almost every city, town and village across the country, war memorials were built. A stone cross rising above a list of names, in memoriam.

Remembering the Fallen

To mark the war's formal conclusion of the signing of the Treaty of Versailles in June 1919, the British government organised a national 'Peace Day'. A 15,000-strong military parade and a silent march past the temporary wood-and-plaster Cenotaph honoured the war dead. The monument became a centre of the nation's grief, and the public spontaneously adorned its base with wreaths in memory of fallen soldiers, which led to calls for a permanent version. The rebuilt Cenotaph, now in Portland stone, was unveiled by King George V on 11 November 1920 during the funeral procession of the Unknown Warrior. The Cenotaph, which stands in the middle of Whitehall, has been the focus of the nation's remembrance ever since.

The fourth verse of the poem 'For the Fallen' by Robert Laurence Binyon (1869–1943), first published on 21 September 1914, has become an ode for remembrance and is recited either before or at the end of a two-minute silence held every year on 11 November and the nearest Sunday.

They shall grow not old, as we that are left grow old:
Age shall not weary them, nor the years condemn.
At the going down of the sun and in the morning
We will remember them.

GRAVE OF THE UNKNOWN WARRIOR

It was also decided to create a special grave containing the remains of an unidentified British serviceman, to honour and commemorate all those who died in British service, but particularly as a monument to the nearly 340,000 soldiers who were missing and had no grave. Conceived by David Railton, a chaplain serving with the British Army on the Western Front, it is Britain's most important war memorial. The selection of the Unknown Warrior – one of those killed whose bodies could not be identified – was a secret process. Once chosen, the Unknown Warrior was transported back from the Western Front, and buried in Westminster Abbey on 11 November 1920.

THE STATE MAKES WARS, AND WARS MAKE THE STATE

Although victorious, Britain had endured a terrible trauma. It was weakened. It had also suffered financially and economically. There was unemployment and dislocation. Academics became pessimistic about the future prospects of the empire with an elite that had suffered a 'Lost Generation'. How would the upper classes, who suffered disproportionately in terms of war dead, be able to lead the empire? There was a desperate hope that the war would provide an example of futility impossible to ignore. It was referred to as the 'War to End All Wars' or the 'Great War'. Perhaps a better world would emerge from the ordeal.

Such optimism struggled to survive contact with news from the Continent. The Austro-Hungarian, German, Ottoman and Russian empires had collapsed. A patchwork of new states emerged, often competitive, angry, bristling with grievance. The spectre of communism stalked the nightmares of the propertied classes. Over the course of the war, over nine million Brits and Irish had put on uniforms and learned to fight. On top of the catastrophic death toll, over two million men had been wounded, and nearly 200,000 had been discharged as invalids.

Government had transformed too. The Defence of the Realm Act (DORA) had been introduced in August 1914 and had given the government a wide range of powers, such as requisitioning property for the war effort. Alcoholic drinks were watered down and opening times were restricted. There were even regulations on buying binoculars and feeding wild animals bread. Conscription had arrived in 1916, as had daylight saving time. Food rationing had been introduced in January 1918 and some foods remained on rations until 1920.

Many now wanted this new activist government to fight poverty and inequality as enthusiastically as it had fought the Germans. There were demands for social reform, welfare provision and equal voting rights. There was a doubling in trade union membership, to 44% of the workforce. Millions of returning servicemen had seen what government could do when it put its mind to it. There was a big increase in state provision, including a dole for unemployed men as a safety net while transitioning back into civilian employment. It was hoped this would help persuade them not to reject the British system in favour of radical alternatives. The Ministry of Pensions had been established in 1916 to provide assistance to war veterans, and by 1921 pension payments had reached 7% of government expenditure. One million ex-servicemen were provided with pension payments that totalled £1.2 billion between 1916 and 1938 – equivalent to around £90 billion in today's money.

'I would say that the people who win concessions, who make things better for the vast majority of the British population, are not the dead servicemen. So this isn't something that's won in return for wartime sacrifice. It's trade unionists and servicemen who have to be persuaded to remain part of the post-war settlement in some way.'

Daniel Todman, Queen Mary University of London

——————— WOMEN'S SUFFRAGE ———————

During the Great War, 25% of British men had been mobilised for military service. To make up for the labour shortage, women took on crucial jobs in factories and fields to support the war effort. The proportion of women in employment rose from 24% at the war's outbreak to 37% by its end, but as men returned from the front these levels fell back to pre-war levels. Nevertheless, women had answered the call in the national hour of need. It was harder than ever to refuse them the vote.

In the early 20th century, two groups had been active in the campaign for women's suffrage: the 'suffragists', who campaigned using peaceful methods including lobbying and meetings with politicians, and the 'suffragettes', led by Emmeline Pankhurst under the Women's Social and Political Union (WSPU). The suffragettes were determined to secure women the right to vote through more robust means, emphasising 'deeds, not words'.

Their unlawful, militant tactics, including attacks on government property, arson of unoccupied houses and churches, and eye-catching acts of civil disobedience, gained them widespread notoriety.

LISTEN TO THE
PODCAST

Modern Warfare

In one of their most famous protests, during the Epsom Derby on 4 June 1913, Emily Wilding Davison dashed out from the crowd enclosure and onto the track. She was struck by the king's horse, and died of her injuries four days later. Her full motives remain unclear. Some suggest she just meant to tie a banner to the king's horse (she had purchased a return ticket home). Nevertheless, following her death the suffragettes considered Davison a martyr for their cause.

Political parties had been debating enfranchisement prior to the war, yet each wanted it to happen on their terms, fearing that widening the voting populace might disadvantage them. The war had frozen the debate; at its outset, Emmeline Pankhurst had called for a halt to suffragette militant actions in order to instead support the British government's war effort.

After the war, this spirit, and the wartime service of women, became the basis for granting some women the vote. In 1918 the Representation of the People Act enfranchised all men over 21 and women aged over 30 who met minimum property qualifications, a discrepancy intended to ensure that, following the huge number of wartime deaths, men did not become minority voters.

But it was hoped that this might prove a stabilising influence. Radical change was feared by those in power. Enfranchising affluent women over 30, who were more likely to have some investment in the system, would hopefully provide a bulwark against revolution. It did mean that younger, poorer women – those who had most likely served in munitions factories or auxiliary forces – were excluded.

'Women were in industry absolutely before the war, in domestic service and in all kinds of industries. The irony is so many of the women who were the munitionettes and everything else didn't get the vote in 1918.'

Naomi Paxton, historian

In the post-war era, many women sought work with the skills they had gained during the war, but they were accused of 'taking ex-servicemen's jobs'. Instead they were forced back into more traditional 'women's work', such as domestic service.

In 1928, the Conservative government extended the vote to everyone aged over 21. It was a step on the way to a more equal society, not a destination. While new industries and professions opened up for women, measures such as the 'marriage bar' (forcing women to resign once married) and unequal pay meant that, by 1931, a working woman's weekly wage in most industries had returned to its pre-war levels of half the male rate. This prompted further protests.

STRIKES, UNEMPLOYMENT AND INTERWAR POLITICS

Britain's economy remained fragile during the 1920s. After something of an economic rebound immediately after the war, Britain struggled with unemployment and the effects of the so-called 'Spanish' influenza pandemic, which in Britain killed an estimated 230,000 people, predominantly of working age. A serious recession occurred in 1920–22, with unemployment rising to 16% and exports at only half their pre-war levels.

Following the collapse of David Lloyd George's coalition government in 1922, and a period of political instability, the Labour Party entered office for the first time in January 1924, albeit as a minority government. This was an upheaval. Many self-styled socialists now held high office at the pinnacle of the world's largest empire.

Another short economic downturn occurred in 1926, resulting partly from Britain's war debts but also from the realigning
of pound sterling with the actual quantity of gold in circula-
tion, an event known as returning to the gold standard. In May
1926 there was a general strike lasting nine days, called by the
Trades Union Congress to prevent wage reductions for 1.2
million coal miners. Unemployment rates remained stub-
bornly high, particularly in the Midlands and north of England,
lingering between 1925 and 1929 at around 10%; in some
areas dependent on traditional sectors of the economy, like
iron, steel and shipbuilding, they were much higher. Economic
growth was sluggish, with Britain growing at just a fraction of
the rate of France and Germany.

The 'Roaring Twenties' did not skip Britain entirely, though.
There was a short economic boom from 1927 to 1929. Labour
returned to power in June 1929, but any ambitions to transform the country were stopped dead in their tracks by the Wall
Street crash that October, leading to the 'Great Slump', as it
was referred to in Britain. By January 1933, the nadir of the
Great Depression, unemployment had soared to 3.5 million.

THE HEIGHT OF THE EMPIRE?

The British Empire reached its maximum territorial extent in
1922, after it took custodianship of former German and
Ottoman colonies. It was said that 'the sun never set on the
British Empire'. This was geographically true; the union flag
fluttered above vast swathes of territory. But the empire's size
could not disguise its weakness. World War One had weakened Britain, and at its close at the Paris Peace Conference
fostered a spirit of self-determination for peoples and nations.

Meanwhile, the Soviet Union, formed in 1922, suggested that the future might belong to the revolutionary socialists rather than traditional European empires.

Irish Independence

One of those nations that asserted its independence was part of the United Kingdom itself. Ireland, the oldest piece of the overseas English empire, would become the first to break away. The question of Irish Home Rule had dominated British politics during the late 19th century. In 1914, Ireland had stood on the brink of civil war as Parliament had approved its devolution, provoking fear and rage in the Protestant community. However, the outbreak of the war saw the plan suspended, and a group of Irish nationalists turned to militancy. At Easter 1916 there was an armed insurrection in Dublin. It was the most significant outbreak of violence in Ireland since 1798, with nearly 500 killed over six days before the rebels surrendered.

The Irish Republican party Sinn Féin won a majority of Irish seats in the December 1918 general election. They refused to sit in Westminster, instead forming their own parliament that declared war on the rest of the UK. By the summer of 1920 the British administration was on the brink of collapse, and heavy-handed tactics and the ill-discipline of British troops were fanning the flames of separatism. Martial law was declared in several Irish counties in December that year. Violence escalated over the next six months, until in July 1921 a truce was declared. Ireland remained

LISTEN TO THE
PODCAST

The Aftermath of
World War One

within the imperial family, but in name only. It gained 'dominion status' as it signed the Anglo-Irish Treaty, on 6 December 1921. Hardline nationalists rejected the treaty and civil war broke out in Ireland, but by 1923 pro-treaty forces had won. Ulster, with a pro-British Protestant ethnic majority, remained in the United Kingdom.

Dominions and the Commonwealth

The Irish Free State thus joined the majority white nations of Canada, Australia, New Zealand and South Africa as a dominion of the British Empire. These nations had been granted greater autonomy over the course of the 19th century, and in 1907 were made dominions. At the 1926 Imperial Conference, this went a step further, as they would be:

'. . . autonomous communities within the British Empire, equal in status, in no way subordinate one to another in any aspect of their domestic or external affairs, though united by a common allegiance to the Crown and freely associated as members of the British Commonwealth of Nations.'

Legislative independence was granted in the 1931 Statute of Westminster, a year that also saw the creation of the British Commonwealth of Nations. Other dominions would later join Britain in fighting World War Two, but Ireland did not. By the late 1930s Ireland was effectively out of the empire, with a president and all the trappings of a sovereign state.

The Restless Empire

While the majority-white nations gained more autonomy, that could not be said of other countries within the British Empire. Much of Africa, Asia and the Australasian islands remained as colonies. Egypt, which had status as a protectorate, declared independence in 1922, but Britain would maintain control over foreign and military affairs without Egyptian consent until 1952.

In India, Home Rule nationalist movements were building. In April 1919, in a shocking act of violence, Brigadier General Reginald Dyer ordered British Indian troops to fire on a crowd protesting against the arrest of two Indian nationalists in Amritsar, Punjab. Hundreds were killed – estimates run up to 1,500 – and around 1,000 injured.

In the words of Winston Churchill, the Amritsar Massacre was 'unutterably monstrous', and it showed how heavy-handed the British could be with their non-white subjects. In 1920, Mahatma Gandhi arranged a campaign of non-cooperation and reorganised the Indian Congress, a nationalist movement founded in 1885, into a mass movement. Mass protests and acts of violence were common in the 1920s, and in 1935 Parliament passed the Government of India Act, which granted some autonomy, but not on the scale of the majority-white dominions.

The British Empire was under pressure, but few could have foreseen just how rapidly it would disintegrate. Following hard on the heels of the Great War, political and cultural transformation and economic collapse came an even greater war. A war from which Britain emerged victorious but also terribly diminished, unable and unwilling to hold its vast imperial holdings together.

——————— THE GATHERING STORM ———————

Traumatised and dislocated, Europe after World War One was a laboratory of political and economic experimentation. New states and old sought to define themselves, meet their populations' demands for a better life and then deal with the tidal wave of the Great Depression. The fascist Benito Mussolini had risen to power in Italy in October 1922, promising radical renewal. The collapse of the German economy in 1929 also propelled Adolf Hitler's National Socialist German Workers' Party into a position of strength, and he was appointed Chancellor on 30 January 1933.

Authoritarian regimes fed off each other's success and thought they could taste a global reordering. In September 1931 Japan invaded Manchuria, in China. Emboldened by the lack of reaction from the world's leading powers, the Italians and Germans also made ever more aggressive foreign policy moves. In March 1935 Hitler rejected another plank of the post-World War One settlement by announcing a massive programme of rearmament. Six months later Mussolini invaded Ethiopia, and the following spring Hitler defied France and Britain by moving military forces into the Rhineland on the border with France.

Britain had no appetite for intervention. In an economic malaise, it could not pay for a large army and a mighty fleet and meet the aspirations of its new voters for a decent standard of living. No one wanted another war; an unofficial 'Peace Ballot' was held in 1935, and 11.8 million voters overwhelmingly signalled their opposition to rearmament and that membership of the League of Nations should be the key factor in deciding British policy. On the right of the political spectrum, it was communism rather than fascism that was considered to be the greatest threat to peace. Relations with the newly formed Soviet Union were icy, and many muttered, 'rather Hitler than Stalin at the Channel ports.' Anxiety grew at the outbreak of the Spanish Civil War in July 1936, when Nationalists fought against the left-wing coalition of Republicans.

In January 1936, King George V died and his son became Edward VIII. However, only months into his reign, he expressed his desire to marry American divorcée Wallis Simpson.

Post-war shifts in British morality had allowed for greater personal freedom, but the Church of England, of which the king was the head, disapproved of divorce – ironic given its own genesis. The cabinet, including prime minister Stanley Baldwin, also opposed the marriage. Edward realised that if the marriage went ahead his government would resign, potentially triggering a general election and jeopardising his status as a politically neutral constitutional monarch.

When it became apparent that he could not marry Simpson and remain on the throne, Edward abdicated, and signed the instruments of abdication at Fort Belvedere on 10 December 1936, witnessed by his brothers – including Prince Albert, Duke of York, who now became King George VI.

Edward, now the Duke of Windsor, married Simpson in France in June 1937. Later that year, the couple visited Nazi Germany, against the advice of the British government. They met Adolf Hitler at his retreat, the Berghof, and gave enthusiastic Nazi salutes. In the months that followed, it seemed possible that Edward's former subjects might be forced to do the same.

Coventry Cathedral in ruins after a night of heavy bombing

Chapter 13

World War Two

When Neville Chamberlain took over as prime minister in May 1937, he hoped that his tenure would be remembered for ambitious domestic reforms. It would not be. Instead his premiership was dominated by the threat of a resurgent Germany and his ultimate failure to contain the ambitions of Adolf Hitler.

Winston Churchill, a former senior minister who languished in the political wilderness during the 1930s, had been an early critic to the menace of Hitler's regime, particularly after its invasion and annexation of Austria in March 1938. Churchill warned repeatedly of a coming war, one for which Britain would not be ready. In September 1938 Hitler had threatened war if parts of Czechoslovakia with sizeable ethnic German populations were not given to Germany. Chamberlain flew to Munich and largely acceded to Hitler's demands in return for an assurance that he had fulfilled all his territorial ambitions. It seemed that war would be averted.

'There's huge euphoria after the Munich Agreement, but that's relief. Within a couple of weeks most people in Britain are beginning to realise that the only way war was avoided was giving in to this bully's demands and that they're probably not going to be his last demands.'

Tim Bouverie, historian

On 15 March 1939 Hitler reneged on the deal and invaded the rest of Czechoslovakia. Chamberlain quickly issued a security guarantee to Poland, Hitler's next likely target. The Germans, in turn, stunned the world with their own security pact; it was with their bitter enemies the Soviet Union. What brought these two former adversaries together was the promise of Polish territory. Germany invaded their Polish neighbour on 1 September. The Soviets pounced from the east a couple of weeks later. In response to the German invasion, the British and French threatened war if Hitler did not withdraw his troops. Hitler refused, calling their bluff. But France and Britain, and their empires, followed through on their threat. Europe and the world were plunged into another catastrophic war.

THE PHONEY WAR AND THE BATTLE FOR FRANCE

While the German Army was occupied in Poland, Britain and France undertook only very limited attacks to support their ally. Instead the western Allies dug defensive positions, hoping to use the time to mobilise and rearm. In the face of overwhelming assaults from both sides, Poland surrendered in early October, and its government went into exile in London.

The Allies hoped to strangle the German economy through the effective World War One strategy of naval blockade, but this was not going to win the war in the short term. There were eye-catching setbacks for the Royal Navy; one of its carriers was sunk within weeks of the start of the war, and then the battleship HMS *Royal Oak* was torpedoed inside the supposedly safe haven at Scapa Flow in October with the loss of 835 lives.

There was fierce fighting at the start of 1940 as the Germans and Allies clashed for control of Norway. The disappointing outcome of the campaign forced Chamberlain's resignation on 10 May. He, and many senior Conservatives, seem to have favoured foreign secretary Lord Halifax to be his successor. But Winston Churchill had stronger support from across the political spectrum. Halifax bowed to the convention that a prime minister ought to sit in the House of Commons and Churchill went to the palace to kiss the royal hand. By that evening he had formed a new coalition government. That same day, the German Army began its invasion of France and the Low Countries.

CABINET WAR ROOMS

Located beneath the streets of Westminster, the Cabinet War Rooms are part of London's underground bombproof bunker complex, where Britain's wartime government operated during World War Two. They became fully operational in August 1939, a week before Britain declared war on Germany, to ensure continuity of government should 10 Downing Street and Whitehall be damaged, and to facilitate quick decision-making between civilian government and military authorities. Throughout the war, Churchill, his cabinet and some 500 civil servants worked, and sometimes slept, there.

Weaving together aircraft, vehicles, artillery and infantry, along with wireless communications, the Germans knocked the Allies off-balance. They sliced through the Ardennes Forest using a warfare method called blitzkrieg (lightning war), striking the Allies where they were least expected. The British Expeditionary Force and a good portion of the French Army marched north into Belgium, and were astonished to find that there was a German armoured column advancing across northern France to their rear. There was no choice but retreat towards the sea. It could not have been more different from the four-year stalemate of World War One. Days after the start of the offensive, German forces had reached the Channel coast and cut the Allied armies in two. It appeared that Hitler had won a stunning victory.

Miracle at Dunkirk

Winston Churchill obstinately refused to accept that this was anything more than a temporary German success. He ordered the navy to do everything it could to rescue Allied troops from the Continent. Operation Dynamo was the miraculous and hastily organised mission to lift beleaguered troops on the coast around Dunkirk. Dozens of warships assisted by 850 requisitioned private boats shuttled back and forward across the Channel. These 'little ships' sailed into legend. They included fishing boats and pleasure craft, and came from ports all over the country, with Ramsgate harbour serving as their main assembly point. Dover Castle's network of medieval and Napoleonic-era tunnels were converted into a makeshift naval base. From there Admiral Sir Bertram Ramsay coordinated the evacuation, assembling ships and crew with only hours of notice.

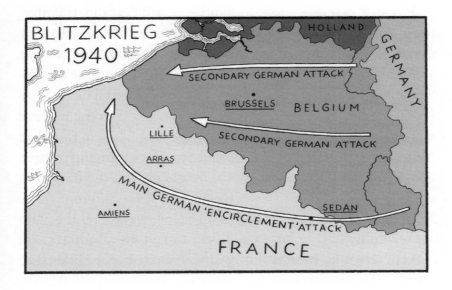

BLITZKRIEG 1940

HOLLAND

GERMANY

SECONDARY GERMAN ATTACK

BRUSSELS

BELGIUM

SECONDARY GERMAN ATTACK

LILLE

ARRAS

MAIN GERMAN 'ENCIRCLEMENT' ATTACK

SEDAN

AMIENS

FRANCE

SUNDOWNER

One of the 'little ships' was *Sundowner*, now housed at Ramsgate Maritime Museum. A motor yacht previously owned by the former second officer of the *Titanic*, Charles Lightoller, it was requisitioned by the Admiralty on 30 May 1940. Lightoller insisted he and his son Roger take the yacht to Dunkirk, together with Sea Scout Gerald Ashcroft, and managed to transport 127 soldiers back to Ramsgate.

Some 338,000 Allied soldiers were evacuated in Operation Dynamo. It became known as the 'Miracle of Dunkirk'. However, the evacuation might have been a propaganda victory, but the Allies had firmly lost the battle for the West. The French Army, considered the most powerful in the world, had capitulated, while the British Expeditionary Force lost 68,000 men and abandoned most of its equipment. France surrendered to Germany on 22 June. Many within Westminster thought the war was lost and believed Britain ought to seek peace terms with Hitler's Germany. But Winston Churchill made a series of superb speeches that set out the case for total war against the Nazi menace no matter what the cost. In one of them, on 4 June 1940, he insisted that if a German invasion came 'We shall fight them on the beaches.'

With the British Army defeated and lacking equipment, Britain looked vulnerable to invasion. Looks can deceive, however; the Royal Navy was powerful and undefeated. For any German invasion to stand a chance of success, Germany would need to wrest control of the English Channel from the Royal Navy – a near impossibility. The only conceivable way they might do so was if the German Luftwaffe was able to gain total air superiority. Then invasion barges might be able to dash across under a defensive aerial umbrella.

In July 1940, Hitler set in motion the preparations for an amphibious invasion, codenamed 'Operation Sealion'. There was huge scepticism among the German High Command about whether they could even launch it, let alone execute a successful invasion. Hitler hoped that the threat of invasion, plus airstrikes on Britain, might force the UK into a negotiated peace.

'I feel myself obliged to make one more appeal to reason to England . . . I do this not as a victor, but for the triumph of common sense.'

Adolf Hitler to the German Reichstag, 19 July 1940

Home Defence Services

Britain built up various services to support the defence of the homeland and the prosecution of the war. Among these were:

- **Home Guard** – the Local Defence Volunteers (LDV) were formed in May 1940 and renamed the Home Guard in July 1940. It was composed mainly of older men ineligible for regular military service, whose role was to act as a secondary line of defence behind the regular army. Far from being a 'Dad's Army', the Home Guard would guard vulnerable beaches, bridges and factories. By 1943 the force numbered some 1.5 million men.
- **Women's Land Army (WLA)** – provided a new rural workforce to boost farming amid a shortage of male agricultural workers and reduced food imports. Initially established in 1917 but disbanded after World War One, the WLA reformed in June 1939. By autumn 1941, over 20,000 women had volunteered, but from December 1941 women could also be conscripted and sent anywhere in the country. 80,000 women were serving in the WLA at its peak in 1944, playing a crucial role in maintaining the nation's food supply.
- **Auxiliary Territorial Service (ATS)** – a women's branch of the British Army had been established in September 1938. Women served as mechanics, drivers, telephonists and anti-aircraft gunners, among other roles, to free up men for front-line service. Princess Elizabeth joined the ATS in February 1945, aged 18 – the first female British royal to become an active duty member of the British Armed Forces – and trained and worked as a mechanic and driver. By June 1945

the ATS had around 200,000 members, drawn from across the British Empire.

THE BATTLE OF BRITAIN

To put pressure on the UK government, the Luftwaffe began daylight bombing raids on British coastal shipping from 10 July, and attacks soon intensified. It was the start of the Battle of Britain, the first battle in history fought solely in the air. Aerial duels or dogfights between German Messerschmitt fighters and Royal Air Force interceptors proved that the German aircraft was formidable. But the new British Spitfire in particular was able to hold its own. Nearly 3,000 air crew would appear on the official list of Battle of Britain participants. Their average age was 20. Alongside British pilots were many from across the empire and beyond. Czechoslovakia and Poland produced a particularly important cohort of airmen. No. 303 Squadron RAF was Polish. Its pilots had flown against the Germans over their own country, and brought that experience to bear in the west. They accounted for more kills than any other squadron, while also suffering the fewest losses.

The Luftwaffe was bigger than the Royal Air Force, but the British had distinct advantages. The Luftwaffe had to travel across the English Channel just to attack their targets, meaning they could spend far less time fighting before needing to return to France and refuel. This also meant that any downed German pilots would become prisoners of war, while British pilots, if they were uninjured, could get a taxi back to their airfield, jump in a different aircraft and rejoin the fight.

Britain also had a secret technology – radar – which could detect German aircraft more than 100 miles out. In the months leading up to the battle, Britain had installed a 'Chain Home' network of 29 'radio direction finding' stations (radar stations) along its southern and eastern coastlines.

CHAIN HOME TOWER

The Chain Home Tower at Great Baddow, Essex is the sole surviving complete Chain Home transmitter tower in the British Isles, and one of just five remaining Chain Home masts. Erected at RAF Canewdon in 1937, it played a vital role in defending London, tracking V1 and V2 flying bombs, before being relocated to Great Baddow in 1956.

Nor was Britain greatly outnumbered in the aircraft types that mattered: advanced fighters like the Spitfire. Large, slow-moving fleets of German bombers were simply prey to these interceptors. Britain was also far better at replacing losses. From the Battle of Britain's beginnings in July, Germany was losing too many aircraft and not replacing them, while Britain was able to replace its downed planes far more effectively. Indeed, Fighter Command actually ended the Battle of Britain stronger than when it began, with about 40% more operational pilots and more aircraft. The Luftwaffe by contrast limped to the end battered and depleted, having lost 30% of its operational strength.

'There was nothing very romantic about it. You talk about knights of the air and jousts, but these sort of one-on-one combats were extremely rare. Largely success was about creeping up on someone from behind and stabbing him in the back and running away before any of his friends could get you.'

Stephen Bungay, historian

Aircraft losses on the biggest days of battle

Date	RAF Losses	Luftwaffe Losses
11 August	17	20
12 August	20	27
13 August	13	47
15 August	32	75
18 August	34	69
30 August	23	23
31 August	37	33
7 September	23	41
15 September	28	56
27 September	29	57

In mid-August, the Luftwaffe switched its focus to the RAF itself by attacking its airfields. While many suffered significant damage, nearly all remained operational. In early September, a frustrated and impatient Hitler changed strategy yet again. He now ordered an all-out assault on London. A huge battle on 15 September saw a large-scale Luftwaffe attack on London eviscerated by the RAF. The Germans realised that their air losses were unsustainable. There would be no air superiority over southern England, and certainly no invasion before the winter.

LISTEN TO THE
PODCAST

The Battle of Britain

Operation Sea Lion was shelved. The fifteenth of September is remembered as Battle of Britain Day.

As the battle tapered off, the Blitz really began. Starting on 7 September, London was bombed for 57 consecutive nights, and other major industrial centres, such as Bristol, Southampton, Birmingham, Sheffield and Liverpool, were also attacked, particularly in November and December in an expression of frustration and rage by Hitler that left many of Britain's cities strewn with fire and rubble. Ordinary people were killed, and neighbourhoods destroyed. On 14–15 November, the medieval city of Coventry was hit hard; 568 lost their lives and its priceless heritage was destroyed, alongside a third of its houses and shops.

COVENTRY CATHEDRAL

Coventry Cathedral's provost, the Very Reverend Richard Howard, had led efforts to protect the cathedral prior to the raid on 14 November. However, these proved futile, and the cathedral was reduced to ruins. The decision to build a new cathedral was taken the next morning. Designed by Basil Spence, it was consecrated in 1962, but the ruins of the original remain as a poignant reminder of the bombing.

This 'Blitz' was intended to destroy Britain's morale and force the British government to surrender, but it did neither. Over the course of the nine-month bombing campaign, some 43,500 British civilians were killed. Britain was bruised, but unbroken, its people more determined than ever to prosecute the war against Hitler.

Britain Stands Alone?

The cliché goes that 'Britain Stood Alone'. It is certainly true that by the spring of 1941 Britain lacked any European allies. But it still had the vast resources of the Empire. It could call upon a quarter of the world's population and resources from a fifth of its landmass. India, Australia, Canada and others all mobilised millions of men over the course of the war. In these opening months of the war, Britain also still had the world's most powerful navy. Despite the early military setbacks, the British Empire was still a global military giant.

———— HITLER TURNS EAST ————

With Britain unbeaten, Hitler turned his gaze to his ideological enemy, albeit temporary ally, in the east – the Soviet Union. The Nazi–Soviet pact of 1939 was a Machiavellian ploy, not a profound change of heart; Hitler always viewed the conquest of a vast eastern empire for the German people as his destiny. Before he could send his armoured columns deep into the Soviet Union he was forced to deal with Greece and the Balkans, which he overran in spring 1941.

LISTEN TO THE
PODCAST

The Great Imperial War

Nazi Germany had by now subjugated most of Europe. Hitler's empire stretched from Brittany in France east to Poland,

and down to the islands of the Mediterranean. Italy, Hungary and Romania were junior partners in his Axis alliance. Not since the days of Napoleon had one power dominated so much of the Continent. Like Napoleon's, Hitler's empire would be short-lived, because, like Napoleon, Hitler invaded Russia.

On 22 June 1941, the German army launched Operation Barbarossa, the biggest land invasion in history. The Soviets were militarily in poor shape after a period of military purges and reorganisation, and by December the Germans were at the gates of Moscow. But despite catastrophic losses over the preceding six months, the Soviets dug in, helped by the bitterly cold winter, and inflicted a stinging defeat on Germany at the gates of their capital.

Churchill had called Russia 'a riddle wrapped in a mystery inside an enigma' back in 1939, and Soviet–British relations were icy. Plans were even drawn up to bomb Soviet oil fields in the Caucasus to prevent them supplying the Nazis. But Operation Barbarossa forced the Soviet Union and Britain into an alliance, and on 12 July the two powers signed the Anglo-Soviet Agreement. Over the next four years, Britain would send the USSR an immense amount of military aid, including:

- 7,411 aircraft
- 27 naval vessels
- 5,218 tanks
- 15 million pairs of boots

Churchill was keenly aware that the involvement of the USA, the world's leading industrial and financial power, would be decisive. The fact that he was half American boosted his confidence that he would be able to convince his mother's homeland to throw its lot in with the Allies. In August 1941, Churchill met US president Franklin Roosevelt to sketch out their vision of a post-war world. Roosevelt stopped short of declaring war but together they issued a joint declaration that made it explicit that they were working towards 'the final destruction of the Nazi tyranny'. It was the first step in the forging of a powerful and enduring alliance.

In October, Roosevelt approved $1 billion in aid to Britain and began providing extensive support to the Soviet Union. Then, on 7 December 1941, the Japanese navy launched a surprise attack on the US Pacific fleet at its Pearl Harbor base. America declared war on Japan the next day. Hitler then made the decision for the Americans by declaring war against them on 11 December. He did not have to. It was a catastrophic decision. He seems to have hoped that Japan might respond to this support from their ally by attacking the Soviet Union. In the space of six months Hitler had pushed both the USA and the USSR into the British corner.

'Hitler's fate was sealed. Mussolini's fate was sealed. As for the Japanese, they would be ground to powder. All the rest was merely the proper application of overwhelming force. The British Empire, the Soviet Union, and now the United States, bound together with every scrap of their life and strength, were, according to my lights, twice or even thrice the force of their antagonists.'

Winston Churchill

The Darkest Hour

Despite the now huge economic advantages of the Allies, early 1942 was the nadir of the war. The Soviet Union was locked in a titanic battle for survival. Britain was on the back foot in North Africa, while in the Far East it faced humiliation. The Japanese army quickly overran Malaya and in February forced the surrender of 85,000 British Empire troops in Singapore – the biggest single defeat in British military history. That same month, a German naval flotilla made a dash through the English Channel without much being done to stop it.

> 'Nothing more mortifying to the pride of our sea-power has happened since the seventeenth century . . . It spelled the end of the Royal Navy legend that in wartime no enemy battle fleet could pass through what we proudly call the English Channel.'
>
> **The Times**

Japan captured the Burmese capital of Rangoon in March and drove the British Army back all the way to India. In June, an eight-month siege of Tobruk in Libya ended in an Axis victory. The string of defeats threatened Churchill's position as prime minister, with grumbling in the press and Parliament about his conduct of the war.

In Europe, though, Britain would take the fight to Germany. At the end of May it conducted its first '1,000 Bomber Raid' on the German city of Cologne, marking a new phase of the air war. Britain would repay the German blitz many times over. Massive fleets of bombers battered German cities to disrupt munitions production, and, they hoped, destroy the will of the German people to go on fighting.

DUXFORD

Duxford was a key RAF fighter base in the Battle of Britain, defending the Midlands and supporting 11 Group's defence of London and southeast England. From April 1943 to October 1945 it became home to the US Eighth Air Forces' 78th Fighter Group, who played a crucial role escorting United States Air Force heavy bombers to targets in Nazi Germany and occupied Europe and conducting ground attacks. Today, Imperial War Museum Duxford is home to aircraft hangars, exhibitions and historic objects, preserving the legacy of those who served and enabling visitors to explore airfields and buildings. Its American Air Museum houses the iconic B-17 bomber, and tells the stories of the Eighth Air Force.

——— THE END OF THE BEGINNING ———

In November 1942 Britain finally won a decisive land victory, at the Battle of El Alamein in North Africa, ending the Axis threat to Egypt and the Suez Canal. The United States also joined Britain in Operation Torch, a series of amphibious landings in northeast Africa that would eventually help trap a quarter of a million Axis troops in Tunisia. Churchill spoke at Mansion House on 10 November, saying enigmatically, 'Now this is not the end. It is not even the beginning of the end. But it is, perhaps, the end of the beginning.'

Something had very decisively ended in Russia too. As the British and Americans began advancing in North Africa, the Soviets had sliced through Axis lines and entrapped what had formerly been the Wehrmacht's finest field army

in the ruins of Stalingrad. On 2 February 1943, the shattered, hungry, frostbitten remnants of that army surrendered. By some measures, the largest and costliest battle in
history had now ended in a catastrophic German defeat.
From here on in on the Eastern Front, Germany would be
on the back foot. It would gamble with a large armoured
assault on Kursk that summer, but no one believed Germany
was capable of delivering a knockout blow against the Soviet
Union.

May 1943 saw the Allied capture of Tunis, which marked the
end of the North African campaign. In July, British, Canadian
and American troops invaded Sicily, followed by mainland
Italy in September. Allied boots were on Axis soil.

By 1943 the American and British air forces had combined
their bomber offensive over Germany: the United States Army
Air Forces (USAAF) would strike by day, and the RAF at night.
In late July a massive Allied attack took place over Hamburg,
destroying over 60% of the city's housing and killing some
37,000 civilians in a giant firestorm. The destruction of
German cities would be one of the war's most morally ques-
tionable Allied strategies, and bombing raids increased in
intensity right to the war's end.

The Special Relationship

By the end of 1943 the Allies clearly had the upper hand. The
south of England resembled a giant armed camp. Over the
course of the war, over two million American servicemen
passed through Britain. American women also served, in roles
such as the American Red Cross or the Women's Army Corps.
The USAAF occupied or built over 200 airfields across the

UK, significantly altering local communities and infrastructure, earning the moniker 'friendly invasion' due to their impact on British life.

THE LOST VILLAGE OF IMBER

The quaint English village of Imber on Salisbury Plain was requisitioned by the War Office in November 1943 to serve as a training ground for US troops preparing for urban warfare ahead of the Allied invasion of Europe. Approximately 150 villagers were evacuated at 47 days' notice, with a promise that they could return six months later or following the war's conclusion. The village became a ghost town, its buildings and streets used only for military exercises. Despite occasional limited access, Imber remains to this day deserted and frozen in time, as residents were never permitted to return. Similar evacuations on parts of the south coast began at the same time, to allow rehearsals for the coming amphibious assault on occupied France.

Such were the numbers of American servicemen heading to Britain that a pamphlet titled *Instructions for American Servicemen in Britain 1942* was issued by the US War Department and distributed to American servicemen. It aimed to give them a crash course in Britishness to smooth any potential sources of friction between the swaggering GIs and the host population.

While American troops were assured that 'the British will welcome [them] as friends and allies' they needed a degree of humility: 'remember that crossing the ocean doesn't automatically make you a hero. There are housewives in aprons and youngsters in knee pants in Britain who have lived through more high explosives in air raids than many soldiers saw in first class barrages in the last war.' Both countries had their strengths and weaknesses:

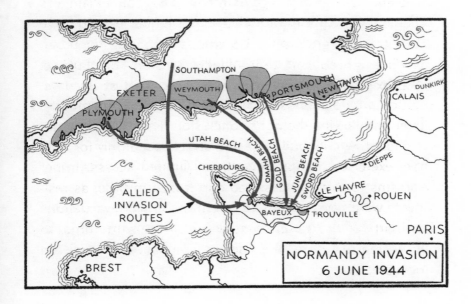

'The British don't know how to make a good cup of coffee. You don't know how to make a good cup of tea. It's an even swap.'

While the Soviets were doggedly beating back German forces in the east, the British and Americans were gearing up for an invasion of Western Europe. After extensive exercises and vast stockpiling of men, machines and supplies in southern England during early 1944, 61,715 British, 21,400 Canadian and 73,000 American soldiers landed on five beaches in

Normandy on 'D-Day' – 6 June 1944. By the end of 11 June (D-Day+5) 326,547 troops, 54,186 vehicles and 104,428 tons of supplies had been landed on the beaches. The liberation of northwest Europe had begun.

SOUTHWICK HOUSE

This 19th-century manor house is the site from which D-Day was launched and coordinated. The village of Southwick had been entirely taken over by the military, and Southwick House itself was used as the advance command post for the Supreme Headquarters Allied Expeditionary Force (SHAEF). In the months leading up to D-Day, the house became the headquarters of the main Allied commanders, with General Eisenhower, Admiral Ramsay and General Montgomery all based there. Eisenhower made his decision to delay D-Day by 24 hours (due to poor weather) in Southwick House's library.

ROAD TO VICTORY

German resistance to the invasion of Normandy was fierce and, while the landings were a success, the important target of Caen was not secured until early August. But then the dam burst. Days later, Allied forces surrounded and destroyed the German 7th army at the Falaise Gap. Paris was liberated on 25 August 1944, after four years of German occupation.

Despite a hopeless situation in both west and east, Hitler would not surrender. German resistance was as tenacious as it was hopeless. Despite Rome falling to the Allies just before D-Day, the Allies in Italy would never reach the Austrian or German borders. A British-led airborne assault on the Netherlands in September was narrowly defeated, as the Germans successfully repelled the northernmost point of the assault in Arnhem. The Germans even launched their last great offensive at the end of December that year. They used low cloud cover to negate Allied air superiority as they drove towards Antwerp. The Allied line buckled but reinforcements prevented a breakout, stabilised the front and then counter-attacked. By the start of 1945 the Allies had liberated nearly all of France and Belgium and were back on the offensive. They were poised for an assault on the German homeland. The most important legacy of Hitler's last offensive was probably that the delay inflicted on the western allies ensured that more of Germany, and its capital Berlin, would fall to the Soviets.

The Red Army was now unstoppable. By the end of 1944 it had overrun Poland, Romania and much of Hungary, and was entering German territory.

The Allies crossed the Rhine in March 1945, and moved through western Germany, but the Soviets were determined to reach the capital of the Reich first. On 2 May, the city fell to the Soviets. Adolf Hitler and other top Nazis killed themselves and, on 8 May 1945, the Germans accepted the Allies' demand of unconditional surrender. Five and a half years of warfare in Europe were finally over.

THE WAR EFFORT

Britain had won, but in relative and absolute terms Britain's national wealth, military power and diplomatic heft had been diminished. Britain had experienced extraordinary levels of mobilisation. World War Two was a total war – close to half of the entire economy had been geared towards the war effort.

Proportion of GDP Devoted to the War Effort

1938	7.4%
1939	15.3%
1940	43.8%
1941	52.7%
1943	55.3%
1944	53.4%

The state had reached into nearly every aspect of national life. Street lighting, land use, food prices and media consumption were all minutely controlled. The government had effectively taken control of the economy. By the war's end, 94% of industrial raw materials were distributed by the state. Ownership of industry, however, had remained largely in private hands. With the coming of peace, many believed the state should retain and even extend this dominant position, to wage war against other enemies: poverty, hunger and want.

LISTEN TO THE
PODCAST

Britain's Fightback

—— THE BIRTH OF THE WELFARE STATE ——

In 1942 the Beveridge Report was published. It was the work of a committee investigating the best way to provide social security. It identified 'Five Giants' – Want, Disease, Ignorance, Squalor and Idleness – that needed to be tackled in post-war Britain. It proved an unlikely bestseller, selling half a million copies within a year. Labour leader Clement Attlee withdrew his party from the wartime coalition soon after Germany's defeat and Britain had its first general election since 1935. Labour campaigned on promising to implement the Beveridge Report's recommendations and build a new 'welfare state'. It won in a surprising, landslide victory over Churchill's Conservatives. Britain's war hero was unceremoniously cast out of office, and Attlee formed Britain's first majority Labour government.

Labour nationalised around 20% of the economy by 1951. The Bank of England and civil aviation came first, in 1946, followed by the coal mines, gas and the railways. Typically workers welcomed the changes, as they earned more and enjoyed higher safety standards.

Money was scarce and Britain needed rebuilding. The winter of 1946/7 was particularly harsh and led to a 10% drop in British industrial output. Four million sheep died in the cold. The meat ration was cut to below its wartime level. Unsurprisingly, the public strongly supported domestic rebuilding over maintenance of the Empire. American aid had stopped abruptly in September 1945, which prompted economist John Maynard Keynes to warn that Britain faced a 'financial Dunkirk', but the Attlee government pressed on with a range of social welfare reforms:

- **Family Allowances Act (1945)** – child benefit provided for the first time.
- **National Insurance Act (1946)** – required everyone of working age (except married women) to contribute to National Insurance, in exchange for unemployment, sickness and widow's benefits.
- **National Assistance Act (1948)** – provided a social safety net for those unable to pay national insurance.

> 'We had not been elected to try to patch up an old system but to make something new . . . I therefore determined that we would go ahead as fast as possible with our programme.'
>
> **Clement Attlee, 1945**

The most striking legacy of the Attlee government was the National Health Service. His government essentially nationalised healthcare, making treatment free for everyone at the point of delivery. It was birthed on 5 July 1948 by Aneurin 'Nye' Bevan, Minister for Health, on his visit to Park Hospital, Davyhulme (now Trafford General Hospital) in Manchester. Britain became the first Western country to offer universal free medical care.

> 'There's the idea that the NHS will start paying for itself, because the nation will get really healthy, and it will be a health service, not an ill health service, and a healthy population won't need it as much. So there's an economic efficiency argument there as well.'
>
> **Jenny Crane, University of Bristol**

Within the NHS's first year, 27,000 hearing aids were issued, and 164,000 medical appliances. There were 6.8 million dental treatments, and 4.5 million pairs of glasses were handed out. Information campaigns taught the British public what was on offer.

Rebuilding Britain

Housing was in short supply. Half a million homes had been destroyed by German bombing during the war, and millions more damaged. Veterans of all the theatres of war wanted to come home and start families. Many felt that the government owed them a roof over their heads.

To meet the demand, Attlee's government launched a rapid house-building programme. Over a million were built, some of them temporary 'pre-fabs'. These were only built to last a decade, but around 8,000 still stand today. There was a 'baby boom' as soldiers returned home to their families, and expanded them. Live births in England and Wales jumped from a low of 580,000 in 1941 to 880,000 in 1947.

While most people yearned to return home after the dislocation of war, a good number wanted to do the opposite and make a clean break. In the first years of peace half a million Brits emigrated and, in early 1948, a Gallup poll found that 42% of English people wanted to follow them. They went largely to Commonwealth dominions such as Canada, Australia, New Zealand and South Africa, searching out cheap land and bigger skies and opportunities. On top of the 400,000 war deaths, this exodus hampered the national rebuilding efforts.

LISTEN TO THE
PODCAST

The Creation of the NHS

To address this, the government encouraged immigration from its colonies with the British Nationality Act of 1948, which extended British citizenship to anyone born in the Commonwealth. One of the more famous arrivals was the *Empire Windrush*, at Tilbury Docks in Essex on 22 June 1948. The ship was carrying 1,027 Afro-Caribbean immigrants and at least two stowaways. While not the first ship to bring West Indians to Britain, this one came to represent the arrival of the 'Windrush Generation'.

India was granted independence in 1947. It was immediately partitioned between predominantly Muslim and predominantly Hindu states. This was accompanied by appalling loss of life and forced migration. South Asians joined displaced Eastern Europeans as other groups of people who sought a life in Britain after the war. In 1931, just under 3% of the British population was born abroad; by 1951 it was approaching 4.5%. A different, multi-ethnic, multicultural Britain was taking shape.

The Barbican Estate, London, in 1971

Chapter 14

The Cold War and Twilight of Empire

'The British Empire in the Far East had depended on prestige.
This prestige has been completely shattered.'
Sir Frederic Eggleston, Australian diplomat (1942)

I mperial Japan was finally defeated by a wonder weapon the
likes of which, just a decade before, had existed only as
science fiction. Japan's American enemy had harnessed the
destructive power of the atom. Two cities, Hiroshima and
Nagasaki, were effectively wiped off the map by two bombs.
The world would never be the same. In August 1945, Japan
surrendered. The world scrambled to come to terms with the
awesome power that now lay in the hands of a species that had
evolved to wield a stick or stone.

Despite the vast cost of World War Two, the British Empire
still appeared to be a strong global power. When the term
'superpower' was coined in 1944, it was meant to apply to
three powers – the USA, USSR *and* the British Empire. In reality, though, the empire was mortally wounded. Britain had
stopped the enemy at the gates of India at Imphal and Kohima
in 1944, and reconquered much of Burma, but otherwise in
Asia the limits of British power had been cruelly exposed;
nearly 200,000 British and imperial troops had been captured

as Japan rampaged through Malaya, Singapore and Burma. The empire's reputation would never recover.

Independence Days

Union flags would come tumbling down flagpoles with a rapidity that shocked even those who had predicted the empire's end. India was first. Attlee's Labour government had come to power in London with a promise of granting Indian independence. The huge Indian army had made a significant contribution to the war effort, but the Indian war experience undermined the British claim to rule the subcontinent effectively and with the consent of its subjects. Some three million Indians had died in the Bengal Famine of 1943. Indians protested against continued British rule through demonstrations and more direct acts of resistance. The British, exhausted after a giant conflict ostensibly fought to safeguard the independence of peoples and states from brutal Axis occupation, did not have the stomach or the wherewithal to enforce their rule over Indians at the point of a gun. India gained full independence on 15 August 1947.

AN IRON CURTAIN

In Europe the victorious 'Big Three' powers had divided up Germany, but this marriage of convenience was soon to unravel. The huge Soviet army, numbering some 11 million in 1945, occupied a devastated Eastern Europe and showed no signs of wishing to leave. Russia had suffered shockingly through both world wars. The trauma of World War One had tipped the country into revolution and civil war, despotism and famine came in its wake. World War Two had taken the lives of 25 million Soviets. Stalin wanted his defensive line as far to the west, and as far away from the Russian heartland, as possible.

It is one of the sad ironies of World War Two that Britain went to war to protect Polish sovereignty, but could do nothing, as the USSR annexed Polish territory after that war and reduced the rest to a satellite state. Czechoslovakia and Hungary followed into a new Eastern Bloc, and the world began to realign around the two dominant superpowers, while Britain began its retreat from the global stage. America was leading the democratic West, while the USSR spoke for the communist world. Both were opposed to the creaking imperialism of France and Britain.

This new 'Cold War' was unofficially declared by Winston Churchill on 5 March 1946. In a speech delivered in Fulton, Missouri, he warned that 'From Stetin in the Baltic to Trieste in the Adriatic, an iron curtain has descended across the continent.' In the US, President Truman warmed to the theme a year later in a speech to Congress by outlining his worldview, which became known as 'The Truman Doctrine'. In February 1947, Britain informed the US that it could no longer support the Greek government as it sought to stave off a powerful communist movement in a civil war. The United States stepped into the power vacuum.

'I believe that it must be the policy of the United States to support free peoples who are resisting attempted subjugation by armed minorities or by outside pressures. I believe that we must assist free peoples to work out their own destinies in their own way.'

US President Truman, 12 March 1947

THE STORY OF ENGLAND

Truman's intentions were clear. America would provide economic and military assistance to any state facing a communist challenge. As it turned out, that included once-mighty Britain, and huge economic support flowed into Britain as well as Western Europe. Known as the Marshall Plan, this was an attempt to show the people of a shattered continent that prosperity lay in choosing a capitalist, democratic future rather than a communist one. Britain was reliant on American finance for its rebuilding efforts.

Economic aid came with a security guarantee. On 4 April 1949, the North Atlantic Treaty was signed in Washington DC, creating NATO. Twelve founding states including the USA, Britain and France bound themselves in a military alliance. Article 5 of the treaty stipulated that an attack on one would be considered an attack on them all, and there would be a joint response. Western Europe would thrive – behind an American military shield.

THE WEST

'The West' is a term commonly used to define the closely aligned American-led, liberal democracies. It is amorphous, a conglomerate of institutions that foster international cooperation, such as the World Bank and International Monetary Fund (founded in 1944), NATO and later the European Economic Community (EEC, founded in 1957), the precursor to the European Union. The United Nations was founded on 24 October 1945 in the United States, but is a comprehensive international organisation, with disparate membership. The legacy of the war can be seen in the make-up of the key decision-making body, the Security Council, on which Russia, China, Britain, France and the United States sit as permanent members.

In Europe there was an uneasy peace. In the Far East the Cold War turned hot. Korea had been divided in two after its liberation from wartime Japanese occupation, with a communist north and an American-aligned south. In June 1950, the north invaded the south. In response, a United Nations force, in reality an American-led Western coalition, drove the North Koreans back to the Chinese border. Unhappy with the proximity of this Western alliance, China intervened, and communist forces then pushed the UN and South Koreans southwards, close to the pre-war border. Months of attritional stalemate followed. An armistice was signed on 27 July 1953, but there has been no lasting peace treaty. Eighty thousand British soldiers served in the conflict, with over 1,000 killed in action.

THE BOMB

Regional and civil wars were internationalised during the Cold War, becoming 'proxy conflicts'. Antagonists pledged allegiance to Washington or Moscow in the hope of receiving arms and money. These regional struggles did not metastasise into global conflicts in part because of the development of nuclear weapons. On 29 August 1949, the Soviet Union had successfully tested its first nuclear bomb. Vast arsenals capable of destroying all life on earth were built up. Direct conflict between superpowers now meant a global Armageddon.

Britain and Canada had actually set up the first nuclear weapons development programme in autumn 1941 under the codename 'Tube Alloys'. This was subsumed into the US-led Manhattan Project in 1943. Britain secured an agreement that America would share the results of this nuclear development, but the United States reneged. The UK revived its own programme and Britain became the world's third nuclear power on 3 October 1952, after a test at Montebello off the west coast of Australia. A month later, the US tested the first thermonuclear device, a hydrogen bomb, which was hundreds of times more powerful than the atomic bombs dropped on Japan.

'It's fair to say that the Soviet government would have been able to create an atom bomb anyway . . . but what espionage did was to accelerate the research and development. It meant that the Soviets didn't have to go through all the failed routes that the British and the Americans did in the Manhattan Project.'

Calder Walton, Kennedy School of Government, Harvard University

ORFORD NESS

The shingled coastline close to the Suffolk village of Orford Ness is now a National Trust nature reserve, but was once the base of the Atomic Weapons Research Establishment (AWRE). In the mid-1930s the research facility had been key to the development of radar, and in World War Two part of it was used as an aerial bombing range. After 1953, six large test cells and many other buildings were constructed to conduct environmental tests on the atomic bomb, designed to mimic the rigours a weapon might be subjected to before detonation. Today the abandoned pagodas and research buildings, which are only accessible via special ticketed tours, are a haunting reminder of Britain's Cold War nuclear weapons development.

MIDDLE EASTERN CRISIS

Britain not only withdrew from south Asia and Greece but also Palestine. Here too the consequences of that withdrawal would be war, partition and a legacy of contested successor states that endures to the present. Having attempted to balance the desire of the Jewish people for a homeland in Palestine with the rights of the Arab inhabitants, Britain left in May 1948. Immediately the Jewish leadership in Palestine declared the establishment of the state of Israel and its Arab neighbours rushed to crush it.

Elsewhere, British interests were undermined by powerful nationalisms. In 1951 Iran nationalised the Anglo-Persian Oil Company (which would later become British Petroleum) in 1951. This prompted the Americans and British to sponsor a coup, in which a more pliable regime was installed – for the time being.

In 1952 the pro-British Egyptian monarchy was overthrown by a military *coup d'état*, and the radical Arab nationalist Gamal Abdel Nasser became president of the new republic. Nasser was opposed to Western interference in the Arab world, and aimed to strike at British interests in the region. In

LISTEN TO THE
PODCAST

The 100-Year Cold War

July 1956, he nationalised the Suez Canal. Britain then struck a secret deal with Israel and France to seize back control by force. Israel struck first on 29 October, and the French and British invaded Egypt two days later.

Israel and its allies achieved their military objectives, but quickly came under heavy international pressure from both the Soviet Union and the USA, as well as the United Nations. US president Dwight Eisenhower threatened to damage the British financial system if the British invaded Egypt and toppled Nasser. The invading powers were forced to back down, and on 7 November they withdrew.

Britain and France's failed intervention exposed their diminished influence as global powers. The Suez Crisis also strained Britain's close relationship with America. Eisenhower was appalled that his allies had attacked without notifying him. The Soviets had just surged into Hungary to stamp out a pro-democracy uprising. Eisenhower believed that the British and French had invited charges of hypocrisy as he sought to unify the Western response to Soviet aggression. Even many Commonwealth countries agreed with America, and the crisis forced the resignation of Conservative prime minister Anthony Eden in January 1958.

THE END OF THE EMPIRE?

The 25-year-old Elizabeth II had ascended to the throne in 1953. While Queen Victoria had presided over the expansion of the British Empire during the 19th century, Elizabeth II's reign would mark its decline. Sudan became the first African nation to achieve its independence, in 1956, and Ghana (then named the Gold Coast) the first sub-Saharan African country a year later. For the next few decades former colonies and dependencies across Africa, the Middle East, the Caribbean and Oceania would all gain full independence.

20 Nations that Left the British Empire 1956–1970

Nations	Year of Independence
Sudan	1956
Gold Coast (Ghana), Malaya	1957
Cyprus, Nigeria	1960
Kuwait, Sierra Leone, South Africa	1961
Jamaica, Samoa, Trinidad and Tobago, Uganda	1962
Kenya, Zanzibar	1963
Gambia, Rhodesia	1965
Barbados	1966
Mauritius	1968
Fiji, Tonga	1970

'Great Britain has lost an Empire, but not yet found a role . . .

'. . . Britain's attempt to play a separate power role – that is, a role apart from Europe, a role based on a "special relationship" with the United States, a role based on being the head of a Commonwealth which has no political structure or unity or strength and enjoys a fragile and precarious economic relationship – this role is about played out.'

Dean Acheson, President Kennedy's
Special Adviser on NATO (1962)

───────── 'NEVER HAD IT SO GOOD' ─────────

Britain's empire might have dwindled but the mood in Britain was one of optimism rather than decline. On 20 July 1957, prime minister Harold Macmillan made a speech in Bedford, proclaiming 'most of our people have never had it so good.' 'Go around the country,' he said confidently, 'go to the industrial towns, go to the farms and you will see a state of prosperity such as we have never had in my lifetime – nor indeed in the history of this country.'

The winds of change were not just blowing through the former colonies. Harold Macmillan had been born in 1894. He had fought at both the Battle of Loos and the Somme during World War One, and served in a variety of political posts in World War Two. In his lifetime, Britain had fought its two greatest conflicts and lost much of its empire. It had experienced post-war austerity and prolonged rationing. But now, in the mid-50s, the economy was growing.

Increasing real wages and cheaper goods led to better living standards. In 1951 there were only 2.2 million cars and a million TV sets. By 1964 there were over 8 million cars and 13 million TV sets. The number of households owning a refrigerator rose from 8% in 1956 to 69% by 1971. International tourism took off, with the first Concorde flight in 1969 and the first jumbo jet landing at Heathrow Airport in 1970. For many, Macmillan's words rang true. They'd never had it so good.

A 'Swinging' Decade?

No other decade in British history has such an instantly evocative and familiar epithet as the 'Swinging Sixties'. Britain had experienced radical swings in morals, behaviour and culture before, but this time the revolution was televised. The contraceptive pill, electronic music and recreational drugs got things 'swinging', but the transformation went deeper. Progressive values were cemented into British life through a series of Acts of Parliament. London's King's Road and Carnaby Street were swing central but unlike previous elite fashion trends this one was disseminated through glossy magazines, film and television. Provincial teenagers were inspired to dress, act and feel like they were part of the movement.

The road to a 'permissive society' was winding, and progress slower and more uneven than it now appears. The Wolfenden Committee was set up to review existing legislation surrounding prostitution and homosexuality, and its findings were published in September 1957. The Conservative government did not implement its recommendations on legalising homosexuality between consenting adults – that would have to wait for another decade – but the wider sense of the report, that the government should draw back from interfering in the personal lives of citizens, helped to shape policies in the years to come.

'I find that much of the legislation for which the Home Office is responsible was drafted and carried through in the emergency of wartime or laced in Victorian corsetry.'

R.A. Butler, Home Secretary, 1959

The contraceptive pill was made available to married women on the NHS in 1961, but its lack of wider availability meant that change was gradual. The watershed year came in 1967, with three major changes in the law governing sexual behaviour carried through by the Labour Home Secretary Roy Jenkins. In that year, often described as the summit of the

'Swinging Sixties', homosexuality was decriminalised and the pill became available to unmarried women. The Abortion Act also legalised abortion in certain circumstances.

As so often, polling from the time makes it clear that attitudes among the wider public lagged behind those of the London elite:

- **49%** – people who disapproved of contraception being used by couples who were not married (1968)
- **16%** – respondents who had a 'tolerant attitude' towards homosexuality (1971)
- **3%** – women aged between 18 and 45 who approved of promiscuous sex (1971)

Censorship was another evolving picture. Sexually explicit literature had also been allowed after the 1959 Obscene Publications Act, as long as it could claim 'artistic merit'. The first major public prosecution under the act came in October 1960, after Penguin Books published an unexpurgated version of D.H. Lawrence's 1928 *Lady Chatterley's Lover*. Penguin won the case, insisting that publication was a public good. Prosecuting barrister Mervyn Griffith-Jones caused some amusement in the courtroom with his opening remarks, asking:

'Would you approve of your young sons, young daughters – because girls can read as well as boys – reading this book? Is it a book you would have lying around your own house? Is it a book that you would even wish your wife or your servants to read?'

The Profumo Affair

In July 1961, Lord Astor hosted a party that may well have proved more shocking to his servants than a paperback.

Skinny-dipping, boozing and excess was the order of the weekend. Christine Keeler, a young model and showgirl, met 46-year-old John Profumo, Secretary of State for War. It was the start of an affair that would shake the establishment to its core. Allegations soon surfaced that Keeler was also intimate with Yevgeny Ivanov, a Soviet naval attaché. By the spring of 1963 they had reached a fever pitch. Profumo tried to staunch the wound by standing up in Parliament on 22 March and stated unambiguously, 'There was no impropriety whatsoever in my acquaintanceship with Miss Keeler.' An investigation soon found that there had been. He had misled Parliament and potentially compromised national security in the febrile atmosphere of the Cold War. The scandal brought down Profumo, who had to resign; and the contagion did not stop there. His boss, Prime Minister Macmillan, also resigned, his health broken by the stress. The Labour Party defeated the discredited Conservatives at the next election.

CLIVEDEN HOUSE

Cliveden House, in Buckinghamshire, is one of the National Trust's most visited properties. Over 500,000 visitors tour its grand rooms and gardens each year. The house as it stands today was built in 1851 for the Duke of Sutherland, but was bought by William Astor for $1.2 million in 1893. Cliveden became something of a sanctuary of political and literary life during the 1920s and 1930s. It was the venue for the party where Christine Keeler met Ivanov and Profumo.

The Profumo Affair eroded 'the Establishment's' semi-mystical reputation for competence. The satirical magazine *Private Eye*, founded in 1961, reflected this ebbing of deference. The public were fascinated by the lurid details, and Christine Keeler was devoured in a frenzy of press attention. Just like so many other fields, the modern media landscape was shaped by the 1960s.

CULTURAL POWER

While Britain's relative economic and military power was waning on the world stage, in the cultural sphere it had one distinct advantage in the new age of consumerism – English was the world's most marketable language, and the United States its biggest market. British bands attained dizzying success across the Atlantic; Brits excelled across the arts generally.

In the burgeoning American film industry, centred on Hollywood, British-born director Alfred Hitchcock's film-making peak came in the late 1950s into the 1960s, and by 1961 he had been nominated for Best Director at the Academy Awards five times – although, somewhat controversially, he never won. Actress Elizabeth Taylor enjoyed her most successful period around the same time, winning Best Actress at the 1960s Academy Awards for her role in *BUtterfield 8* and becoming the world's highest-paid movie star. Dashing British spy James Bond made his first outing in *Dr. No* in 1962, and Scottish actor Sean Connery would gain global fame with four more Bond films in the 1960s.

The 'British Invasion' of America was led by pop and rock groups such as the Beatles, the Rolling Stones and the Who, and British artists topped the American Billboard chart for half of both 1964 and 1965. The Beatles scored their first UK number one hit with 'From Me to You' in April 1963. They went on to have another 16 number ones before the decade was out, the final coming with 'The Ballad of John and Yoko' in 1969. In America they had 20 number ones, starting with 'I Want to Hold Your Hand' (1964) and ending with 'The Long and Winding Road' (1970). This chart-topping record has never been surpassed.

Their appearance on *The Ed Sullivan Show* in 1964 drew a record-breaking 73 million viewers, igniting 'Beatlemania', and their infectious charm and catchy tunes captivated American youth. In 1967, the Beatles released *Sgt. Pepper's Lonely Hearts Club Band* – a defining cultural moment in the height of the 1960s, heralding the album era and 1967's 'Summer of Love'. This groundbreaking album showcased the Beatles' exploration of new soundscapes, songwriting techniques and studio innovations, transforming popular music into an artistic medium and bringing counterculture into the mainstream.

In sport, too, England was excelling. England also hosted and won the eighth FIFA World Cup in 1966. Thirty-eight million people across Britain watched the final and heard commentator Kenneth Wolstenholme's legendary concluding words, 'Some people are on the pitch. They think it's all over – it is now!' English people took to the streets in celebration of beating West Germany 4–2 after extra time. The *Daily Mirror* wrote that, 'Nothing has ever gripped the entire nation like this World Cup', and celebrations went on for months afterward.

——————— THE SHADOW OF THE BOMB ———————

While affluence and liberalisation had led to greater personal freedom, there was at the same time an inescapable sense of deep foreboding. The proliferation of the nuclear arms race between the superpowers reached its most dangerous point in the early 1960s with the Cuban Missile Crisis.

In autumn 1962 the United States uncovered Soviet ballistic missiles in Cuba and blockaded the Soviet-aligned island nation. A tense stand-off between the two superpowers led the world to the brink of nuclear war. The British government could only wait, and there was a feeling of helplessness at Westminster in late October as the crisis unfolded.

The Cuban Missile Crisis was averted by a diplomatic agreement, but public anxiety over the possible Armageddon had reached its highest point. By 1962 the United States had amassed nearly 30,000 nuclear warheads, and the USSR had close to 4,000. Such a huge stockpile could destroy the world many times over, and meant any exchange would lead to the two nations' mutually assured destruction. Schoolchildren across Britain were taught to 'duck and cover' under their desks in the event of an H-bomb exploding in their vicinity. In 1963 the government printed 500,000 copies of *Civil Defence Handbook no.10: Advising the Householder on Protection Against Nuclear Attack*, which was criticised in Parliament for containing 'remarkable understatements'.

LISTEN TO THE
PODCAST

The Cuban Missile
Crisis

'The average householder who reads what to do in the event of imminent nuclear attack, and is told, if driving a vehicle, that he should "Park off the road if possible; otherwise alongside the kerb", will not form the impression that the civil defence measures taken by the Government are of any value whatsoever.'
    Emrys Hughes, MP for South Ayrshire, 2 December 1963

The Campaign for Nuclear Disarmament had been formed in November 1957, drawing considerable public interest and support from well-known people. The annual Aldermaston March, which had been held over Easter since 1958, peaked in 1963; as many as 100,000 people filled Trafalgar Square and the protest turned violent.

Mass Protest

Mass protest was a consequence of war-weariness and the growing American Civil Rights movement, which inspired marginalised groups worldwide to demand equality. More and more, people were organising themselves to speak out against government. America's involvement in the Vietnam War coincided with the growth of its Civil Rights movement, and protests erupted on a global scale. In London on 17 April 1968, 30,000 anti-war protestors descended on the American embassy in Grosvenor Square, and the march turned into a riotous clash with the police, with 200 people being arrested and 50 hospitalised.

In Northern Ireland, deep-seated religious and political divisions between Protestant Unionists and Catholic Nationalists had persisted since Ireland's partition from the United Kingdom in 1921. Catholics sought an end to discrimination

THE STORY OF ENGLAND

imposed by the Protestant-dominated government and police. These increasing tensions ignited the start of a 30-year period of violence known as 'The Troubles' in Northern Ireland from 1968 (up until the Good Friday Agreement of 1998), with events like 'Bloody Sunday' in 1972, where British troops killed 14 demonstrators in a scenario reminiscent of earlier Anglo-Irish violence.

Meanwhile in England, MP Enoch Powell's 1968 'Rivers of Blood' speech condemned the volume of post-war immigration to Britain and warned of societal breakdown due to multiculturalism. By that year, Britain's foreign-born population had risen to 5%, close to three million. Powell's inflammatory rhetoric sparked controversy and condemnation, leading to his dismissal from the Conservatives.

Nevertheless, progressive social change initiated in the later 1960s continued into the next decade. The 1970s saw an expansion of the Women's Liberation Movement, which advocated for women's self-realisation and protest. Free contraceptive services were introduced from 1 April 1974, and the Sex Discrimination Act 1975 prohibited workplace discrimination against women. By 1971, 53% of women aged 16 to 64 were in employment. However, inequality persisted. Although it was passed in 1970, the Equal Pay Act took five years to take effect, and women were often still expected to fulfil the role of primary caregiver alongside full-time employment.

--------- **THE DECADE OF DISCONTENT** ---------

On 18 June 1970, Edward (Ted) Heath unexpectedly defeated Harold Wilson's Labour government and became prime minister. Decimalisation was introduced in February 1971, replacing

Britain's complex system of pounds, shillings and pence and better aligning Britain's monetary system with international standards.

The 1970s was a traumatic economic decade. It featured the highest ten-year average rate of inflation in English history since the medieval period, while seeing the return of unemployment, a major recession and ultimately 'stagflation' – economic stagnation and inflation combined – which particularly impacted young people and public service workers. The conditions triggered widespread protests, power cuts and strikes in a power struggle between trade unions and the government that affected the entire nation.

Britain was still heavily reliant on coal for energy, and faced severe disruption during a two-month strike called by the National Union of Mineworkers (NUM) in January 1972, which was prompted by stagnant mining wages and the NUM's demand for a 43% pay rise. This led to a state of emergency, with planned blackouts to conserve energy. Despite a deal being struck soon after, soaring inflation levels soon wiped out the monetary gains the workers had made.

The European Economic Community (EEC) had been established in 1957, heralding a new era of closer collaboration in Europe. Britain had applied for membership in both 1961 and 1969, but had been vetoed, and its manufacturing industries had struggled to compete internationally as a result. Britain finally joined the EEC in January 1973. Initially, membership did not deliver the anticipated economic benefits, which led to Britain's reputation as the 'sick man of Europe' compared to the growing economies on the Continent.

Shortly after joining the EEC, Britain faced a further energy crisis triggered by an Arab oil embargo in response to countries supporting Israel in the Yom Kippur War. To conserve limited coal supplies amid impending NUM strike threats, the prime minister announced commercial electricity restrictions; from 1 January 1974 usage was only allowed during specific hours over three consecutive days each week. Essential services like hospitals and supermarkets were exempt, but the policy led to business layoffs and closures. TV broadcasts ceased at 10.30 p.m., and people resorted to candles and torchlight, blankets for warmth and boiling water for washing.

Media opposition to the NUM strike contributed to perceived public backing for the government's hardline stance against union power. Fearing that concessions would embolden the miners, in February 1974 Heath called a snap election, hoping to garner public support. Instead, it ended his tenure and Labour managed to form a minority government under Harold Wilson. Wilson promptly increased miners' wages by 35%, and ended the three-day working week on 7 March 1974. However, by 1975, with rising wages and energy shortages, inflation had soared to nearly 25%, while the economy had contracted by 2.5% in 1974 and another 1.5% in 1975. Britain was humiliated when in 1976 Chancellor Denis Healey requested a £2.3 billion loan from the IMF, the largest loan provided by the organisation until then, in exchange for some £3 billion of public spending cuts.

BRUTALISM AT THE BARBICAN

British buildings of the 1970s leave a visual legacy of the decade. During the 1950s, 'Brutalism' emerged as a cost-effective post-war architectural style, with similarities to building projects in Eastern Europe and the Soviet Union. Steel and labour shortages led to greater use of reinforced concrete. The Barbican Estate, which began construction in 1965, was built in the Brutalist style in the war-torn area of Cripplegate. The estate contains 2,000 residential homes and Europe's largest performing arts centre. Many of Britain's new universities and 1970s housing projects were also built in the Brutalist style.

The 'Winter of Discontent'

There was a lull in strike action in the mid-1970s, but Britain faced a new crisis in summer 1976 when drought led to critical water shortages. Nevertheless, Queen Elizabeth II's Silver Jubilee in 1977 brought a wave of patriotic celebrations, harking back to the World Cup win a decade earlier.

By late 1978, the Trades Union Congress (TUC) was once more demanding higher pay amid rising inflation. This combined with the coldest winter in 16 years prompted public sector workers up and down the country to go on almost general strike. The turn of the year was labelled the 'Winter of Discontent'. Rubbish piled up as binmen refused to work, while some hospitals could only accept emergency patients.

'It turns very bad indeed when that mood of striking spreads across to the public sector, which isn't something we'd encountered on a national level before. You started getting hospital porters closing down hospitals, and school caretakers closing down schools, and rubbish piling in the streets, and the famous *Daily Mail* headline, "Now they won't even let us bury our dead", because mortuary workers were on strike in Liverpool, and also in Sedgefield. It was those strikes I think that really hit home

LISTEN TO THE
PODCAST

The Winter of
Discontent

with the Winter of Discontent, because these were public services, and the people most affected were those who rely on public services. So it's the poor and the working class who are most hard-hit by the Winter of Discontent.'

Alwyn Turner, University of Chichester

The 1979 election saw the Conservatives secure victory over James Callaghan's Labour, with the election slogan 'Labour isn't working'. Leading this change was Britain's first female prime minister, Margaret Thatcher.

THATCHERISM

'I can't bear Britain in decline. I just can't. We who either defeated or rescued half Europe, who kept half Europe free, when otherwise it would be in chains. And look at us now.'

Margaret Thatcher, 1979

Thatcher sought to end Britain being at the mercy of trade unions, as witnessed in the 1970s, and lessen the role of the state through deregulation. One of her first moves was to lower the top rate of income tax from 83% down to 60%, and she also granted over five million local authority tenants in England and Wales the right to buy their homes through the 1980 Housing Act. Public spending was also briefly reduced.

But recession, doggedly high inflation and rising unemployment would lead to quickly dwindling popularity polls, and by the end of 1981 72% were dissatisfied with the government and 65% against Thatcher as leader. There was a brief moment of national jubilation with the wedding of Princess Diana and Prince Charles in June 1981, but Thatcher was also aided by two important external events: in March 1981, the former reforming Labour home secretary of the 1960s, Roy Jenkins, led the 'Gang of Four' in defecting from Labour and creating the new Social Democratic Party, which briefly went ahead of Labour in opinion polls. Then, in April 1982, the military junta in Argentina launched an invasion of the Falkland Islands.

Thatcher responded boldly, dispatching a naval task force of 127 ships to retake the islands. The Falklands War would last 74 days before ending in an Argentine surrender on 14 June. The war was Britain's biggest military commitment since Korea, and victory saw Thatcher win a landslide re-election in 1983. With her party strengthened at Westminster, she turned her attention to the trade unions.

In March 1984, the National Coal Board proposed closing 20 of the 174 state-owned mines and cutting 20,000 of the 187,000 associated jobs. Two-thirds of the country's miners, led by the NUM under Arthur Scargill, downed tools. The strike culminated in violent confrontation at the 'Battle of Orgreave' in June that year, where South Yorkshire Police charged protestors on horseback, leading to 123 injuries and 94 arrests. Thatcher refused to yield to union demands, likening the dispute to the Falklands War and referring to 'the enemy within'. Prepared for a long fight, this time the government had already gathered significant coal stockpiles, and after a year of hardship the striking miners returned to work in March 1985.

Thatcher also faced another 'enemy within': the Irish Republican Army, who were fighting for a united Ireland.

Seventeen people had been killed and over 50 injured in bomb attacks in London between 1982 and 1983, and on 12 October 1984 the IRA attempted to assassinate members of the British government staying in the Grand Hotel, Brighton, for the Conservative Party Conference. Thatcher was in the hotel when the bomb detonated at 2.54 a.m., but escaped unharmed. Five people were killed, including one of her MPs, and another 31 injured. Undeterred, Thatcher addressed the Conference at 9.30 a.m. the following day, denouncing the attack as an assault on democracy and proclaiming, 'all attempts to destroy democracy by terrorism will fail'. Immediately afterwards, her popularity soared.

Despite these ongoing troubles, by the mid-1980s Thatcher's approach to the economy was leading to growth, which between 1984 and 1988 averaged 4.7%; but it was also leading to a country of 'haves and have-nots', with working-class unemployment remaining high as heavy industry shut down. Chancellor Nigel Lawson's 'Big Bang' of allowing foreign firms into the City of London led to an economic boom against a backdrop of three million (12%) being unemployed. But Britain had turned from its industrial past into a service-led economy, with unemployment almost halving by 1989, and the nation moving away from its uncomfortable moniker of the 'sick man of Europe'. Culturally, the decade would also see a second 'British Invasion', with British acts topping the US Hot 100 music charts for even longer than in the 1960s.

THE END OF THE COLD WAR

There had been a Cold War détente from the late 1960s to late 1970s, but tensions resurfaced following the Soviet Union's invasion in Afghanistan from 1979 to 1989. US president Ronald Reagan, also a popular deregulating conservative, challenged what he saw as the 'evil empire' through hawkish rhetoric, and vastly increased American defence spending, raising it to over a trillion dollars for the first time.

Anxieties about nuclear annihilation resurfaced, and in 1980 the government published an amended pamphlet of its *Protect and Survive* campaign. The TV film *Threads* was broadcast on BBC Two before a debate on *Newsnight* on 23 September 1984 to 6.9 million viewers. It illustrated the aftermath of nuclear war in horrific detail, and was the first film to depict a nuclear winter.

'Protect and Survive . . . was a government leaflet accompanied by films, although the films were never released, which said you will be basically left to your own devices if it happens. There will be no public shelters as it was during the blitz. You will be left to yourself at home. So therefore you have to, very 1980s, very Thatcherite, take responsibility, sort yourself out, don't expect us to help you. You'll be left at home, fortified at home. So board up the windows or brick up the windows, reinforce the exterior walls with sandbags or with wardrobes, packed with boxes of books and clothing.'

Julie McDowall, historian

YORK NUCLEAR BUNKER
Built at the height of the Cold War in 1961 and an open secret, York Cold War Bunker operated within a national network of bunkers as a nerve centre, ready to observe and

report on nuclear explosions, and assess radiation and fall-out in the event of a nuclear attack. It was not designed to withstand a direct hit, but played a role as part of the UK Warning and Monitoring Organisation system. It is the most modern English Heritage managed site, and open to the public for guided tours.

Fears lessened after the rise to power of Mikhail Gorbachev in the USSR in 1985. The Soviet Union was being left behind by the fast-modernising economies of the West, and he set about introducing a series of social and political reforms known as perestroika (restructuring) and glasnost (openness). He also made often unexpected concessions that led to arms reduction agreements. A historic summit between Gorbachev and Reagan in Reykjavik in October 1986 paved the way for the signing of the Intermediate-Range Nuclear Forces Treaty which in turn led to the dismantling of thousands of nuclear missiles in Europe.

Just two years later, the fall of the Berlin Wall in November 1989 symbolised the end of the Cold War era. Peaceful revolutions across Eastern Europe and the collapse of communist regimes heralded the triumph of democracy and capitalism over communism. Gorbachev's decision not to intervene militarily marked the end of Soviet dominance in Eastern Europe, breaking up the USSR and ushering in a new era of international relations.

The Soviet Union's dissolution came hand in hand with, in Britain, the shrinking

LISTEN TO THE
PODCAST

How to Prepare for
Nuclear War

of the state and the waning of socialist sentiment. But despite victory in a long struggle against an ideological enemy, Thatcher would soon be out of office, as Churchill had been at the end of World War Two. Thatcher had enjoyed a third general election victory in 1987, but a cornerstone policy of introducing a 'community charge' led to her political demise. When this 'poll tax', as it became derisively known, was introduced in 1990, it led to a riot on Trafalgar Square that March. Upon the resignation of chancellor Nigel Lawson and foreign secretary Geoffrey Howe in November, Thatcher faced a leadership challenge from Michael Heseltine and resigned. The longest-serving Conservative prime minister of the 20th century stepped down from leading a much-changed Britain.

Epilogue

When communism collapsed, the American political philosopher Francis Fukuyama published an essay titled 'The End of History?'. It argued that, with the disappearance of the last meaningful political alternative, liberal democracy had won, and was the only feasible mode of organising our societies. With a constitution reaching back into the Middle Ages, amended through the upheavals of the 17th century, and with expansions to the franchise through the 19th and 20th centuries, the representative democracy forged in England and Britain appeared to be on the right side of history. Western nation states had conquered the world, they had abandoned autocratic monarchy, defeated tyrannical alternatives in Europe and outlasted the communist experiment.

James Bond went on extended leave. With the Soviet Union gone, the British spy and symbol of soft power had nothing to do. Six years passed, the longest gap in the franchise's history, as producers figured out where to take the story. He returned in *GoldenEye* (1995), in which rogue Russians threatened the world order through 'hacking' the new-fangled Internet. Critics dismissed it as too fantastical even for that franchise . . .

The World Wide Web was invented by an Englishman. While its origins lay in the American military, Tim Berners-Lee published the first website in December 1990, and it is now generally agreed that this is when we passed into a new age. One not of bronze, iron or steel but of information. Not since the invention of the telegraph in 1851 had the speed of information exchange been so suddenly transformed. Internet adoption in the early 1990s was slow; it took too long to connect and exchange that information on legacy networks and low-powered computers. But over the following decades the web grew and grew. It transformed and further globalised the world economy, it revolutionised work, leisure time, dating, politics and, well, everything. Whether for work or pleasure, Britons now spend over 60 hours a week online.

The threat of nuclear destruction appeared to be gone. The Internet was changing everything. From 1992 through to the economic crisis beginning in 2007, Britain experienced a remarkable 16 consecutive years of economic growth, and average earnings rose by 30%. The Channel Tunnel, a fantasy of Napoleon, became a reality in May 1994, joining Britain to the Continent for the first time since the inundation of Doggerland and slashing travel time to France for freight and travellers alike. Britain also stepped politically closer to Europe, becoming a member of the new European Union and joining the Single Market when it was created in 1993.

After nearly two decades in power, the Conservative government was defeated by Tony Blair's New Labour in 1997. Blair had distanced the reformed Labour party from its radical past and its relationships with the trade unions. He believed elections would be won in the centre ground, and he was proven right; he won two consecutive landslide victories, as well as a narrower one in 2005. He became the longest-serving Labour prime minister in the party's history, and matched Margaret

Thatcher for the most consecutive election wins. 'Things can only get better', Labour's adopted song for their 1997 campaign went, and for a decade they broadly seemed to do so.

Northern Ireland had been torn apart by sectarian violence since the 1960s. There were bombings in Manchester and London in 1993 and 1996. In August 1998, the Real Irish Republican Army, a splinter group of the IRA, planted a car bomb in Omagh, killing 29 people and injuring hundreds. This seriously threatened to derail the Northern Ireland peace process, which had formally begun in the early part of the decade. But peacemakers prevailed. The Good Friday Agreement was signed on 10 April 1998 with signatories from across the political spectrum from Ireland, Northern Ireland and the United Kingdom. It brought to an end 30 years of violence in Northern Ireland.

Internationally, Britain often acted alongside the US as an adjutant world police officer. When Iraqi dictator Saddam Hussein invaded Kuwait in August 1990, a 42-nation coalition, led by the US but including Britain and France, drove Iraqi forces out of the nation; but Hussein would remain in power, paving the way for a more controversial invasion of Iraq itself in 2003. Britain would also intervene militarily in the Yugoslav Wars as part of NATO in 1995, and again in 1999.

If the British Empire's birth can be traced to the reigns of Elizabeth I and her successor James VI and I, perhaps its end was symbolised by the return of Hong Kong to China on 1 July 1997. There are other islands and fragments of territory that still fly the Union Jack but the departure of Hong Kong, a rich, dynamic city of millions that had been a British colony since 1842, felt like the end of a chapter. Its people were promised a high degree of autonomy for the next 50 years under 'one country, two systems', but the Chinese reneged on this promise. Perhaps this was an early sign of a more active rebuttal of western political ideas; many fear that this tightening grip on Hong Kong is a precursor to conflict over the future of Taiwan.

This Story of England ends at the turn of the millennium. Plenty of history has happened since, but we will leave it to the journalists to write the first draft. The English story remains, as it always has been, shaped by our position in Europe and the world, our neighbours, climate, sea and resources.

The great moments in English and British history tend to stem from its interactions with mainland Europe. In prehistory waves of immigrants used the land bridge to settle; metalworkers arrived, bringing the Bell Beaker. The Romans invaded and transformed Britain's trajectory and, as they left, Jutes, Angles and others filled the void. Englishness was forged as these cultures met, fought, traded, exchanged and intermarried. The sea that almost completely surrounds England has been a bridge rather than a barrier. The boundaries of Englishness have expanded into Ireland, Wales, Scotland and parts of France, and contracted as Vikings forced England's founder Alfred to cling to his desperate refuge in the marshes of Somerset. England has been large and small, powerful and weak, conquered and conqueror. Yet England has endured. For centuries it has been subsumed in much larger political entities, yet to many of its inhabitants it commands a more visceral allegiance than the composite kingdom of which it is a part. It is a small place, but its story, this story, is enormous. Its language is now the world's language. Its faith is practised by tens of millions across continents. Its customs have been adopted by distant peoples, inspired in part by those foundational English texts like Magna

Carta and the Bill of Rights. Its industrial innovations changed the lives of everyone on the planet, and the atmosphere above and around them. Everyone thinks their home is special. Everyone thinks their story has had an outsized influence of the human story. And in the case of the English, they are right.

Acknowledgements

This book, like History Hit itself, is the result of collaboration. We are a band of history geeks who broadcast history on every platform available. The idea of a history of England was born out of a five-part podcast series on *Dan Snow's History Hit* in 2023 which we called, imaginatively – *The Story of England*. An accompanying three-part documentary series was also broadcast on History Hit's subscription on-demand TV channel.

These programmes were recorded as a road trip around England with support from English Heritage. The podcast series was presented by Dan Snow, produced by Mariana Des Forges and James Hickmann and edited by Dougal Patmore. The documentary series was presented by Dan Snow, directed by Bill Locke, produced by Annie Woodman, filmed by Nathan Williams and edited by Levi De Sousa. The programmes were adapted and added to create this book. James Carson was editor, with contributions from Tristan Hughes, Matthew Lewis, Lily Johnson, Kyle Hoekstra and Amy Irvine. Jen Bennett got us over the finish line.

Picture Acknowledgements

Images within the book:

p. xvi: © Simon Bradfield / iStock / Getty Images Plus
p. 2:   © The Natural History Museum / Alamy Stock Photo
p. 18:   © David Clapp / Stone / Getty Images
p. 34:   © CM Dixon / Print Collector / Getty Images
p. 60:   © Hulton Archive / Getty Images
p. 62:   © Universal History Archive / Universal Images Group via Getty Images
p. 88:   © Manor Photography / Alamy Stock Photo
p. 110:   © Matthew Lewis
p. 132:   © Bridgeman Images
p. 134:   © Gibson Blanc / Alamy Stock Photo
p. 158:   © Bildarchiv Monheim GmbH / Alamy Stock Photo
p. 180:   © Pete Scott
p. 210:   © Leslie Brown
p. 238:   © Windmill/Robert Hunt Library / UIG / Bridgeman Images
p. 240:   © Peter Trulock / Fox Photos/Hulton Archive / Getty Images
p. 266:   © Bettmann / Getty Images
p. 290:   © Central Press / Getty Images
p. 318:   © Evening Standard / Hulton Archive / Getty Images

First 8-page inset:

p. 1 above: © The Natural History Museum / Alamy Stock Photo
p. 1 below: © Gary Cox
p. 2 above: © Philip Selby
p. 2 below: © Adam Burton / Alamy Stock Photo
p. 3 above and below: © Colchester and Ipswich Museums Service: Colchester Borough Council Collection
p. 4 above and below:© Jim Scott
p. 5 above: © Jenna Thomas
p. 5 below: © CPA Media Pte Ltd / Alamy Stock Photo
p. 6: © Pictorial Press Ltd / Alamy Stock Photo

Index

Illustrations are denoted by the use of *italic* page references.

INDEX

More from History Hit!

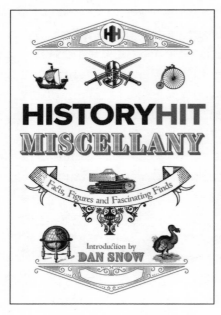

History Hit Miscellany
9781399726009

History Hit Guide to Medieval
England
9781399726139

You can subscribe to History Hit at historyhit.com/subscribe.